BEHIND CLOSED DOORS

Behind Closed Doors

What Company Audit is Really About

Vivien Beattie

Stella Fearnley

and

Richard Brandt

Foreword by Sir David Tweedie

Based on research sponsored by the Institute of Chartered Accountants in England and Wales

Published by
PALGRAVE MACMILLAN
Houndmills, Basingstoke, Hampshire RG21 6XS and
175 Fifth Avenue, New York, N.Y. 10010
Companies and representatives throughout the world

PALGRAVE MACMILLAN is the global academic imprint of the Palgrave
Macmillan division of St. Martin's Press, LLC and of Palgrave Macmillan Ltd.
Macmillan® is a registered trademark in the United States, United Kingdom
and other countries. Palgrave is a registered trademark in the European
Union and other countries.

ISBN 0–333–74784–4

This book is printed on paper suitable for recycling and
made from fully managed and sustained forest sources.

A catalogue record for this book is available from the British Library.

Library of Congress Catalog Card Number: 00–053042

Printed and bound in Great Britain by
Antony Rowe Ltd, Chippenham and Eastbourne

This publication is the outcome of research sponsored by the Centre for
Business Performance at the Institute of Chartered Accountants in England
and Wales (ICAEW). The views expressed are those of the authors and are
not necessarily shared by the Institute or its Centre for Business Performance.

I dedicate this book to my mother and father, Joyce and Bill Urquhart. In their different ways, they have both given me enormous support and encouragement throughout my life.

Vivien Beattie

We thank our families for their tolerance and support throughout the writing of this book.

Stella Fearnley and Richard Brandt

Contents

List of Figures

List of Tables

Preface

The audit of public companies is a very private activity. All that the outsider is aware of is the existence of a (usually clean) external audit report that says that the financial statements represent a true and fair view. Periodically there is a highly publicised company collapse and there are allegations of audit failure. This book uncovers, for the first time, what really goes on behind the closed corporate doors. It reveals the true extent of the effort that goes into finalising the financial statements of a public listed company and the generally high level of expertise and integrity within the UK auditing profession.

It does this by identifying a varied group of six UK public companies that had recently experienced audit interactions involving significant accounting issues. Matched interviews with both the finance director and the audit engagement partner were conducted and analysed using grounded theory methods. This method of analysis is designed to establish the factors that influence the nature and outcome of these audit interactions. It supports a rich understanding of the principal parties and their motivations, their relationship, the contextual factors that influence the interaction process and the strategies adopted, and the critical factors that determine the quality of the financial reporting outcome and the ease with which it is achieved.

'Earnings quality' may be a relatively recent term, but concern with this issue has been a central theme for the accountancy profession for decades. The impact that the auditor has on earnings quality is also central and associated with this are well-publicised concerns regarding auditor independence. The findings of this book inform both debates.

V.B.
S.F.
R.B.

Acknowledgements

The financial support of the Centre for Business Performance of the Institute of Chartered Accountants in England and Wales is gratefully acknowledged. We would also like to thank the twelve participants who were willing to talk to us about their audit experiences so frankly.

V.B.
S.F.
R.B.

List of Abbreviations

AEP	Audit Engagement Partner
AICPA	American Institute of Certified Public Accountants
APB	Auditing Practices Board
ASB	Accounting Standards Board
CAJEC	Chartered Accountants Joint Ethics Committee
CCAB	Combined Committee of Accounting Bodies
CEO	Chief Executive Officer
DTI	Department of Trade and Industry
EC	European Community or European Commission
EU	European Union
FD	Finance Director
FEE	Fédération des Experts Comptables Européens
FRC	Financial Reporting Council
FRRP	Financial Reporting Review Panel
FRS	Financial Reporting Standard
ICAEW	Institute of Chartered Accountants in England and Wales
ISB	Independence Standards Board
MAS	Management Advisory Services
NAS	Non-Audit Services
NASD	National Association of Securities Dealers
NED	Non-Executive Director
NYSE	New York Stock Exchange
POB	Public Oversight Board
PwC	PricewaterhouseCoopers
SEC	Securities and Exchange Commission
SECPS	Securities and Exchange Commission Practice Section
SPR	Second Partner Review
UITF	Urgent Issues Task Force

Foreword

In a speech (September 2000) to the National Association of State Boards of Accountancy, Chairman Arthur Levitt, of the Securities and Exchange Commission quoted from an author of the 1960s:

> 'accountants began to take on the corporate mentality, to think of themselves no longer as independent, critical, perhaps even judicial examiners, but as part of management, members of the corporate "team" … "It was a question of role definition." Accountancy was losing its soul, then, the way so many souls are lost – by definition and by degree.'

Chairman Levitt concluded:

> 'I believe the time has come for the profession's own broader membership … to stand up and take back what some are trying to take from them: the pride and privilege of serving the American public and its investors as the most rigorous, objective, and independent accountants in the world; it's time that the profession's own take back the cause and determine the course; it's time that the profession's own take back the spirit of the franchise that America's investors bestowed upon them long ago.'

The decline in the standard of British auditing was probably most marked in the mid to late-1980s. Schemes were developed, many in the City of London, which, while not contrary to the (then) accounting standards or the law, were at the edge, and some of us would say beyond, the limits of acceptability. In the absence of a strong accounting standards regime the true and fair view proved to be a double edged sword. It consists not only of accounting standards but also accepted practice. Some of the accounting schemes were accepted by one or two major firms of auditors and consequently moved within the corpus of practice covered by true and fair. From that moment auditors were powerless to reject the schemes by qualifying the accounts. This situation, in part, led ultimately to the formation of the Financial Reporting Council and its two attendant bodies, the Accounting Standards Board (which in turn created the Urgent Issues Task Force) and the Financial Reporting Review Panel. What was needed, however, was a sea-change in the attitude of the profession. As Mr Levitt has put it, it was time that the profession's own took back the cause.

The will for change in the 1990s was manifest. The Board would not have succeeded in its programme of reform had it not been backed enthusiastically by auditors, finance directors and users of accounts. While the Auditing Practices Board set out to define best practice, the new generation of auditors developed more backbone and began to question practices that previously would have been accepted.

This fascinating book pulls aside the veil over the audit process and shows to those who have not been involved the difference between good and bad auditors. It shows in its case studies the highly competent auditor imbued with integrity (deemed to be the 'crusader' or the 'safe pair of hands'). In contrast, it reveals 'the accommodator' and the 'truster' – the former bending to the client's wishes, forgetting that the auditor's role is to serve the public not management's interest, the latter tending to leave his client alone assuming all will be well. Fortunately, evidence was not presented of the incompetent or rogue auditor, although the accommodator came very close.

The cases highlight, too, the need for accounting firms to match engagement partners with management. It is senseless sending along a newly qualified partner to deal with a highly experienced senior finance director who could set out to intimidate the younger accountant.

Questions are also raised about the appointment of auditors and the use by finance directors of the threat of putting the audit out to tender. This, of course, raises issues of corporate governance and whether executive directors should have the power to appoint or fire auditors.

The case studies are anonymous – which is as well for the auditor who allowed overvalued stock to be written down over three years – for goodness sake! In better cases, however, it reveals the standards to which all auditors should aspire. The encouraging conclusion is that, despite the exceptions, both the profession and the quality of its audits are fundamentally sound.

This book will be fascinating for those involved in audit and who know the dynamics of the meetings between company management and auditor. It should be a stern lesson for those auditors who still do not reach the required level of independence from management. For those to whom the audit is something of a mystery, it shows how a good audit and a good auditor is a vital safeguard in ensuring transparency and investor protection.

I was encouraged by this readable study. It shows the audit profession in a much stronger position than it was ten years ago and clearly on the way up. For those auditors who do not match the best, the appropriate standard is clearly visible. Independence from management can be achieved, it should be achieved, and, for the sake of the auditing profession, it must be achieved or the societal purpose of the audit is lost and with it the accounting profession.

September 2000   SIR DAVID TWEEDIE
Chairman of the Accounting Standards Board
London

Part I
The Background

1 Introduction and Regulatory Framework

1.1 WHAT THIS BOOK IS ABOUT

This book penetrates the closed world of the discussions and negotiations that take place between the finance director and the auditor of companies. It is out of this interaction process that the audited financial statements ultimately emerge. The book examines six case studies where the authors were able to have in-depth, matched interviews with both the finance director (FD) and the audit engagement partner (AEP) of listed UK public companies. These reveal, perhaps for the first time, the pressures on both parties and the effects on their interaction. These interviews were carried out in 1996 and 1997 and, therefore, reflect the economic and regulatory environment of that time. However, although the regulatory environment has changed since then, the fundamental issues that emerge remain unaffected by the passage of time – in particular the quality of earnings and auditor independence.

1.2 FUNDAMENTAL ISSUES FACED BY THE ACCOUNTANCY PROFESSION

1.2.1 Structural and procedural changes in the accountancy profession

Everyone is now acutely aware of the phenomenal pace of change in the business environment. The information technology revolution has resulted in the globalisation of the world's capital markets and many businesses. In an economy that is increasingly knowledge-based, businesses (including the accounting 'industry') must be flexible and adaptable to survive and prosper. Given this trend towards globalisation, and the move for harmonisation and possibly convergence of accounting and auditing standards in the European Community (EC) and world-wide, we do not restrict our discussion to the UK environment. In particular, we refer to significant events in the US, since this country dominates world markets.

Within the accountancy profession, a series of mergers among the major international firms resulted in the Big Five by 1998. This has led to

increasing concentration within the external audit market. This is especially the case among listed companies, where 82 per cent were audited
by the Big Five by 1998. Among the very top listed companies, the FTSE
100, this figure stood at 99 per cent in 1999 (i.e., one company was
audited by a non-Big Five firm) (*Accountancy*, 1999). A concern is that
this oligopolistic concentration of market share may be anti-competitive.

Another structural change has been the increase in revenue from non-
audit services, especially management advisory services (MAS). In the
US, audit and accounting fees contributed only 34 per cent to total revenue
in 1998 for the Big Five (down from 70 per cent in 1976), while MAS
contributed 40 per cent (up from 15 per cent) (Turner, 2000). It is not that
the absolute level of accounting and audit fees in declining, it is simply
that audit revenues have remained remarkably flat, certainly since 1990,
with a very significant growth in MAS revenues since 1994 (Antle, 1999).[1]
In the UK, the picture is remarkably similar (not surprisingly, as the Big
Five are global firms). Figures calculated using the annual survey of financial performance by the leading firms show that, for 1998/99, audit and
accounting represented 36 per cent of total revenue and consulting represented 28 per cent (*Accountancy Age*, 1999).[2] Moreover, FTSE 100 auditors now generate more than twice as much fees from non-audit work for
their clients as they do from the audit – only three years ago, in 1996,
audit fees were narrowly ahead of non-audit fees (*Accountancy*, 1999).
A number of firms are now considering separating their consultancy arms.

Finally, there is ample evidence of growing commercialisation within the
accountancy profession, which is most visible among the major firms. In the
face of extreme competitive pressures, developments in information technology, and rising client expectations, the top firms have re-engineered the
audit process to emphasise its 'added-value' qualities (Percy, 1997). This
allows them to offer, *inter alia*, benchmarking and risk analysis services
(see, for example, Bell *et al.*, 1997, who document KPMG's Business
Measurement Process approach, which focuses on understanding the
client's business). Thus, the auditor is progressively adopting an advisory
role, in addition to the traditional monitoring role, a development that several commentators caution against (e.g., Hatherly, 1997; Williamson, 1998).
There is, in particular, a concern that auditor independence is not possible in
the face of the 'added-value' or 're-engineered' audit (e.g., Jeppeson, 1998).

---

[1] The existence of stagnant audit fees suggests that there is effective price competition,
despite concerns about the anti-competitive impact of increasing concentration.
[2] These percentages are based on only three of the Big Five, as PricewaterhouseCoopers
(PwC) and Arthur Andersen did not provide a breakdown.

Moreover, these 'new audit methodologies' represent a shift away from compliance-based audit procedures towards a highly judgemental process (Hatherly, 1999). This is not welcomed by all.

The profession as a whole is also seeking to expand the scope of its services. In the US, the American Institute of Certified Public Accountants (AICPA) has been at the forefront of these efforts. A special committee developed the concept of 'assurance services', a broad set of services (including the traditional financial audit) designed to improve the quality of information (AICPA, 1997). The principal new service opportunities include, *inter alia*, risk assessment, business performance measurement, information systems reliability and electronic commerce. Moreover, the top firms are also entering into strategic alliances with companies.

1.2.2 Public concerns regarding the quality of financial reporting and audit

The traditional financial audit exists to provide the external user with confidence in the financial statements (APB, 1995). A 'robust independent audit process' is, therefore, fundamental to the integrity of financial reporting which is, in turn, fundamental to confidence in the capital markets (APB, 1994). While this has been recognised for many years, it has become a critical imperative due to major changes in the accountancy profession and the environment in which it operates. Throughout 1998, 1999 and 2000, regulatory bodies on both sides of the Atlantic have put the issues of quality in financial reporting and audit at the very top of their agendas.

In 1998, Arthur Levitt, Chairman of the Securities and Exchange Commission (SEC),[3] gave a now famous speech in which he pointed to erosion in the quality of earnings and, therefore, the quality of financial reporting (Levitt, 1998). He stated that many in corporate America were operating in the grey area between legitimacy and outright fraud, where accounting was being perverted and the integrity of financial reporting was being lost.

The debate continues to focus on the role of auditors in producing high-quality financial reporting, with the spotlight on auditor independence. Auditor independence concerns have existed for many years, though this has grown as the level of non-audit services provided by auditors to their

---

[3] An independent federal regulatory agency with authority to prescribe the form and content of financial statements filed by companies whose securities are traded in the US capital market.

clients has grown. As a result, the SEC and the AICPA set up a private-sector Independence Standards Board in 1997. A concern with the role of audit committees and with 'audit effectiveness' is more recent. In 1999, the Blue Ribbon Committee on Improving the Effectiveness of Corporate Audit Committees made ten recommendations, one of which made explicit reference to the *quality*, not just the *acceptability*, of the company's financial reporting (NYSE/NASD, 1999). In the UK, the Institute of Chartered Accountants in England and Wales (ICAEW) set up a review of auditor independence in 2000, headed up by Ian Hay Davison (*Accountancy*, 2000).

1.3   THE REGULATORY FRAMEWORK IN THE UK

In 1991 the Financial Reporting Council (FRC) and its subsidiaries were established to address concerns in the UK about the quality of financial reporting. This was considered necessary because the previous regime was perceived to be inadequate (CCAB, 1988). Accounting standards were flexible, compliance was poor, and no effective enforcement mechanism operated against directors who breached accounting standards. The ability of auditors to withstand pressure from directors to breach accounting standards (Whittington, 1989) was questioned and 'creative accounting' (Griffiths, 1986; Smith, 1992) was rife. As a result, there was widespread abuse of the system, which undermined the credibility of UK financial reporting and the credibility of auditors (Whittington, 1989; Tweedie and Whittington, 1990). The object of the reform process was to improve the standard of financial reporting in the UK. The Accounting Standards Board (ASB) became responsible for standard setting, the Urgent Issues Task Force (UITF) became responsible for providing authoritative guidance on emerging problems and the Financial Reporting Review Panel (FRRP) became responsible for the enforcement of the regulatory framework for financial reporting in respect of large companies.

The establishment of the FRC was part of a wider range of regulatory reform, involving the development of a framework for corporate governance (Cadbury Report, 1992; Hampel Report, 1998; Turnbull Report, ICAEW, 1999), which resulted in a vastly expanded annual report, the emergence of audit committees, and such concepts as the separation of duties between chairman and chief executive and an emphasis on the need for non-executive directors. The Department of Trade and Industry (DTI) introduced a new regime for the regulation of auditors, and new regulations for auditor independence (ICAEW, 1991) also formed part of this revised framework. In 1999, the Chartered Accountants Joint Ethics Committee

(CAJEC) issued the draft of a review of these ethical guidelines, but the basic framework is unchanged (CAJEC, 1999). Currently (2000), further changes are in train. The accounting profession's regulatory activities are to be subject to independent oversight by a Review Board (see CCAB, 1998 and DTI, 1998); regulation of securities listing has moved from the Stock Exchange to the Financial Services Authority; and revision of company law is also in process.

For the future, in the changing circumstances of ever-increasing globalisation of financial markets and the search for global standards, the twin concerns for earnings quality and for the effectiveness of the audit process remain as insistent as they have ever been. The USA, in particular, is concerned with threats to auditor independence caused by the expansion of audit firms and with the problems of agreeing internationally accepted standards of reporting.

1.4   RESEARCH APPROACH

This book reports the findings of a two-stage study of auditor–client company interactions involving UK listed companies. Using a combination of quantitative and qualitative methods, the interactions between the two primary parties in the auditor–client company relationship – finance directors (FDs) and audit engagement partners (AEPs) – is explored. Stage one, the quantitative stage, undertakes a questionnaire survey of 300 FDs and 307 AEPs. This survey establishes the frequency with which, over a three-year period, an extensive set of 46 audit and audit-related issues is discussed, is negotiated, and results in a change to either the accounting numbers or disclosures. Response rates were 51 per cent and 80 per cent, respectively. This large-scale survey allows the extent, nature and outcome of interactions to be assessed for the population as a whole. A summary of the findings from this stage is presented in Chapter 3.

The focus of this book is, however, stage two, the qualitative stage, which presents six cases across a range of company sizes and industries where a substantial amount of discussion and negotiation occurred. In-depth, matched interviews were conducted with both principal parties to the interactions. During these interviews, the specific nature of the key accounting and non-accounting issues was identified, contextual factors were established and the dynamic process of interaction (including the influence of other parties) was uncovered. Although the cases relate to a particular point in time, and hence a specific economic and regulatory environment, the fundamental issues that emerge are shown to be generic and insensitive to the passage of time.

1.5   OUTLINE OF BOOK

This book has been organised in three parts, as follows:

Part I comprises Chapters 1 to 3. Chapter 1 provides an introduction and background to the accounting regulatory framework in the UK. Chapter 2 reviews the relevant academic literature relating to the auditor–client relationship. Specific areas covered include the regulatory dilemma of creative compliance, the auditor–client company relationship, the demand for audit, audit quality, audit quality attributes, buyer types, the role of commitment, auditor independence; second partner review, corporate governance and audit committees, and the audit effectiveness. Chapter 3 summarises the results of the questionnaire which provided the introduction to these six FDs and their AEPs. This first stage of the study shows the frequency of discussion of 46 accounting and audit-related issues; the frequency of negotiation about these issues; and the frequency of resulting changes to the accounting numbers and disclosures.

Part II comprises Chapters 4 to 10. Chapter 4 reviews the theoretical and empirical literature from non-accounting sources that discusses the general issues arising from conflict and negotiation. A model of the generic negotiation process is presented and the unique features of negotiation in an audit setting are discussed. The few empirical studies that relate to negotiation in audit settings are also outlined. The chapter then explains how the case companies were selected and approached, states the broad approach taken to the analysis, describes how each case was written up, offers a preliminary within-case analysis, and presents an overview of the general context and the interaction issues in each of the six cases. It also offers a short explanation of the interview methods used and sets out the six case studies. Chapters 5 to 10 present the findings from the interviews. These six chapters tell the story of each case as described by the interviewees, including numerous direct quotations. A description of the background setting in which the interaction takes place is included, together with an outline of any technical accounting 'problem'. The process of interaction and resolution, seen from the perspective of each party, is documented. Full within-case analysis of the key influences, parties and strategies adopted is provided at the end of each chapter, together with a brief summary of what the case tells us about the audit process.

Part III comprises three chapters. Chapter 11 begins with an explanation of grounded theory and how we use it on the cases. It then provides a summary overview of the six cases. Chapter 12 presents a cross-case grounded theory analysis of six matched cases. It also offers a taxonomy of seller types that is developed from the case evidence. The degree to which the cases fit the generic negotiation process model presented in Chapter 4 is considered. Finally, Chapter 13 presents our conclusions, including the implications for policy and our recommendations.

2 The Auditor–Client Relationship

2.1 OVERVIEW

The audit firm–client company relationship (hereafter auditor–client relationship) is an extremely complex one, as discussed in section 2.3.[1] The overall relationship between the two organisations is the aggregate of a series of two-party and group relationships, between individuals from both organisations and third parties (e.g., regulators). The primary audit relationship is, however, normally that between the FD and the AEP.

A number of disparate strands of literature are relevant to an investigation of this relationship, and will be reviewed in this chapter, although there is very little literature that directly addresses the relationship empirically from a behavioural perspective (see section 2.4). The literature reviewed is predominantly academic and some readers may prefer to skim this chapter or indeed omit it altogether. However it provides a valuable theoretical framework which informs the rigorous analysis of the six case studies presented in this book.

2.2 THE REGULATORY DILEMMA: CREATIVE COMPLIANCE

In the UK, a mixture of state and self-regulation governs accounting, although the emphasis is on self-regulation (with state oversight) by the profession. This basis of regulation was reviewed in the late 1980s in the Dearing Report (CCAB, 1988) and again in the late 1990s (DTI, 1998). Both times, a broadly self-regulatory approach has been confirmed. This is despite the widely held belief that this approach lacks authority and effective sanctions and that this failure could be remedied by invoking the 'might of law'.

McBarnet and Whelan (1991 and 1992) are legal scholars who provide a valuable analysis of different regulatory control strategies in terms of 'formalism'. Formalism implies a narrow approach to control, i.e., the use of clearly defined, highly administrable rules. They argue that a strategy of

---

[1] Strictly, the term 'client' refers to the company's shareholders; however, it is often used to refer to the company's managers (the shareholders' agents).

anti-formalism was adopted by the newly formed Accounting Standards Board (ASB) post-Dearing in an explicit bid to restrain creative accounting. They explain that the danger of formalism (whether implemented through tight rules set by the profession or the law) lies in the exercise of 'creative compliance', which is the use of rules to escape control without actually violating those rules. Examples of these avoidance and manipulation devices from the 1980s era include the use of non-subsidiary subsidiaries and the use of the 90 per cent test in classifying leases.

Consequently, the ASB introduced a shift toward general principles. This involved stressing the overriding purpose of financial accounting in terms of the true and fair view, the use of broad criteria and the avoidance of tight definitions, and a continuing reliance on the professional bodies to implement the regulatory framework. However, the strategy of anti-formalism has its own inherent problems. It is criticised on the grounds of legitimacy, it being argued that citizens have the right to know exactly what is prohibited in advance of behaviour, rather than in retrospect. It is argued that broad rules are imprecise, over-inclusive and can result in outrageous results. It is also argued that anti-formalism will not result in effective control because it is impossible to implement. McBarnet and Whelan (1999) point out that the law is a double-edged sword – both 'an instrument of control but also a basis for arguing escape routes from it'. They conclude that controlling creative accounting ultimately depends on instilling a business ethic of compliance with the spirit of the law.

The outcome of these debates appears to have been a drift (or push) back to formalism throughout the 1990s in the UK. Many accounting standards now include detailed guidance notes (explanatory paragraphs) in addition to the broad principles (e.g., FRS 15). In essence, the cases described and analysed in this book demonstrate how people dance around the margins, irrespective of where these margins are set by regulators.

2.3   THE AUDITOR–CLIENT COMPANY RELATIONSHIP

An audit engagement requires the accountancy firm (a registered auditor) to undertake a review of the company's operations and conduct detailed audit procedures with a view to preparing an audit report. For listed companies, the audit will involve an audit team, headed by the AEP. To obtain the information and access necessary to conduct the audit, this team will have contact with employees at various levels within the client company and also the board of directors (executive and non-executive). However, as the audit is primarily a financial audit, it is the company FD who is normally the most senior, principal point of contact for senior members of the audit team. Thus, the primary audit relationship is normally that between the FD and the AEP. The audit report, addressed to the company's shareholders (who, strictly, are the clients), states whether or not, in the auditors' opinion, the company's financial statements give a true and fair view and have been properly prepared in accordance with the Companies Act 1985. This audit report appears in the company's annual report and accounts. A positive opinion affords a 'clean audit report' deemed to be critical by company management and capital market participants.

2.4   PAUCITY OF RESEARCH INTO THE PRIMARY RELATIONSHIP

Despite the importance of these communications, no studies have, to date, empirically examined these interactions between the AEP and the FD. Clearly, it is imperative that these interactions be examined as a *dynamic, context-sensitive process.* Yet research into the auditor–client company interface tends to be highly abstract, adopting an analytical or experimental approach (see, for example, Fellingham and Newman, 1985; Fisher *et al.*, 1996). Most of the empirical research that does exist is based on economic rationales that fail to recognise behavioural aspects of the relationship. These empirical studies either analyse large data-sets of publicly available information regarding audit report qualifications and company characteristics with a view to making inferences about aspects of the audit process, or conduct postal questionnaires to elicit the views of interested parties. The former is indirect, while the latter, though direct, fails to capture the dynamic aspects of the process and provide background context. Consequently, the insights gained are limited and unreliable.

Existing approaches to the study of the auditor–client company relationship undoubtedly reflect the difficulties associated with gaining access to real-life settings (Dye, 1991, footnote 3). This book, as its title states, takes the reader behind these closed doors to find out what company audit is really about. In other words, we look inside the black box out of which the audit opinion emerges to understand *how* it emerged. What were the critical issues? How were they resolved? What were the critical influences? In the case of extreme conflict, which party held the balance of power?

The urgent need for academic research of this type is well-recognised. In a recent review of the theory and empirical research into auditor independence, Kleinman *et al.* (1998, p. 36) conclude that 'the field needs a theory capable of describing the nature of interactions between the auditor and client firms'. In a similar vein, in 1999 the SEC issued a call for research into a variety of auditing and accounting issues facing it (call reproduced in *Accounting Education News*, 1999). One of the topics listed was 'what key factors influence the decision-making process when an auditor is confronted with difficult and contentious accounting issues?'. This book is an attempt to develop a theory capable of answering the question posed by the SEC.

2.5   THE DEMAND FOR AUDIT

Wallace (1980) has examined the demand for audit, using economic analysis. She identifies three related sources of demand: agency (or stewardship) demand, information demand and insurance demand. Agency theory investigates the agency relationship that exists between the company directors (agents) and the company shareholders (principals).[2] The distinguishing characteristic of an agency relationship in the audit context is that the shareholders engage the directors to perform some service on their behalf that involves delegating some decision-making authority to the directors. Because of goal conflict, and because it is difficult for the shareholders to observe the directors' behaviour (due to information asymmetries), there is concern that the directors will maximise their own self-interest at the expense of the shareholders. This is referred to as 'the agency problem'. Because of rational expectations, shareholders anticipate this and reduce the amount that they are willing to pay for the company's securities. This is referred to as 'agency costs'. To reduce these costs, principals or agents may write contracts to restrict the agent's actions, giving rise to monitoring and bonding costs, respectively. The theory predicts that the monitoring role of an audit can reduce agency costs attributable to the self-interested behaviour of directors. Thus, even in the absence of a statutory requirement to do so, companies with high agency costs will tend to volunteer to undergo an audit to bring those costs down.

The information demand for audit is closely related to the agency demand, since it also arises from information asymmetries.[3] The selection of credible auditors signals management's honesty and quality to interested parties. It also reduces agency costs via the monitoring function. The insurance demand for audit recognises that the auditor's professional liability exposure serves to indemnify investors and creditors against financial losses.

---

[2] This theory, as it applies to a company, was developed by Jensen and Meckling (1976).
[3] The information demand for audit was originally explored by Dopuch and Simunic (1980, 1982).

Clearly, this demand will be curtailed if the law is changed to permit audit firm partnerships to have limited liability.[4]

These three sources of audit demand give rise to a demand for a quality-differentiated audit, i.e., different 'levels' of auditing are required.[5] Essentially, higher-quality audits are demanded by companies with higher agency costs, greater information asymmetries, and greater risk of financial loss. In these circumstances, higher-quality audits may also be expected by shareholders.

2.6   AUDIT QUALITY

From a strictly economic perspective, the quality of an audit can be defined as the probability that 'a given auditor will *both* (a) discover a breach in the client's accounting system, and (b) report the breach' (DeAngelo, 1981a, p. 186, emphasis in original). Thus, audit quality depends on both technical competence and independence.[6] DeAngelo (1981a) argues that auditor size acts as a proxy for audit quality, since larger firms have reduced incentives to lower audit quality opportunistically in order to retain any single client. This is because a large firm's economic dependence on any single client is, relative to a small firm, lower. Moreover, auditors with a greater number of clients have 'more to lose' by failing to report a discovered breach. Consequently, consumers (i.e., shareholders, lenders, other capital market participants, and other stakeholder groups) rationally use auditor size as a surrogate for audit quality.

2.7   AUDIT QUALITY ATTRIBUTES

Some understanding of the factors that influence the nature of the auditor–client relationship is provided by empirical studies that examine client's view of audit quality attributes and the closely related concept of client satisfaction.

In the US, Schroeder *et al.* (1986) found that auditor committee chairs rated audit *team* factors as more important than audit *firm* factors. The top five factors were:

- partner and manager attention to the audit;
- planning and conduct of the audit;

---

[4] In the UK, audit firms have been permitted to incorporate (and thereby enjoy limited liability) since 1991 (under §25 of the Companies Act 1989).
[5] This is the so-called 'product differentiation hypothesis'.
[6] The concept of auditor independence has proved to be very difficult to define (see section 2.10.1).

- communication between audit team and management;
- independence exhibited by audit team members; and
- firm provisions to keep auditors up-to-date technically.

Auditors' views were generally very similar to those of the audit committee chairs. Carcello *et al.* (1992) surveyed three key groups – preparers, sophisticated financial statement users and audit partners. The five highest-rated attributes across the three groups were:

- very knowledgeable audit team;
- active engagement partner;
- high ethical standards – audit team;
- partner knowledgeable about client industry; and
- frequent communication – auditors and management.

Most recently in the US, Behn *et al.* (1997) relate client satisfaction to audit quality attributes. They asked controllers of the Fortune 1000 companies to rate their auditor on the 12 audit quality attributes identified by Carcello *et al.* (1992) and to rate their level of satisfaction with both the audit firm and the audit team. The satisfaction measures were modelled as a function of the 12 quality attributes, in addition to variables to capture the presence of a new auditor, the controller's work experience, client size and audit opinion. The model explained 61 per cent of the variation in client satisfaction. Six audit quality variables had a significant positive association:

- responsiveness to client needs;
- active involvement by executive of audit firm;
- effective and ongoing interaction with the audit committee;
- appropriate conduct of audit field work;
- industry expertise; and
- prior audit team and firm experience with the client.

Interestingly, but perhaps not surprisingly, there was a significant negative association between auditor scepticism and client satisfaction, indicating the difficult task that auditors face in balancing client preferences with societal and professional expectations. There were also significant positive associations between recent auditor change and finance controller work experience with the current auditor, indicating that controllers were inclined to select their former employer as auditor. Behn *et al.* conclude 'the overall pattern of results highlights the important roles of communication and relationships in promoting client satisfaction' (1997, p. 7).

In the UK, Beattie and Fearnley (1995) appears to be the only academic study of auditor characteristics published to date. They survey the finance directors of 210 listed companies to elicit the importance of 29 potentially desirable auditor characteristics. The top five characteristics were:

- integrity of firm;
- technical competence of firm;
- quality of working relationship with audit partner;
- good reputation; and
- technical competence of audit partner.

These findings indicate the critical importance of the AEP's people skills and technical skills in addition to audit firm characteristics.

2.8   BUYER TYPES

Beattie and Fearnley (1998a, pp. 12–13) note that the economic theory of auditor choice is recognised to be under-specified, in that not all of the relevant factors have been identified. They suggest that, by augmenting the economic theory of auditor choice with insights from the marketing and psychology disciplines, a more complete understanding of auditor choice will be created.

They observe that the analysis of market structure and competition based on brand choice and switching models has received considerable attention in the marketing literature. Research in this area has adopted one of two approaches, depending on whether product alternatives or consumers are grouped. Recently, models that simultaneously group consumers and brands have been proposed. McCarthy *et al.* (1992) is a typical example of this line of research. Service marketing research, in particular that relating to professional services, has revealed the importance of the *relationship* between the buyer and the seller, relative to characteristics of either the buyer or seller in isolation (Gronroos, 1990; Sharma, 1991). The potential for new insights into buyers' behaviour is offered by this 'relationships approach' which classifies relationships (in the present case, auditor–client relationships) based on buyer type (Sharma, 1994). The concept of buyer types was developed by marketing researchers, who have always recognised the need for classification (Sharma, 1994). It is argued that buying behaviour falls into distinct categories, based upon the buyer's needs, attitudes and beliefs.

Sharma (1994) identifies, based on interviews, four buyer types (the bargainer, the loyal, the confused, and the competent) based on two dimensions of buying situations: piecemeal versus project and price versus quality. A distinctive characteristic of the audit service (compared with

Table 2.1   Key characteristics of buyer types

The grudger
- Sees little value in audit
- Resents audit
- Cost-minimiser
- Unhelpful to auditor
- Possibly a bully

The status-seeker
- Sees some value in audit
- Seeks to enhance external parties' perceptions of company by association with audit firm of acknowledged status

The comfort-seeker
- Sees significant value in audit
- Wants thorough examination of systems
- Wants assurance that annual reports will attract no adverse criticism
- Senior directors use auditor as a confidential sounding-board
- Comfort 'chain' exists

The resource-seeker
- Sees significant value in audit
- Wants technical advice on financial reporting matters
- Wants business ideas
- Wants compliance-related non-audit services (e.g., tax, accounting)
- May also want non-compliance-related non-audit services (e.g., corporate finance, due diligence)

Source: Beattie and Fearnley, 1998a, p. 51. Reproduced with the permission of the Institute of Chartered Accountants in England and Wales.

other professional services) is that it is a legally required regulated service, which can be purchased only from a licensed supplier.

Based on their earlier survey findings and related factor analysis (Beattie and Fearnley, 1995), and detailed interviews with twelve companies that had conducted a competitive tender and/or changed auditor (Beattie and Fearnley, 1998b), Beattie and Fearnley (1998a) inductively derived four audit buyer types: the grudger, the status-seeker, the comfort-seeker, and the resource-seeker. They offer a characterisation of the four buyer types as shown in Table 2.1.

2.9   THE ROLE OF COMMITMENT

De Ruyter and Wetzels (1999) also draw upon the relationship marketing literature. They use it to examine commitment in auditor–client relationships. They present a conceptual model of both parties' commitment that links two aspects of commitment to its antecedents and consequences. The two forms of commitment are *calculative commitment* (an instrumental dimension that evaluates costs and benefits) and *affective commitment* (an attitudinal construct that captures the affective orientation towards and value congruence with the business partner) (Gundlach *et al.*, 1995). The six antecedents are: shared values and norms: perceived service quality; trust; interdependence; service portfolio (the availability of a full range of business advisory services); and client orientation (the attention give to client needs at the level of the auditor–client interaction). The two drivers of continuance intentions are co-operation and opportunistic behaviour (behaviour of one party that endangers a relationship for the purposes of taking advantage of a new opportunity).

De Ruyter and Wetzels conduct an empirical study into these links based on clients of a leading audit firm in the Netherlands. A postal questionnaire sent to 213 clients is used to measure the model's variables and subsequent modelling shows the direction and strength of the links between these variables. In terms of antecedents, the expected positive relationships between affective commitment and service quality, trust, and interdependence were found, as was the expected positive relationship between calculative commitment and trust. However, unexpectedly negative links between calculative commitment and both service quality and service portfolio were found. In terms of consequences, it was found that relationships characterised by affective commitment exhibit more co-operative behaviour and less opportunistic behaviour, while relationships characterised by calculative commitment exhibit less co-operative behaviour.

2.10   AUDITOR INDEPENDENCE

2.10.1   The concept and its importance

In section 2.6, it was explained that auditor independence is one of the twin pillars of audit quality. The reality and perception of auditor independence is fundamental to public confidence in financial reporting. A new private-sector Independence Standards Board (ISB) was set up in the US in 1997. The EC has sought to establish a common core of independence principles via a Green Paper (EC, 1996) and with the help of the Fédération des Experts Comptables Européens (FEE) (FEE, 1995, 1998). In 1998, the European Parliament approved a resolution broadly supporting the EC Green Paper. In response, the Commission set up a Committee on Auditing composed of government experts. One of the new Commission's principal tasks was to examine the set of core principles on independence developed by the European accountancy profession (EC, 1998, §3.4). Draft proposals were published in March 2000 (EC, 2000). The concept of independence has proved, however, to be difficult to define precisely (Antle, 1984, p. 1; Schuetze, 1994, p. 69). Representative definitions are: 'the conditional probability of reporting a discovered breach' (DeAngelo, 1981a, p. 186); 'the ability to resist client pressure' (Knapp, 1985); 'an attitude/state of mind' (AICPA, 1992; Moizer, 1994, p. 19; Schuetze, 1994, p. 69); a function of character, with the attributes of integrity and trustworthiness being key (Magill and Previts, 1991); and an absence of interests that create an unacceptable risk of bias – the AICPA White Paper definition (AICPA, 1997).

A subsidiary issue is whether independence is an absolute concept (as implied by the structure of current relevant SEC regulations and the AICPA Code of Professional Conduct) or is a matter of degree, with recent empirical evidence supporting the latter view (Bartlett, 1993). Furthermore, since third parties are unable to observe directly independence *in fact*, the *appearance* of independence assumes prime importance. This is recognised explicitly in most current professional conduct codes (e.g., AICPA, 1992, para. ET.55) and in the EC Green Paper (1996, para. 4.8).

2.10.2 Models of independence

Models of auditor independence are based either on the analysis of economic incentives or the analysis of power. Kleinman *et al.* (1998, pp. 6–9) identify two versions of each type. DeAngelo's (1981b) economic model is perhaps the most widely known. Audit firms obtain revenue directly from the auditee, with directors in many countries having de facto control over the appointment and remuneration of the auditor. Further, incumbent auditors earn client-specific quasi-rents which, by providing an incentive to 'cheat' to retain the client company, intuitively lower auditor independence. A countervailing force is the existence of similar rents from other auditees, which may be lost if the auditor is 'caught' (DeAngelo, 1981b, pp. 189–90). The relative strength of these incentives clearly depends upon the significance of the auditee to the audit firm's portfolio, the perceived riskiness of the client and the risk of getting 'caught'. These incentives can operate at firm, office, and partner levels.

Antle's (1982, 1984) economic model draws upon mathematical agency theory. Both client management and the auditor are assumed to be effort averse and utility maximising. Management has incentives to misrepresent the financial condition of the company and, in the absence of some form of restraint, the auditor will not expend effort to identify and report this.

These economic models, by their very nature, have very limiting assumptions. The power models of Goldman and Barlev (1974) and Nichols and Price (1976) take a more complex view of auditor–client interactions than the utility maximisation models. They focus on the parties' resources and moderating variables such as pressure from the auditor's role set, litigation, reputation loss. However, both models are restricted to the analysis of a single period.

2.10.3   Studies of perceived auditor independence

No formal 'theory' of auditor independence exists and thus, to date, analytical models concerning independence are very limited. Research has focused upon identifying the factors that potentially influence independence based on rational argument, and assessing their impact upon *perceived* independence since independence in fact is unobservable. Factors affecting independence generally fall into two broad categories: economic factors and regulatory factors. Since the general setting within which auditor independence perceptions are formed is subject to continuous change, policymakers must constantly address new threat factors and seek new regulatory safeguards.

Empirical studies date from the mid-1960s (Schulte, 1965) and typically employ a mail questionnaire approach. Early studies, conducted before (or just after) more rigorous ethical guidelines on independence issues were put in place by many countries in the 1970s, focused on specific auditor–client relationships in the four areas of fees, personal relationships, financial involvement, and conflicts of interest. Several of these relationships, which twenty years ago were considered acceptable, have now been proscribed in many countries for many years (e.g., ownership of shares in client).

Since then, studies have focused on the impact of changes in the economic and regulatory environment in which accounting and auditing takes place and in which independence perceptions are formed. The four principal factors believed to impact auditor independence are: the economic dependence of the auditor on the auditee, competition within the external audit market, the provision of non-audit services (NAS) by the auditor, and the degree of laxity of the regulatory framework. Each is now considered briefly, in turn.

High levels of market competition are generally argued to increase the auditor's economic dependence (AICPA, 1978). In recent years, competition has increased due to excess supply and the removal of solicitation restrictions in many countries. This can be reflected in the budget pressures faced by auditors (Bartlett, 1993, pp. 57–8), tender threats by auditees (Moizer, 1994, pp. 19–20), and competitive pricing by auditors (ICAEW, 1995).

The provision of NAS by incumbent auditors is the factor which in recent years has been debated most intensively by policy-makers, the accountancy profession, practitioners, and academics. Clearly, NAS provision increases the economic bond between the auditor and auditee; however, joint provision may be efficient due to knowledge spillovers. Joint provision is thus generally favored by both auditors and auditees. No direct evidence that NAS provision by the auditor impairs auditor independence has been uncovered by various congressional committees and professional commissions (e.g., AICPA, 1978, 1979). This does not, however, preclude an impact upon *perceived* independence, due to a decline in the monitoring value of the audit.

Regulatory factors concern both accounting and auditing. It is argued that independence is most threatened where all auditors do not agree on the preferred accounting treatment, due to the flexibility of accounting standards (Knapp, 1985; Magee and Tseng, 1990). Key existing or proposed aspects of audit regulation argued to promote independence are: the existence of unlimited legal liability for auditors (Farmer *et al.*, 1987, p. 5); strong enforcement of standards; effective discipline of companies and auditors; control over the appointment and remuneration of auditors being taken from directors (ICAS, 1993, p. 57; APB, 1994); and the existence of an audit committee (Cadbury Report, 1992).

In addition to these principal factors, a wide variety of other factors have been discussed. These include, *inter alia*, long periods of tenure which are argued by some to reduce auditor independence (Mautz and Sharaf, 1961, p. 208; Beck *et al.*, 1988; Teoh and Lim, 1996); the auditee's financial condition (Knapp, 1985), which is argued to be negatively related to independence, due to the changing legal exposure; the degree of acculturation to audit firm norms (Farmer *et al.*, 1987); unpaid fees (Stamp and Moonitz, 1978); existence of audit committee and disclosure of non-audit fees (Teoh and Lim, 1996); and financial interest in auditee, most forms of which are prohibited in many countries (Pany and Reckers, 1980; Dykxhoorn and Sinning, 1982; Lindsay *et al.*, 1987). The impact of factors upon perceived auditor independence is, ultimately, an empirical question. Moreover, the nature and impact of factors may be affected by changes in the socio-economic and regulatory environments and, therefore, may not be stable either over time or across countries.

In some cases, the questionnaires present a list of factors to be assessed individually. In other cases, a limited number of factors are combined in 'case studies' with a repeated-measures, fixed-effects design, allowing investigation of interaction effects. Thus, the type of stimulus provided to the subjects could range from a statement of the factor, to a brief (typically one-line) description of a specific auditor–client relationship resulting from the factor, to a fairly extensive (typically one-half to one page) case study covering several factors. The factors examined are, in most studies, restricted to potential *threats* to independence, with potential *enhancement* factors not being considered.

The type of response required also varies, depending, to some extent, on the type of respondent. Some studies ask directly whether the factor/situation described would affect their perception of the auditor's independence (or their ability to withstand pressure from the client), while other studies ask how a particular decision (e.g., audit judgement, lending decision, investment decision) would be affected. Responses are captured as either simple dichotomous variables (i.e., independent/not independent) or an importance score (typically a five or seven-point Likert scale). Studies using binary (i.e., yes/no) responses typically investigate the issue of group consensus (defined in terms of a simple majority) for individual factors. Studies also vary in focus, with some investigating only one factor in detail, while others cover a subset, and yet others are based upon professional guidelines/rules. Analysis takes the form of descriptive statistics, combined with statistical tests of differences. All limited factor, factorial analysis of variance (ANOVA) studies have shown significant between-subjects differences in responses (e.g., Lindsay, 1990). Typically, four-factor models explain less than 30 per cent of the total variation in perceptions.

The UK studies are worthy of particular mention in relation to the case studies presented in this book. Firth's (1980) study was conducted at a time when radical change to the independence framework was being debated. Firth examined 29 specific auditor–client relationships related to fees, personal relationships, financial involvement with (or in the affairs of) clients, and conflicts of interest. Subsequent changes to the UK regulatory framework have since prohibited these and many of the other relationships studied by Firth.

The more up-to-date study by Beattie, Brandt and Fearnley (1998, 1999) surveys users, preparers and auditors after many of the significant changes in the UK regulatory framework had occurred (see section 1.3). They identify a large set of 45 economic and regulatory factors for investigation, which are reduced to 14 underlying factors for the finance director group and 15 underlying factors for the audit partner group.

The principal threat factors are found to relate to economic dependence (at firm, office, *and partner* level) and non-audit service provision, while the principal enhancement factors relate to regulatory changes introduced in the early 1990s (the existence of an audit committee, the risk of referral to the Financial Reporting Review Panel (FRRP), and the risk to the audit firm of loss of Registered Auditor status).

2.10.4 Studies of actual auditor independence

Actual auditor independence has been indirectly investigated empirically in a number of ways using publicly available data, using the experimental markets methodology, and (in a unique study) via direct questioning of auditors themselves. Each of these US studies will now be considered briefly, in turn.

Studies that use publicly available data tend to focus either on audit report qualifications or auditor sanctions. Neither Barkess and Simnett (1994) nor Roush *et al.* (1992) find evidence of a link between NAS provision and the type of audit report issued. St Pierre and Anderson (1982) examine the characteristics of 129 lawsuits against auditors in the US between 1960 and 1976. Of the 334 alleged errors involved, only eight (2 per cent) concerned auditor independence directly. To address the potential bias arising from the analysis of only published cases against auditors, St Pierre (1984) analyses a sample of complaints against auditors in the US at the state board level. Consistent with prior evidence, a very small proportion (seven out of 1,639) concerned auditor independence.

Using the experimental markets methodology, Dopuch and King (1991) find no evidence of a link between NAS and auditor independence. Finally, the study by Pearson (1987) is, to the best of our knowledge, unique, in that he uses a mail questionnaire to investigate actual independence impairment directly. The responses of 120 practising Certified Public Accountants (CPAs) were obtained using a randomised response technique to ensure anonymity. The percentages of respondents admitting to at least one act of 'auditing by conversation', pursuing engagements without the necessary expertise, and agreeing to inappropriate client requests/demands were 30 per cent, 22 per cent, and 10 per cent, respectively, suggesting that independence is compromised in a significant number of cases.

2.10.5 The influence of the auditor's personal attributes

A final strand of research focuses on the auditor's personal attributes, rather than outside influences, in the formation of individual judgements.

This research draws upon moral psychology to investigate the cognitive process underlying ethical reasoning and judgement formation. Ponemon and Gabhart (1990) use Kohlberg's stage model of moral development and ethical cognition to examine an auditor's implicit reasoning in the resolution of an independence conflict. This well-validated model distinguishes three levels of ethical cognition:

- *pre-conventional* – where the individual places self-interest well above the common interests of society and is sensitive to penalty attributes;
- *conventional* – where the individual conforms to the rules of society and is sensitive to affiliation attributes; and
- *post-conventional* – where the individual forms a judgement conforming to ethical principles and not to society's rules.

The findings of an experimental study using 119 audit partners and managers show that a systematic relationship between auditors' measured ethical cognition and hypothetical and audit conflict scenarios and their resolution of an independence conflict exists.[7] They also found that independence judgements are significantly influenced by factors relating to penalty and are less sensitive to affiliation factors (i.e., living up to what is expected by people). There was also a systematic relationship between ethical cognition and auditors' priority rankings of factors influencing auditor independence. In particular, subjects at the preconventional level of ethical cognition ranked freedom from pressure to retain client and existence of legal liability significantly higher than subjects at the conventional level.

Windsor and Ashkanasy (1995) extend Ponemon and Gabhart's (1990) study by including economic and personal belief variables, in particular client management bargaining power and belief in a just world, in addition to the level of moral reasoning development. Three styles of auditor decision-making emerged:

- *autonomous* – auditors who were responsive to personal beliefs and were more likely to resist client management power;
- *accommodating* – auditors who responded to both personal beliefs and client management power and who were least resistant to client management pressure; and
- *pragmatic* – auditors who were responsive to client management power, irrespective of beliefs.

These three styles correspond to individuals with high, mid, and low levels of moral reasoning, respectively.

---

[7] This basic result is confirmed in a later study by Sweeney and Roberts (1997).

The contingent influence of organisational culture, i.e., the moral atmosphere of the audit firm, is also being explored by researchers, although no clear results have yet emerged (Ashkanasy and Windsor, 1997; Sweeney and Roberts, 1997).

2.11 SECOND PARTNER REVIEW

It is generally believed that second partner review (SPR) is an internal monitoring mechanism that audit firms can introduce to improve actual (and perceived) auditor independence. Since its inception in the US in 1977, the SEC Practice Section (SECPS) has required all members to institute SPRs on all listed company audits (AICPA, 1986). These are pre-issuance reviews, as opposed to peer review, which occurs after the audit report is issued. However, firms can and do exercise considerable latitude in the internal policies and procedures that govern this process. Mautz and Matusiak (1988) have argued that the SECPS should specify:

- the responsibility of the concurring reviewer (they argue that the existence of a concurring reviewer in no way reduces the responsibility of the AEP; each has *different* responsibilities);
- the scope of work to be performed (they suggest that peer review standards provide a suitable model, whereby all key audit areas of the engagement be reviewed in depth);
- the timing of the review and role of the reviewer (they argue that it should be a cold review performed upon completion of the audit and that, to ensure objectivity, the reviewing partner should not also act as a consultant to the AEP); and
- reviewer qualifications (they argue that the reviewer should have prior experience of listed company audits and familiarity with the industry of the client company and have authority at least equal to that of the AEP).

In the UK, regulatory guidance on the issue of SPR is very recent. January 2000 saw the issuance of an exposure draft of a revised Statement of Auditing Standards 240 *Quality Control for Audit Work* (APB, 2000). A key new feature is the proposal that firms should undertake an independent (i.e., second partner) review of listed company audits before issuing the audit report (240.10 and 240.11). Additional requirements are that firms establish procedures to facilitate consultation in relation to difficult or contentious matters (240.6) and to deal with conflicting internal views (240.12). The proposed statement seeks to achieve a balance between individual and collective responsibilities, between personal accountability and teamworking, and between building quality into process and monitoring the results.

Matsumura and Tucker (1995) develop an analytical model of SRP. This single-period model assumes auditors to be economically rational and self-interested. Their example of this model demonstrates that SPR can cause the AEP to report with greater independence. Using the parameters specified in this example, Tucker and Matsumura (1997) experimentally test their model's predictions and find that SPRs do remove a considerable amount of bias.

2.12 CORPORATE GOVERNANCE AND AUDIT COMMITTEES

2.12.1 Corporate governance

The term 'corporate governance' has become widely used only relatively recently (e.g., Tricker, 1984) and the topic has developed as a multi-disciplinary research area. Corporate governance can be defined as the examination of the 'structures and processes associated with production, decision-making, control and so on within an organisation' (Keasey and Wright, 1993, p. 291). The two key aspects of governance are:

- supervision and monitoring of management performance i.e., the need for governance mechanisms to motivate management towards increasing business wealth (the *enterprise* aspect); and
- ensuring accountability of management to shareholders and other stakeholders (the *accountability* aspect).

These elements are closely linked and introduce both efficiency and stewardship dimensions to corporate governance.

The supervision of directors is effected through a variety of mechanisms: shareholders, debtholders, the market for corporate control, non-executive directors, executive remuneration, and compensation. The accountability of directors is effected by means of auditors, audit committees and executive remuneration (Keasey and Wright, 1993, p. 292). For the purposes of this book, we focus in this section on the financial reporting and accountability aspects of corporate governance, in particular the role of auditors and audit committees.

The need for supervision and accountability arises because of the divorce of ownership from control in modern corporations. The Anglo-American system, which is grounded in self-regulation and market sanctions, has in recent years been shown to have several weaknesses (e.g., creative accounting; unexpected business failures; short-termism).

2.12.2 Corporate governance reporting requirements

In 1991, the Cadbury Committee was set up by the Financial Reporting Council (FRC), the London Stock Exchange and the accountancy profession to address the financial aspects of corporate governance. It reported in 1992 (Cadbury Report, 1992). The Cadbury Report argued that the low level of confidence in financial reporting and auditing was caused by:

* the absence of a clear framework whereby the directors reviewed the company's internal controls;
* the looseness of accounting standards; and
* pressures on auditor independence.

The report's recommendations were presented as a voluntary Code of Best Practice. Compliance with the code was, however, made obligatory by the London Stock Exchange for listed companies after June 1993. In the area of financial reporting, the Code's recommendations are intended to improve the quality of communication between the company, its auditors and its shareholders. It is recommended that:

* the board of directors include a significant number of independent, non-executive directors and that an audit committee comprising independent directors be formed;
* that the audit committee should:
    (i) review financial statements before submission to the full board;
    (ii) ensure adequate resources for the internal audit function and co-ordination of that function with the external auditors;
    (iii) appoint and assess the remuneration of the external auditors; and,
    (iv) discuss the results of the audit with the external auditors;
* that the board report on the effectiveness of internal controls and the company's going concern status and that the external auditor review this report.

The Stock Exchange listing rules require that companies make a statement of compliance with the Code in their annual report and that the auditor review this statement. Further, the APB requires that a report on this review is issued to the company management and strongly recommends that this report be included in the annual report.

Since the Cadbury Report, there have been, to date, three further corpo-rate governance reports. The Greenbury Report (1995) focuses on directors' remuneration and requires extensive disclosures on this matter. The Hampel Report (1998) was a general review of corporate governance matters, as had been called for by the Cadbury Report. Its main thrust was that share-holders should accept greater responsibility for corporate governance and many commentators expressed disappointment that the scope of its propos-als were not wider. The Hampel Report was concerned that too much emphasis was being placed on accountability at the expense of enterprise and therefore sought to introduce general principles rather than detailed propositions (Short *et al.*, 1999). This can be seen as a move towards anti-formalism (see section 2.2).

A principal contribution of the Hampel Report was to prepare a Com-bined Code that consolidated the work of the Cadbury and Greenbury Committees with its own work (Committee on Corporate Governance, 1998). The Combined Code includes 14 principles of good governance and 45 best practice provisions. These are grouped under four headings:

- directors;
- directors' remuneration;
- relations with shareholders; and
- accountability and audit.

Of these provisions, 19 derive from Cadbury, a further 8 from Greenbury, and the remaining 18 from Hampel. The Combined Code is now appended to the London Stock Exchange Listing rules. This requires companies to make a narrative statement in their annual report on how they have applied the 14 principles. Directors must also include a compliance statement in respect of the provisions, seven of which must be reviewed by the auditor (APB, 1998a).

Following the issuance of the Combined Code, APB Bulletin 10 (1998a) which has persuasive rather than prescriptive status, reviews auditors' responsibilities in relation to corporate governance and their communication to users of the annual report. It is recommended that a statement of auditors' responsibilities in relation to the whole annual report be included in the annual report. This would eliminate the need for a separate auditors' report on the directors' compliance statement in the annual report. In relation to internal controls, and in anticipation of the guidance from the Turnbull Report (ICAEW, 1999), auditors are advised to seek an explanation from directors as to how they have ensured that their review procedures have cov-ered operational and compliance controls and risk management. If the audi-tors are unable to conclude that the directors' statement is substantiated, then they must report this in their report on the financial statements. In relation to the independence of non-executive directors, the APB advise that it is sufficient for auditors to confirm that an audit committee has been formed, has a written terms of reference, and comprises a majority of independent non-executive directors as identified in the annual report.

Most recently, the Turnbull Report (ICAEW, 1999) on internal controls has been published. This is an area that previous reports had either not addressed or not addressed successfully. The report proposes that the board should, as a minimum, disclose whether or not there is an on-going process for identifying, evaluating and managing the company's key risks that is regularly reviewed by the board and accords with the guidance. The board should also disclose how it has reviewed the effectiveness of the process.

2.12.3   Audit committees

The Cadbury Report highlighted the value of audit committees as an internal monitoring device supportive of good corporate governance. Audit committees were seen as a mechanism to ensure that 'an appropriate relationship exists between the auditor and the management whose financial statements they are auditing' (para. 5.7). By 1995, all FTSE 100 companies and all but four of the FTSE mid-250 companies had established audit committees (Conyon, 1995). How effective these audit committees have been in enhancing financial reporting, as yet, is unclear in the UK (Collier, 1996; Spira, 1998). However, recent research in the US does provide some evidence of a positive link between the presence of an audit committee and more reliable financial reporting (Kalbers and Fogarty, 1993; McMullen, 1996).

A recent PwC survey of Chief Executive Officers (CEOs) and audit committee chairmen of the FTSE 250 companies has revealed 10 characteristics that the 'best' audit committees have in common:

- non-executive directors with relevant industry experience;
- at least some members with a sound grasp of current developments in financial matters;
- openness to regular training;
- distinct appointment policies and criteria, succession planning and membership rotation;
- clear delineation between their role and that of the full board;
- clear brief and strategies for setting an appropriate control culture within their organisations;
- regular, clearly structured meetings held at least four times a year;
- regular flow of relevant, timely information from company executives;

- at least annually, a private meeting between each of the external and internal audit leaders; and
- self-assessment procedures (Hughes, 1999).

In the US, the National Association of Corporate Directors convened a Blue Ribbon Commission on Audit Committees in 1999, tasked with preparing practical guidance on audit committee duties and how to discharge them effectively (NACD, 2000).

2.12.4 Communication between external auditors and audit committees

Individually, external auditors and audit committees each have a significant role to play in ensuring directors' accountability. They can also be mutually reinforcing, given the right communication links between them. The APB has noted the potential importance of audit committees in both enhancing the value of external audit to shareholders and helping to reinforce auditors' objectivity and commitment to high-quality auditing (APB, 1996, *Next Steps*). The Hampel Report (1998, para. 6.9) stated that audit committees form 'an essential safeguard of auditor independence and objectivity'.

For these reasons, the APB (1998b) issued a non-mandatory briefing paper that comments on the structure and content of external auditors' communication with audit committees with a view to assisting in the development of good practice. Several key comments relate specifically to the auditor–client management relationship:

- direct communication between the auditors and the audit committee may on occasions be necessary as a means of anticipating and facilitating the resolution of potentially contentious issues (§2.8);
- in most circumstances, the auditor's discussion with the audit committee will include a commentary on any material differences of view between auditors and management that arose during the audit, and how these differences were resolved (§3.15); and
- it may be helpful to discuss the accounting policies applied by the company, any changes in the accounting policies and give a commentary on the overall degree of prudence consequent upon those policies and the overall transparency, clarity and quality of the annual report (§3.16).

In the US, increased auditor contact with audit committees was one of the recommendations of the Blue Ribbon Committee on Improving the Effectiveness of Corporate Audit Committees (NYSE/NASD, 1999).[8]

2.13 AUDIT EFFECTIVENESS

Recently in the US the Public Oversight Board's (POB) Panel on Audit Effectiveness issued an Exposure Draft (POB, 2000). Interestingly, their findings and recommendations are based, in part, upon in-depth reviews of the quality of a significant number of public company audits. Their principal recommendations fall into five areas:

* the conduct of audit (definitive auditing standards, comprehensive and vigorous audit methodologies, and effective peer review);
* leadership and practices of the audit firms (professional leadership, professional development, personnel management and time pressures on auditors);
* auditor independence – non-audit services (the panel members could not agree whether an exclusionary ban was desirable; pre-approval of significant non-audit services by the audit committee recommended);
* governance of the auditing profession (unify the profession's self-governance system under a strengthened POB); and
* international (recommended that audit firms implement uniform audit methodologies world-wide and recommended to the International Federation of Accountants (IFA) that the self-regulatory structure of the international auditing profession meet certain important criteria).

---

[8] Unfortunately, one of the first studies to investigate this requirement (using experimental methods) finds that it does not mitigate against the tendency of auditors to accept a client-preferred, aggressive method of accounting when engagement pressure is high (Kadous *et al.*, 1999).

3 Questionnaire Stage of Study

3.1 OVERVIEW

In this chapter, we present a summary of the questionnaire stage of our study, in which 153 FDs and 244 AEPs comment on the frequency with which 46 audit and audit-related issues are discussed, are negotiated, and result in a change to the accounting numbers and/or disclosures. First, the methods used are outlined, then the results are summarised.

3.2 METHODS

This chapter provides a summary of the questionnaire stage of the study. A full account of the sample selection, research instrument, questionnaire administration procedures, and results can be found in Beattie, Brandt and Fearnley (2000).

Two samples, one of listed company FDs and one of listed company AEPs, were selected. To provide a specific context within which to respond, AEPs were asked to respond with reference to one specific listed company client; specifically, 'the listed company for whom they act as engagement partner which generates *the largest total recurring fee* (*including non-audit services*) in their listed portfolio' (emphasis in original). Respondents were asked to indicate which of 46 itemised issues had 'been the subject of discussion and/or negotiation between you and your auditor/client X over the last three years, and whether any of these discussions or negotiations resulted in any change to you/your client's proposed accounting numbers or disclosures'. For the FD sample of 300, 153 usable responses were received, representing a response rate of 51 per cent. For the AEP sample of 307, 244 usable responses were received, representing a response rate of 80 per cent.

Discussion can involve the simple exchange of information or a debate that occurs without either party having a preconceived view that it wishes to persuade the other party to agree to. The mean number of issues discussed was 15 for the FDs and 18 for the AEPs.[1]

3.3 RESULTS

The ten issues relating to the production and audit of annual financial statements that are most frequently discussed by the auditor and auditee are given in Table 3.1. The frequencies and ranks are given for the FD and AEP samples combined and separately, with issues being listed in decreasing frequency for the combined sample. It is clear that the level of discussion activity over the three-year period could reasonably be described as high: four issues are discussed by more than 50 per cent of FD respondents and 12 issues are discussed by more than 50 per cent of AEP respondents. The rankings for the FD and AEP samples separately are very similar, although there is a general tendency for AEPs to indicate more frequently than FDs that discussion took place.

Of these issues cited by FDs (AEPS), 4(4) relate to compliance, 1(2) relates to audit-related matters, 1(3) relates to accounting principles and practice, 2(1) relates to the balance sheet and 2(–) relates to disclosure. The high ranking of issues ranked 1, 2 and 5 by the combined groups is to be expected, given that they were new requirements and apply to all companies. In addition, the disclosure of directors' remuneration packages and stock options (ranked 2 and 3 by FDs and AEPs, respectively) is an extremely sensitive issue for directors, due to the media attention it attracts.

The high ranking of nature and content of management letters (ranked 3 and 2 by FDs and AEPs, respectively) is also to be expected. Management letters are one way in which value can be added to the audit, with points relating to internal controls and accounting policies being most valued by companies (Manson *et al.*, 1994). Management letters can, however, include implicit or explicit criticism of the executive directors. In consequence, the high incidence of discussion can be seen as a behavioural response to the personal, sensitive nature of the issue.

It is also interesting to note some of the issues which do *not* rank highly (not shown in table). For example, despite the now widespread acceptance of the importance of accounting for the environment (Gray *et al.*, 1993), environmental liabilities/contingencies rank a lowly 41 and 40 by FDs and AEPs, respectively, while, despite the well-documented expectation gap,

---

[1] The medians fell only slightly below the mean values, indicating a fairly symmetrical distribution. The standard deviation was 8 for both groups, indicating a high level of variation among respondents.

Table 3.1   Ten most frequently discussed issues

Rank[1]	Issue	% indicating discussion took place				
		FD and AP samples combined (n = 397)[2]	FD sample (n = 153)	AP sample (n = 244)	FD sample rank	AP sample rank
1	Timing of implementation of new regulatory requirements (FRSs, Cadbury, etc.)	84.4	80.4	86.9	1	1
2	Statements in the annual report concerning compliance with the Cadbury Code of Best Practice re disclosure of directors' remuneration packages and stock options	74.3	72.5	75.4	2	3
3	Nature and content of management letters	73.0	64.7	78.3	3	2
4	Goodwill	54.4	43.8	61.1	13 =	4
5	Statements in the annual report concerning compliance with the Cadbury Code of Best Practice re existence and composition of audit committee	53.7	51.6	54.8	4	8
6 = a	Deferred tax assets/liabilities	52.6	48.4	55.3	6 =	7
6 = b	Extent of audit of internal control	52.6	42.5	59.0	16	5
8 = a	Reorganisation costs	50.9	49.0	52.0	5	10
8 = b	Stock Exchange reporting requirements	50.9	40.5	57.4	17	6
10	Group matters: fair values on acquisition	49.4	43.8	52.9	13 =	9

[1] Issues are ranked in decreasing frequency for the combined FD and AEP samples.
[2] FD = finance director; AEP = audit engagement partner.

Table 3.2   Ten most frequently negotiated issues

Rank[1]	Rank from Table 3.1	Issue	% indicating negotiation took place				
			FD and AEP combined samples (n = 397)[2]	FD sample (n = 153)	AEP sample (n = 244)	FD sample rank	AEP sample rank
1	8 =	Reorganisation costs	27.0	15.0	34.4	5 =	1
2	34	Unexpected audit-related fees	26.2	24.2	27.5	1	3 =
3	10	Group matters: fair values on acquisition	23.4	17.0	27.5	3	3 =
4	3	Nature and content of management letters	22.9	10.5	30.7	7	2
5	32 =	Level of non-audit fees from incumbent auditor	20.2	20.3	20.1	2	7 =
6	39	Attempts to renegotiate agreed audit fees	19.4	16.3	21.3	4	6
7	15	Stock and work-in-progress	18.1	15.0	20.1	5 =	7 =
8	22	Group matters: reorganisation costs on acquisition	16.6	7.8	22.1	11	5
9	1	Timing of implementation of new regulatory requirements (FRSs, Cadbury, etc.)	15.4	9.8	18.9	8	9 =
10	6 =	Deferred tax assets/liabilities	14.9	8.5	18.9	9 =	9 =

[1] Issues are ranked in decreasing frequency for the combined FD and AEP samples.
[2] FD = finance director; AEP = audit engagement partner.

ability to detect fraud and other irregularities ranks only 39 and 35 by FDs and AEPs, respectively.

The mean number of issues negotiated was 3 for the FDs and 6 for the AEPs.[2] The ten most frequently negotiated issues are reported in Table 3.2, whose format is identical to that of Table 3.1, with the addition of a column showing the comparable ranks from Table 3.1 (see second column). The extent of negotiation is reasonably high: two issues are negotiated by more than 20 per cent of FD respondents and eight issues are negotiated by more than 20 per cent of AEP respondents. As in the case of discussion, the rankings for the FD and AEP samples separately are very similar, and there is a general tendency for AEPs to indicate more frequently than FDs that negotiation took place.

Of these issues, accounting principles and practice issues and audit-related issues dominate. The high rank of reorganisation costs, fair values on acquisition and reorganisation costs on acquisition indicates that, despite Financial Reporting Standard (FRS) 3, reported earnings can still be 'managed' to some degree – the bottom line used by the City has simply moved down to 'super-exceptionals' (Griffiths, 1996, ch. 1). The high rank of stock and work-in-progress and deferred tax assets/liabilities may be attributed to their highly subjective nature relative to other accounting issues (Griffiths, 1996, chs 5 and 13).

Out of the 46 issues examined above, 35 could give rise to changes in the accounting numbers and/or disclosures, whereas the 11 audit-related matters could not. The mean number of issues giving rise to a change in the accounting numbers was 1.3 for the FDs and 3.4 for the AEPs.[3] The mean number of issues giving rise to a change in the disclosures was 2.9 for the FDs and 6.1 for the AEPs.[4]

The frequency with which changes to the financial statements arose from discussion and/or negotiation is reported in Table 3.3. Once again, our initial impression is that the audit process has a significant impact upon corporate financial statements: more than 10 per cent of respondents indicated a change to the accounting numbers for 10 issues, with the corresponding number of issues being 23 for a change to disclosures. Naturally, the top ten issues resulting in changes to the accounting numbers relate to

---

[2] The medians fell only slightly below the mean values, indicating a fairly symmetrical distribution. The standard deviation was 3 for the FDs and 5 for the AEPs, indicating a reasonably high level of variation among respondents, especially APs.

[3] The median values were 0 and 3, respectively, while the standard deviations were 1.9 for the FDs and 3.0 for the AEPs, indicating a reasonably high level of variation among respondents.

[4] The median values were 2 and 5, respectively, while the standard deviations were 3.4 for the FDs and 4.7 for the AEPs, indicating a reasonably high level of variation among respondents.

Table 3.3 Frequency of changes to accounting numbers and disclosures resulting from discussion and negotiation

Issue	Rank for change to accounting numbers	Rank for change to disclosures	Rank from Table 3.2	% indicating change to accounting numbers					% indicating change to disclosures				
				FD and AEP samples combined (n = 397)²	FD sample (n = 153)	AEP sample (n = 244)	FD sample rank	AEP sample rank	FD and AEP samples combined (n = 397)²	FD sample (n = 153)	AEP sample (n = 244)	FD sample rank	AEP sample rank
Reorganisation costs	1	3	1	25.4	9.2	35.7	4	1	26.2	13.7	34.0	5 =	3
Group matters: fair values on acquisition	2	4	3	21.2	10.5	27.9	3	2	22.4	12.4	28.7	7	4
Stock and work-in-progress	3 =	28	7	16.1	12.4	18.4	1	7	6.5	3.9	8.2	25 =	28
Goodwill	3 =	8 =	12	16.1	7.2	21.7	5 =	3	18.6	6.5	26.2	20 =	6
Group matters: merger or acquisition accounting	5 =	8 =	11	14.4	5.2	20.1	9	4	18.6	11.8	23.0	8 =	9
Deferred tax assets/liabilities	5 =	16	10	14.4	7.2	18.9	5 =	6	13.6	7.8	17.2	15 =	14
Operating and finance leases	7 =	6	19	13.6	7.2	17.6	5 =	8	19.6	11.8	24.6	8 =	7
Group matters: reorganisation costs on acquisition	7 =	11 =	8	13.6	4.6	19.3	10 =	5	16.1	8.5	20.9	13 =	11
Off-balance sheet items	9	5	13	11.8	6.5	15.2	8	9 =	20.4	7.8	28.3	15 =	5
Liabilities	10	29	14 =	10.6	3.3	15.2	15 =	9 =	5.0	2.0	7.0	30	29
Prior year adjustments	11	24	26	9.1	11.1	7.8	2	18	9.3	6.5	11.1	20 =	25
Group matters: subsidiary undertakings	12 =	21	20 =	8.1	4.6	10.2	10 =	12 =	10.8	5.9	13.9	23	20 =
Debtors	12 =	32	18	8.1	3.3	11.1	15 =	11	3.0	3.3	2.9	28 =	32
Fixed assets	12 =	25 =	20 =	8.1	4.6	10.2	10 =	12 =	9.1	7.2	10.2	18 =	26 =
Deferred pension or other post retirement benefit assets/liabilities	15	10	27	6.8	2.6	9.4	18 =	14	16.6	7.8	22.1	15 =	10

Table 3.3 Continued

Issue	Rank for change to accounting numbers	Rank for change to disclosures	Rank from Table 3.2	% indicating change to accounting numbers					% indicating change to disclosures				
				FD and AEP samples combined (n = 397)[2]	FD sample (n = 153)	AEP sample (n = 244)	FD sample rank	AEP sample rank	FD and AEP samples combined (n = 397)[2]	FD sample (n = 153)	AEP sample (n = 244)	FD sample rank	AEP sample rank
Investments	16	27	22 =	6.5	3.9	8.2	14 =	15 =	8.8	6.5	10.2	20 =	26 =
Group matters: associated undertakings	17 =	17 =	25	6.0	4.6	7.0	10 =	20 =	13.4	8.5	16.4	13 =	15
Contingent contracts (e.g., consignment stock, sale and repurchase/ leaseback, factoring, etc.)	17 =	20	24	6.0	2.6	8.2	18 =	15 =	11.3	7.2	13.9	18 =	20 =
Capital issues of debt or equity convertibles	19	23	29	5.5	2.6	7.4	18 =	19	10.3	3.9	14.3	25 =	18 =
Regularity of fixed asset revaluations	20	25 =	33	5.3	0.7	8.2	25 =	15 =	9.1	3.9	12.3	25 =	14
Timing of implementation of new regulatory requirements (FRSs, Cadbury, etc.)	21	1	9	4.5	0.7	7.0	25 =	20 =	41.8	29.4	49.6	1	1
Issues arising from the requirement to comply with the Companies Acts and Accounting Standards not specifically itemised in the questionnaire	22	13	17	4.3	1.3	6.1	22 =	22	15.4	9.2	19.3	12	12
Statements in the annual report concerning compliance with the Cadbury Code of Best Practice re disclosure of directors' remuneration packages and stock options	23	2	14 =	3.8	1.3	5.3	22 =	23	36.0	26.1	42.2	2	2

Post balance sheet events	24	17 =	30 =	3.3	2.6	7.3	18 =	24	13.4	9.8	15.6	11	16 =
Contingencies other than environmental	25	19	30 =	2.8	3.3	2.5	15 =	27	12.3	3.3	18	28 =	13
Environmental liabilities/ contingencies	26	30	38	2.5	1.3	3.3	22 =	25	3.5	1.3	4.9	32	30
Stock Exchange reporting requirements	27	7	30 =	2.0	0.7	2.9	25 =	26	18.9	11.8	23.4	8 =	8
Information provided to, or other form of communication with, a regulator (e.g., Bank of England, Financial Reporting Review Panel, etc.)	28	31	41	0.8	0.7	0.8	25 =	28 =	3.3	2.0	4.1	30 =	31
Brands	29	33	44 =	0.5	0.0	0.8	30 =	28 =	1.8	0.7	2.5	33 =	33
Related party transactions	30 =	22	36	0.3	0.7	0.0	25 =	31 =	10.6	4.6	14.3	24	18 =
Going concern	30 =	15	34	0.3	0.0	0.4	30 =	30	13.9	13.7	13.9	5 =	20 =
Statements in the annual report concerning compliance with the Cadbury Code of Best Practice re existence and composition of audit committee	32 =	11 =	37	0.0	0.0	0.0	30 =	31 =	16.1	17.0	15.6	3	16 =
Statements in the annual report concerning compliance with the Cadbury Code of Best Practice re existence and composition of remuneration committee	32 =	14	39 =	0.0	0.0	0.0	30 =	31 =	14.4	15.0	13.9	4	20 =
Maintenance of proper accounting records	32 =	34	43	0.0	0.0	0.0	30 =	31 =	0.5	0.7	0.4	33 =	34
Fraud and illegal acts	32 =	35	46	0.0	0.0	0.0	30 =	31 =	0.0	0.0	0.0	35	35

1 Issues are ranked in decreasing frequency for change to accounting numbers for the combined FD and AEP samples.
2 FD = finance director; AEP = audit engagement partner.

accounting principles and practice or balance sheet areas, whereas the top ten issues resulting in a change to disclosures also included three compliance issues. The FD and AEP rankings were once again very similar.

In response to an open-ended question regarding the factors influencing the outcome of interactions, respondents referred to:

- the client's general attitude, in particular their wish to 'stick to the rules';
- the need for compromise, i.e., to balance technical accounting considerations with commercial considerations;[5]
- the influence of third parties, in particular audit firm technical departments and client audit committees;
- fear of referral to the FRRP;
- the threat of audit qualification; and
- the quality of the auditor's argument in support of their position.

3.4   SUMMARY

This chapter has presented evidence from a postal survey of FDs and AEPs concerning the extent, nature, and outcome of interactions between these two primary parties. The level of interaction activity is characterised as 'high'. Four issues are discussed by more than 50 per cent of FD respondents and 12 issues are discussed by more than 50 per cent of AEP respondents. By comparison, two issues are negotiated by more than 20 per cent of FD respondents and eight issues are negotiated by more than 20 per cent of AEP respondents. Compliance issues are found to dominate discussions, while accounting and fee issues dominate negotiations. In aggregate, auditor/auditee interactions have a significant impact upon the content of financial reports, the mean number of reported changes to the accounting numbers (disclosures) being 1.3 (2.9) and 3.4 (6.1) for the FD and AEP groups, respectively.

The level of discussion revealed suggests that the traditional agency model of audit is an inadequate characterisation of the activities of external auditors in relation to the client company. The auditor is found to be a source of support and advice, with the final accounts generally resulting from a co-operative effort. However, in the case of significant accounting issues, and where the main parties are unable to agree, third parties (i.e., audit firm technical department, independent internal second opinion, audit committee, and (indirectly) the FRRP) are influential in the final outcome. This indicates that, at the negotiation stage, interactions involve multiple parties.

---

[5] For example, one FD commented 'the outcome of negotiations have satisfactorily taken into account technical and commercial considerations', while an AEP remarked 'it is left to the auditor to make commercial judgements on the issues at the end of the day'.

Part II
The Case Studies

4 Introduction to the Case Studies

4.1 OVERVIEW

In this chapter, we first present relevant prior research on negotiation, most of which relates to non-audit settings. We then describe the research methods used for the matched interview stage of the study. We first describe how the six case companies were selected and approached, and the interview techniques used. We then give an introductory explanation of the method of analysis used for the six cases (a more detailed explanation is provided in Chapter 11, prior to the cross-case analysis). The final section presents an overview of the six cases that follow in Chapters 5 to 10.

4.2 NEGOTIATION AND CONFLICT IN A GENERIC SETTING – THEORY

The generic process of negotiation, studied across a wide range of settings, has been the subject of detailed analysis in the social sciences. The concepts used in this literature require careful definition. *Negotiation* is defined as 'processes of interaction between disputing parties whereby, without compulsion by a third-party adjudicator, they endeavour to come to an interdependent, *joint decision* concerning the terms of agreement on the issues between them' (Gulliver, 1979, p. 79, emphasis in original). A *dispute* arises 'when the two parties are unable and/or unwilling to resolve their disagreement' (Gulliver, 1979, p. 75). Negotiation encompasses *bargaining*, which 'consists of the presentation and exchange of more or less specific proposals for the terms of agreement on particular issues' (Gulliver, 1979, p. 71).

The problem faced by negotiators is that of 'being interdependent while having interests which are in contrast to those of the other party' (Mastenbroek, 1989, p. 56). In addition, 'negotiating presumes a certain symmetry in the balance of power' (Mastenbroek, 1989, p. 63). *Power* can be defined as 'the ability of one actor to overcome resistance in achieving a desired result' (Brass and Burkhardt, 1993). *Conflict* can be defined as 'the interaction of interdependent people who perceive the opposition of goals, aims, and (/or) values, and who see the other party as potentially interfering with the realization of these goals (aims, or values)' (quoted in Nicotera, 1993).

For the purpose of our study, we use Gulliver's (1979) analytical framework. This framework captures economic, social, and psychological aspects of the negotiation process. It has been developed from actual cases which span a wide range of social, cultural and economic contexts and we consider it to be the most appropriate for this research. It is a non-game model that recognises the general processes in negotiation that create and sustain the internal dynamics. Two distinct, though interconnected, processes occur simultaneously – a *cyclical process* and a *developmental process* (Gulliver, 1979).

The *cyclical process* involves the ongoing exchange of information between the parties (perhaps incorporating information from third parties). The kind of information exchanged depends on the current phase of negotiation, and may include information about procedural rules, appeals to norms, factual information, threats, and promises. When a party receives information, they assess it, adjust their own preference set and their expectations of the other party, and revise their overall strategy. They then make a tactical decision about what information to pass to the other party (Gulliver, 1979, p. 84). Typical tactics are:

- to concentrate on obtaining further information;
- to change the subject matter of the information exchange when a current issue seems threatening;
- to focus on the affective tone of the relationship;
- to match the behaviour of the other party, i.e., offer antagonism for antagonism;
- to offer opposing behaviour to that of the other party; and
- to make concessions. (Gulliver, 1979, pp. 109–11).

As stated above, the kind of information exchanged depends upon the negotiation phase involved. Factual data, recourse to norms, threats and promises may all be exchanged.

The *developmental process* occurs through successive iterations of this cycle, as they drive the negotiation through a number of overlapping phases. Each phase has a particular focus of attention, typically: formulation of agenda and working definitions of the conflict issues, preliminary statements of demands and offers, narrowing of differences, and final bargaining. The causes of convergence and the nature of the outcome can often be explained in terms of appeals to norms and other sources of power. It is the conversion of *potential power* into effective persuasive strength (not actual power) which is important (Gulliver, 1979, ch. 6). Table 4.1 represents this

Table 4.1 The developmental process in negotiation

Stage	Label	Description
1.	Agenda definition	May occur through discussions specifically focused on this goal or emerge from early information exchanges
2.	Exploring the field (emphasis on differences)	Each party reiterates and develops initial stands; information exchanged often deliberately imprecise because expectations and preferences incomplete and inconsistent and want to avoid restrictive commitments; assertive rejection, rather than reasoned argument, of the other's case, and shows of strength, typical; concentration on differences and concomitant antagonism
3.	Narrowing differences (emphasis on tolerable agreement)	Shift in orientation towards co-operation; parties become increasingly clear about dimensions of dispute and their preferences; where there are multiple issues, each with several attributes, common negotiation strategies are: – agenda method – issues taken one-by-one – agree on key issues and focus on them – reduce issues to a common objective, e.g. money – identify and deal with easy issues first – engage in the trading of issues
4.	Preliminaries to final bargaining	Search for a viable bargaining range within which parties are willing to accept any outcome rather than have no agreement; refine persisting differences; test trading possibilities; and (perhaps) develop a bargaining 'formula'
5.	Final bargaining	The exchange of more or less specific, substantive proposals; preference sets and expectations are fairly clear, so proposals are either a determined reiteration of position or a concession; possible situations range from the clearing up of minor details, through considering remaining differences, to no viable range yet discovered; convergent concession-making is the predominant behaviour

cyclical process in terms of five stages.[1] In the event of failure to reach agreement in the audit context, the auditor may qualify the audit report, communicate with shareholders, and/or either not seek reappointment or resign.

We selected this particular framework because it is less abstract than game-theoretic approaches, which are now discussed briefly. The early decision-theoretic approach (Kinney, 1975a,b) does not address the impact of the auditor's behaviour on the manager's reporting decisions. The more recent Fellingham and Newman (1985) game-theoretic approach does permit the auditor's testing strategy to influence the manager's reporting decisions. For many parameter values, a Nash equilibrium strategy, rather than a co-operative strategy, is the predicted outcome.[2]

These models have generally been tested using experimental methods. For example, Fisher *et al.* (1996) test the Fellingham and Newman (1985) model, and find that the model generally fails to predict a significant proportion of observed auditor and client behaviour, with the observed behaviour involving mutual co-operation. These models are acknowledged to be 'highly stylized and abstract away from some of the important and interesting features in the extant auditing environment' (Fisher *et al.*, 1996, p. 157). Recently, Hansen and Watts (1997) report on the first empirical test of the two alternative approaches using archival accounting data, finding that the game-theoretic model better describes the auditor–manager interaction.[3]

Alternative non-game models fail to consider features that, *a priori*, we would expect to be important in the audit conflict context; features such as norms, values and beliefs, power and third-party influences.

4.3   NEGOTIATION STRATEGIES IN NON-AUDIT SETTINGS – EMPIRICAL STUDIES

Many empirical studies of bargaining focus on outcomes and contextual factors, leaving the actual bargaining process as a black box. Kipnis and Schmidt (1983) provide a useful review of studies that look inside this black box and investigate the exercise of 'influence' (tactical actions).

---

[1] Gulliver (1979) includes a further 3 stages: the search for an arena precedes agenda definition, and ritualisation of outcome and execution of outcome occur after final bargaining. These stages have been omitted here as they are not expected to be of great significance in the audit context. The precise number of stages in negotiation models varies.
[2] A co-operative game theory model is explored by Hatherly *et al.* (1996).
[3] This study uses audit fee data and data on the incidence of five earnings management techniques for 112 UK companies.

They question the utility of deductively derived schemes for classifying influence on the grounds that they are neither mutually exclusive nor exhaustive and that they blur the distinction between potential influence and actual influence.

Kipnis *et al.* (1980) undertake an empirical study of managerial use of influence within organisations. They first asked managers to describe actual incidents and from this constructed a questionnaire containing 58 influence tactics. Responses to this questionnaire were factor analysed to reveal seven dimensions of influence. Kipnis and Schmidt (1982) develop a new scale to measure these seven influence strategies:

- reason – the use of facts and data to support the development of a logical argument;
- coalition – the mobilisation of other people in the organisation;
- ingratiation – the use of impression management, flattery, and the creation of goodwill;
- bargaining – the use of negotiation through the exchange of benefits or favours;
- assertiveness – the use of a direct and forceful approach;
- higher authority – gaining the support of higher levels in the organisation to back-up requests; and
- sanctions – the use of organisationally derived rewards and punishments.

4.4 NEGOTIATION IN AUDIT SETTINGS – EMPIRICAL STUDIES

As explained in section 2.4, there are very few studies that provide direct evidence in relation to auditor–client interactions. Gibbins and Newton (1994) investigate the response to accountability relationships in public accounting firms. They recognise that the public accountant has multiple sources of accountability, including hierarchical superiors and clients. They predict nine response strategies to accountability situations – five are final actions and four are information gathering delay responses: routine action; uninformed compliance; grudging compliance; adjusted compliance; defensive non-compliance; persuasion; self-discovery; external discovery; and self-support.

Using a questionnaire in which public accountants were asked to disclose accountability situations, they find that the most frequently occurring responses were, in descending order: routine actions (28.2 per cent); persuasion (17.1 per cent); defensive non-compliance (16.5 per cent); adjusted compliance (8.2 per cent); external discovery (8.2 per cent); self-discovery

(7.8 per cent); self-support (4.9 per cent); grudging compliance (4.1 per cent); non-defensive non-compliance (1.6 per cent); and uninformed compliance (0.8 per cent).

Of most direct relevance to the present study is a working paper by Gibbins *et al.* (1999). Ninety-three experienced Canadian public accounting firm partners responded in the context of a specific negotiation example selected from their experience. Client perceptions were not surveyed. They conclude that negotiation is important, frequent and context-sensitive.

They find that agreement was reported to have been reached somewhere between both parties' original positions in 41 per cent of cases, on the auditor's original position in 32 per cent of cases, and on the client's original position in 4 per cent of cases. A new solution was generated in 16 per cent of cases. The two factors said to be of most importance to the negotiation were 'accounting and disclosure standards' and 'audit firms' accounting expertise'.

4.5   HOW THE CASE COMPANIES WERE SELECTED AND APPROACHED

This part of our book contains the individual case studies and their associated within-case analysis. These cases were identified from the questionnaire study, the key findings of which are reported in Chapter 3. As part of the questionnaire, respondents were asked whether they were willing to be interviewed to enable us to explore with them, in greater depth, the responses that they had made. Of the 153 FD respondents, 23 indicated willingness to be interviewed. The questionnaires received from these respondents were reviewed, and six FDs who indicated high levels of negotiation and discussion were approached for interview. An effort was made to select companies representing a range of company sizes, industry sectors and audit firms (Eisenhardt, 1989). In analysis of this type, the recommended optimum number of cases is four to ten (Eisenhardt, 1989). All six respondents agreed to see us. A request was made for permission to record the interview. Written assurances were given at the same time that neither the interviewee nor the company would be identified or identifiable in any subsequent publication.

Two of the principal researchers were involved in conducting the interviews. Both have extensive experience in the audit of listed companies and therefore were able to identify with and fully understand the issues being discussed. Before the interviews took place, we studied the company's annual reports for the period covered by the questionnaire to familiarise ourselves with the company and its activities and to pick out, where possible, the issues referred to in the questionnaire responses.

No standard interview guidelines or questions were developed as each case was different. FDs were asked to 'tell the story', from their perspective, of the discussions and negotiations with their auditors referred to in their questionnaire responses, and encouraged to raise any other issues they wanted to (Thompson, 1988). The interviewer employed both neutral, conversational prompts and a laddering technique. This technique requires that the interviewer keeps asking 'why?', working backwards to antecedent conditions and forwards to anticipated effects (Brown, 1992, p. 293). Where necessary, subsidiary prompts used were:

- who got involved in the various stages of the interaction (e.g., FD, audit committee, main board)?
- what was the role of the audit committee?
- were negotiations conducted informally or at formal meetings?
- what information was exchanged?
- how did the information you received alter your preferences, your expectations of the other party, your strategy (if at all)?
- were any threats or promises made?
- what was the tone of the exchanges?
- were you happy with the outcome?

To support the accuracy of the interviewee's statements, reference was made to the company's annual reports where the outcomes of some of the discussions and negotiations were observable, thus providing assurance about the reliability of the evidence collected (Yin, 1984, p. 80).

At the close of each interview, we asked the FD for permission to interview the audit partner with whom the discussions and negotiations had taken place. (Without the client's permission, no AEP would talk to us because of professional confidentiality rules.) All the FDs interviewed gave their consent, and in all cases the key contact was the audit firm's designated AEP, confirming that this was the primary relationship. In one case, however, the condition was that the FD also wanted to be present. We asked the interviewee to effect an introduction to the AEP, before contacting the AEP direct and conducting a similar interview with them.

We did not have questionnaire responses from the AEPs on which to base the interviews. The contents were therefore drawn from the FD's questionnaire responses and additional comments. Each AEP was asked to 'tell the story' from his perspective about the issues which had been discussed with his client and was also encouraged to add any other information he considered relevant. We were very careful not to give any indications to the AEPs

of what the FDs had actually said about any of the issues. The same laddering techniques as referred to in the FD interviews were used and similar
references were made to the company's annual reports for a second confirmation of the reliability of what we were told. All the interviews except one
were recorded and fully transcribed. One AEP was unwilling to be
recorded, so extensive notes were taken during the meeting and dictated
immediately afterwards.

4.6   BROAD APPROACH TO THE ANALYSIS

The transcripts from the cases were first reviewed and decisions taken
about the approach to the analysis and theory development. This was
recognised to be a four-stage process:

- telling the story of each case;
- within-case analysis;
- cross-case analysis; and
- building theory from cross-case analysis.

This approach is consistent with the use of the grounded theory methodology, which is described more fully in Chapter 11.

4.7   WRITING UP EACH CASE (MATCHED PAIR OF
         INTERVIEWS)

Each interview transcript was input into, and then printed out from, the
NUD-IST data analysis package to facilitate coding and cross-referencing
between the matched pairs of interviews. The package was not used
beyond this stage because the subject matter of each case was very indi-
vidualistic. By means of an iterative process, the key events and issues
referred to by the interviewees in each case were identified and written up
as a chronological story that reflects the differing perspectives of both
interviewees on the issues (Hansen and Kahnweiler, 1993).

As confidentiality assurances had been given to the interviewees, certain
distinguishing features about the companies have been omitted and
changes made to information provided about the company and its activities
in order to protect its identity. The omissions and changes do not alter the
substance of the stories. Changes necessitated by ethical considerations
such as these have been made in other accounting research projects (e.g.,
Anderson-Gough *et al.*, 1999, p. 47).

In the cases where a continuing business relationship still exists between the two parties, particular care has been taken to ensure that each party is comfortable with the remarks about his peer being included in the story. Although the companies themselves would not be identifiable, we were conscious that the interviewees could recognise each other, and we have no wish to undermine any business relationship. Other than very minor edits to improve clarity, which were suggested by the interviewees themselves, no other changes have been made to the material taken from the original transcripts.

4.8 PRELIMINARY WITHIN-CASE ANALYSIS: ATTACHING LABELS TO THE KEY CATEGORIES

After the contents had been agreed with the interviewees, we recognised that in order to carry out our analysis, a classification system had to be developed by which common labels would be attached to the key concepts contained in each case. This was not straightforward because every case was different.

4.8.1 Labelling the concepts described in the stories

We first considered the nature of the concepts described by our interviewees. These are readily identified as being either of a descriptive or of an interactive nature. The descriptive concepts, which provide background information about each company, its policies and *modus operandi* in relation to accounting and corporate governance issues, have been labelled *contexts*. The interactive concepts, which describe the discussions and negotiations which took place, have been labelled *interactions*. The results of the interactions have been labelled *outcomes*.

4.8.2 Preliminary analysis of the contexts

At an early stage in the analysis, we identified four contextual factors that we thought might influence the nature and outcome of the interactions. These preliminary factors were:

- the size of the company;
- the quality of the primary relationship (between the FD and the AEP);
- the existence of an audit committee; and
- the company reporting style.

We have attached gradings to the second and fourth of these factors. The quality of the primary relationship is graded from *poor* to *very good*. The company reporting styles is graded from *aggressive* to *very conservative*. Because of confidentiality constraints we have referred to company size as being merely larger or smaller. For the same reason, the size of the audit firm is not disclosed. The existence of an audit committee is either *yes* or *no*, but attached to *yes* is an indicator as to whether it is (or is perceived to be) effective.

4.8.3   The interactions

The interactions themselves are divided into those that have a financial reporting outcome and those that do not. (Some of the interactions relate to matters associated with the performance or management of the audit, and others to the management structure within the company i.e., corporate governance issues.)

We then considered how further to label the interactions. The audit and corporate governance interactions are simply labelled *audit* and *corporate governance*. Labelling the financial reporting interactions was more complex. We wanted to classify the interactions by *type*. We have based our labels for these interactions on the classification scheme used by Brandt *et al.* (1997) in their analysis of the FRRP's activities, i.e., *recognition, measurement, classification in a primary statement and disclosure*. *Recognition* concerns the boundaries of an entity as reported in its primary statements. *Measurement* concerns the value to be attached to an asset or liability. *Classification* refers to the location where accounting numbers are disclosed in a primary statement. *Disclosure* relates to the information content of the financial statements over and above the primary statements. To this we have added *fundamental accounting principle*, which covers such issues as prudence and going concern.

Having identified these seven classes of interaction issue, we made use of two further descriptive labels. The first, *compliance*, applies to interactions where the regulatory framework prescribes how the issue should be treated. The second, *judgement*, applies where the issue is a matter of judgement, such as a valuation or a provision, where no prescriptive pronouncements can be made.

4.8.4   The outcomes

Having attached labels to the interactions themselves, we then considered the nature of the outcomes of the interactions. These have been graded from *good* to *poor*. The outcomes of the non-financial reporting interactions are a matter of judgement. For the financial reporting outcomes, we have been able to attribute grades according to whether the outcome complies fully with the regulatory framework as it stood at the time (regardless of whether there is room for improvement in the framework). Outcomes that comply have been graded from acceptable to good. Anything below this has been graded *poor*. Included in poor outcomes are cases that we believe demonstrate *creative compliance* (see section 2.2).

4.9   WITHIN-CASE ANALYSIS

Having established a preliminary, basic set of categories and labels to use for the contexts, interactions and outcomes, we were then able to begin the in-depth, within-case analyses. For each case, we separately identified the general contextual factors that appeared to influence the nature and outcome of all the interactions. These are described in the text and also shown in diagrammatic form.

In addition, each interaction for each case has been analysed separately and appropriate labels attached to its type and outcome. The specific contextual factors that appeared to influence the interaction have been identified and, where the interaction was complex, this has also been represented in diagrammatic form. This within-case analysis leads to the identification of concepts, categories, sub-categories and relationships specific to the interactions occurring in a single case setting.

A conclusion is attached to each chapter, which highlights the key issues that emerge from the case.

4.10   SUMMARY OF CASES

To help us (and our readers) assimilate the key features of each case, we prepared an overview of the general context and interaction issues in each of the six cases (see Table 4.2). Obviously, certain aspects of this table emerged only during the analysis stage. Each chapter is titled using the (*changed*) first names of the interviewees. For simplicity, the company case name is derived from the initials of the interviewees.

Table 4.2 Overview of cases

Case name	Names	Co. size	Quality of primary relationship	Audit committee?	Co. reporting style	Key interaction issues	Issue type[1]
NS	Nick & Simon	Larger	Very good	Yes – old committee perceived ineffective; new committee perceived effective	Had been aggressive: desire to moderate	1. Refinancing – going concern issue 2. Treatment of leases 3. Negotiation over fees	FP R A
TJ	Thomas & James	Smaller listed	Poor	No	Resistant to increasing stringency of regulatory framework (FD & chairman)	1. Stock obsolescence provisions 2. Treatment of product development costs under FRS3 3. Treatment of restructuring costs under FRS3 4. Events surrounding the sale of the group	M C C A
MP	Michael & Paul	Larger	Very good	Yes – perceived effective	Very conservative; very sensitive to criticism	1. Accounting issues relating to an acquisition 2. Control and accounting issues re treasury function	M M & CG
CRA	Colin, Richard & Andrew	Larger	Very good	Yes	Culture respectable; senior accountants fairly aggressive	1. Accounting for Neweng acquisition 2. Accounting for Cleanup acquisition 3. Depreciation policy for Cleanup sites 4. Finance leases 5. Restructuring provisions	R & M R & M M M R

					Issues	Code
RC	Robert & Charles	Larger	Fair	Yes – perceived effective	Respectable	1. Accounting for resale of businesses acquired — M 2. Accounting for stock & defective products on acquisition — R, M & D 3. Accounting for reorganisation costs on acquisition — R 4. Disclosure of reorganisation costs — D
DA	Dennis & Alan	Smaller listed	Good	Yes	Resistent to increasing stringency of regulatory framework (chairman); desire to fully comply but not be at forefront of reporting practice (FD); respectable	1. Accounting for assets on disposal — M 2. Accounting for assets on acquisition — M 3. FRS3 disclosures — C 4. Last minute adjustments — M 5. Chairman's attitude to goodwill — R 6. Compliance with Cadbury — D

[1] Code: FP = fundamental principle; R = recognition; M = measurement/valuation; C = classification in a primary statement; D = disclosure; CG = corporate governance; and A = audit.

5 Nick and Simon (NS plc)

'In the top five of the highest risk clients'

5.1 BACKGROUND TO THE CASE

Along with many other organisations this group experienced serious financial difficulties during the recession, but fortunately managed to survive. It has used the same audit firm for many years.

Towards the end of the 1980s, the group had a strong balance sheet and was in a position to finance further growth. Encouraged by the strength of the balance sheet and the easy availability of borrowings, the board embarked upon a programme of expansion which mainly involved acquiring businesses in related industry sectors. Although the problems could not have been predicted, the decision to expand and take on extra borrowings was unfortunate. The economic downturn followed soon afterwards, and the group entered the recession with high borrowings. As the recession deepened and interest rates rose, it had difficulty in servicing these debts. Further funding was obtained and the group's accounting function was reorganised. As part of this reorganisation Nick was recruited as finance director.

At about the same time Nick joined the group, Simon took over as the audit engagement partner. His predecessor, who was older, remained involved with the company as a general service partner in order to maintain continuity in the relationship with other senior board members. Both Nick and Simon are in their forties.

On joining the group, Nick was concerned to find it close to insolvency. He also felt that the accounting function and the management information systems could be improved. The group had relied heavily on its auditors for much of the routine work involved in the preparation of the annual accounts and this had led to high fees. As a priority he arranged meetings with the lenders who agreed to support the group for a further two years. As the end of this period approached, the group was hovering at the limit of its debt covenants[1] and the existing lenders were not prepared to extend the

---

[1] Debt covenants are undertakings to a company's bankers regarding the level of debt and the agreed timetable to reduce it. A company may also undertake to keep its balance sheet within certain key accounting ratios.

facilities on the same terms. Therefore a new process of negotiation had to be undertaken to obtain further funding. Because of the group's recognised problems this proved to be a complex and time-consuming exercise which took several months to bring to a conclusion. The process also involved changing some of the board members. Simon and other specialists from his firm were extensively involved in advising on some aspects of this process.

In addition to the process of obtaining finance to keep the group going, Nick and Simon reviewed the group's accounting policies. This was driven by the need to comply with the changing regulatory framework, particularly the ASB's new accounting standards, and also by Nick's wish to adopt more conservative accounting policies.

The changes to the composition of the board led to a culture change which affected, among other things, the membership and role of the audit committee. The new audit committee wished to improve the value for money obtained from the audit fee.

5.2 THE KEY ISSUES FOR NICK AND SIMON

Both Nick and Simon had become involved with the group at a critical time in its development. Nick was completely new to the group's problems but Simon had the advantage of his firm's previous experience. Neither could be held responsible for past events. They had common goals, albeit with different motivation. Neither wanted the group to fail (Nick would lose his newly acquired job and possibly his reputation: Simon's firm would lose a client and both the firm and Simon personally risked reputation damage). Also both wanted to adopt more prudent accounting policies to reassure potential lenders and to ensure that the accounts complied with the changing regulatory framework being introduced by the ASB. The overriding influence running throughout this case was the group's struggle to survive and the efforts required to achieve this.

We interviewed Nick and Simon separately. Three interactions and one contextual influence emerged during the discussions which covered three accounting periods in all. These are described in the order below to maintain the flow of the story.

- renegotiation of the financing arrangements and year-end going concern problems (*interaction NS1*);
- the changing role of the audit committee (*context NS(a)*);
- the need for accounting reform in the group (*interaction NS2*);
- negotiations over audit fees (*interaction NS3*).

Interactions one and two had outcomes which affected the group financial statements. Interaction three did not, as it was audit related.

5.3   INTERACTION NS1: RENEGOTIATION OF THE FINANCING ARRANGEMENTS AND THE YEAR-END GOING CONCERN PROBLEMS

When Nick joined the group he engaged with the banks almost immediately having realised that it was almost insolvent. With the chief executive he arranged for the existing facilities to be consolidated and renewed for another two years. However, during this period the group from time to time breached its debt covenants. Apart from the group's continuing precarious position, this meant that the going concern issue had to be specifically addressed in respect of the year-end accounts and the audit report.[2] However, the extension of the facilities Nick had negotiated shortly after his appointment expired soon after the end of the third year and a new arrangement had to be negotiated. This arrangement, which took several months to sort out, was initially delayed because the lenders insisted on changes to the composition of the board before they were prepared to proceed. Because of the delay that this caused, the accounts were held back until the deal was settled. The group was not financially viable until the new arrangements had been agreed.[3]

As far as Nick was concerned, the continuing negotiation of financing arrangements with the group's lenders was primarily his responsibility. The whole process was lengthy and time-consuming:

> '[*Shortly after joining the group*] ... it was quite clear to me that if we didn't do something pretty rapidly, the group was heading for liquidation, so I got the lending group together, because that was fragmented and said "Look guys, we're all in this together. We've got to sort something out", and then we went into the special care department of the bank and agreed a programme of disposals for two

---

[2] The going concern problem arises whenever there are inadequate finances or loans to enable a business to continue. In the absence of assured facilities for twelve months after the accounts are approved by the directors, the auditor must either refer to the fundamental uncertainty in the audit report, or, if the company's circumstances are so serious that the going concern basis is no longer appropriate as a basis for the preparation of the accounts, the auditor would issue a qualified report with an adverse opinion to this effect.

[3] Until new financing arrangements are agreed, a company can continue only because the lenders choose to permit it. When a company is in breach of its borrowing arrangements, secured lenders can put it into receivership.

years, and [*another audit firm*] sitting on everything we did, every moment of the day' (Nick).

The existing borrowing facilities were consolidated and extended for a further two years. Although the auditors were not directly involved in the day-to-day problems they were kept informed:

'Now the re-engineering was not really a function of the auditors, or a responsibility of the auditors in any way, but obviously we kept them abreast of what was going on' (Nick).

Simon acknowledged this and recognised Nick's initial problems:

'I think one of his first meetings, and it proved to be one of the most difficult, was actually with his bankers, and what they said was they had to agree and negotiate ... a consolidation of all their banking arrangements. And because they were unhappy with the way [*the group*] was trading and the way it was looking ... they signed that agreement which took them through a 2-year period ... that gave them facilities, subject to them not breaching the covenants for two years' (Simon).

Despite this agreement, going concern problems still arose for the directors and auditors at the first two year-ends, because the group had breached its debt covenants. Agreement had to be obtained from the lenders for their continuing support, before the audit report was signed:

'We were then broadly in a position for [*years one and two*] to be able to sign off on the basis that, although they had been in breach of the covenants, they were not when we signed off. The covenants had to be renegotiated before we could sign off' (Simon).

Year three was the vital year. The existing facilities expired soon after the year-end, leaving the group without adequate support for the future, and the existing lenders were unwilling to extend the facility as it stood. This was a major issue for both Nick and Simon:

'It was a joint problem if you like, because we had a situation potentially where we were ... not refinanced ... we didn't have necessarily sufficient funds guaranteed from the lenders beyond the twelve-month period after completion of the accounts. I mean that was the nub of the issue and at the state of the company's position the banks wouldn't commit to a longer lending period because ... we were gobbling up the two years that they'd agreed to' (Nick).

Renegotiation of the financing arrangements was critical to the group's future viability. Because of the seriousness of the issue Nick had started the renegotiation process in good time but had hit a snag:

> 'We were actually going to refinance six months earlier than we did ... [*the lenders*] wouldn't accept the existing board ... they chucked us back and said, "You had better change your board before you come back to us again" ' (Nick).

Simon commented on the changes to the board:

> 'They brought in a new chairman and other non-executive changes ... anybody that was associated with the old guard was asked to leave ... that's typical of a company that goes through ... this. For want of a better phrase some one's got to carry the can and heads roll when something like this happens. The chief executive and finance director are effectively promoted and given a new role ... once you've done that the composition of the board totally changes ... you get a new direction' (Simon).

The negotiation of the arrangements to keep the group afloat took many months to complete. Simon's firm was heavily involved in the process.

> 'It was a full-time job for us [*for eight months*]. It was stop, start, stop, start. The deadline was changed. We made many presentations to the full board, to the audit committee, to sub-committees of the board. We had documents like these ... reports that set out exactly what the working capital position was ... they were probably updated eight, maybe ten times over the period. And every time those reports were re-issued to people, not just to Nick but to the rest of the board as well' (Simon).

Although Simon's firm was not involved in the negotiations with the banks, they took a leading role in moving things forward:

> 'In terms of the other advisors we were not in the driving seat, but our documents would be circulated to the others. We were very much a focal point of ... summarising what these new banking arrangements meant in terms of covenants and whatever. So from that perspective we were leading it' (Simon).

Simon emphasised the difficulty of getting consensus for the arrangements:

> 'No one was under the illusion that there was a half-way house here ... you have to get everybody's concurrence to this otherwise the thing doesn't run, and that's why they are so complicated and they take so long to do ... you have to

get every bank in line, every creditor involved, and there has to be a consensus' (Simon).

Because of the delay caused by the boardroom changes, the group reached the year-end before the deal was completed. This presented a going concern problem in respect of the accounts:

'So when we got to the end of [year three] we were actually in a very difficult position ... from the accounts point of view' (Nick).

Not having the finance in place provided a major problem for Simon as auditor:

'We couldn't have signed off ... the accounts in the way in which they were eventually presented simply because the company wasn't a going concern without that banking agreement in place ... now this was so far-reaching that we couldn't have possibly indicated what the changes to the balance sheet or operations would have been if they hadn't got the revised banking agreement. So it was so fundamental that we couldn't have given any intermediate-type position' (Simon).

Simon explained this to the whole board:

'The way we explained it to Nick and the board was that first and foremost, it's the directors' responsibility of course. I mean they have to prepare the accounts and the first obligation is on them, for them to get comfortable with the fact that the whole group is a going concern ... and we come after that. Once you as a board come up with your plan for re-financing, we'll then look at it and we get comfortable as well' (Simon).

Nick felt that the board had done its best to keep the company going and was upset at the prospect of a qualified audit report:

'It would have been a disaster ... because I think we'd managed our way through the ... two to three years very effectively ... and we've managed to keep a lot of people reasonably comfortable in difficult circumstances' (Nick).

He believed that it could undermine future financing prospects:

'The issue as far as the auditors were concerned was one which was understandable from a textbook perspective. One had then to put a live situation judgement on it as to whether, given all the evidence the company would carry on or not. And of course it would have been devastating for us to be faced with the prospect of a qualified report that this was not a going concern, because of the limited funding available for the company' (Nick).

He also recognised that the situation was so bad that Simon had no choice:

> 'It wasn't as if it was one of those debatable areas. It was quite clear that they had to. No question about it ... I mean shareholders should be aware if that was the situation. The danger was that it was a situation which would actually have destroyed the company if we'd let it happen' (Nick).

Therefore, rather than issuing the accounts when the group was not financed, another strategy was adopted:

> 'Now in fact this thing all resolved itself in the end because we actually held the accounts back until we re-financed ourselves' (Nick).

They had avoided committing themselves in advance to a date for the preliminary announcement of their results with the Stock Exchange:

> 'We don't have to advise them until fifteen days before you make an announcement, and there was so much uncertainty, there was no way I was going to stick my neck on the block. ... If you say, "I'm going to announce the results on this day", and then you go back and say, "Well, problems, there's a problem, we're delaying it." Everybody says, "Oh, problem!" So there's no point in notifying it' (Nick).

Of course the going concern problem remained until the deal was in place:

> 'We weren't in a position to sign off on those accounts until the banking agreement had been put in place ... and therefore the group's a going concern, and therefore we can sign off' (Simon).

This was successfully completed and the accounts were delayed by only two months. Simon acknowledged that the process had been challenging for him and his firm, both from a risk management point of view and from the technical complexity of the accounts.

> 'It was in the top five of the highest risk clients, because it was likely to go bust at any moment. You couldn't get any more risky than [the group] was ... As it gets back to a degree of normality then our risk reduces. ... It was probably one of the most complicated sets of accounts I've ever been involved with. I mean it had absolutely everything in, in terms of accounting disclosures' (Simon).

5.4 CONTEXT NS(a): THE CHANGING ROLE OF THE AUDIT COMMITTEE

An audit committee had been established to comply with the Cadbury Code.[4] Following the changes to the composition of the board its role had changed significantly. Nick acknowledged that the original audit committee had not been very effective:

'We had a problem with the audit committee ... There is a big danger with audit committees and remuneration committees and all the rest of them, depending on how the board is constructed. If you've got a board which is basically a group of people who were, quite bluntly, friends of the chairman, who were appointed because they would do what the chairman wanted, then one individual effectively runs the company. You create audit committees, remuneration committees, which meet all the requirements. They are potentially just cosmetic exercises and I have to say that's what we really had here' (Nick).

Simon was less critical but recognised that the original audit committee lacked technical accounting expertise:

'Until the end of the refinancing they did not have another accountant on the audit committee ... I mean they did rely on Nick and ourselves. This is where we probably had a wider role because there were no accountants on the audit committee. They did depend on us effectively to say, "Look, this is what you should be doing" and they took our word for that, and that's what you'd expect in terms of advisors and auditors' (Simon).

He also accepted that the original committee had been faced with some difficult problems:

'There were a lot of issues being raised, not only by us but by Nick. ... It was an aftermath ... of the problems of the past ... the audit committee's role was to some extent different ... I mean there were just such a wealth of issues to deal with in terms of trying to unravel them, that you can always be more robust ... take a stronger line or whatever ... but at the end of the day all those issues were resolved, and they were resolved in a way that had got them through' (Simon).

Nick was less sympathetic:

'It was a pretty weak, pretty weak committee' (Nick).

---

[4] Named after its chairman Sir Adrian Cadbury, the Committee on the Financial Aspects of Corporate Governance reported in December 1992. This report included 'The Code of Best Practice' which was commonly referred to as the Cadbury Code and was mainly directed at governance of listed companies.

After the boardroom changes the committee became more effective:

'It's totally different now. It's got [*Mr. XX*] as chairman and [*Mr. YY*] is on it and it's a proper committee. I mean it functions as it should. They're independent board members now. There's no group of yes-men so, yes, a totally different situation' (Nick).

Simon also observed improvements with a technically competent chairman, but recognised that the committee had a different role from that of its predecessor:

'There is now a chairman of the audit committee ... more attuned to specific accounting issues and the technical debates. I think that the issues they've had to deal with are totally different to the issues that the predecessor committee had to. What they're now dealing with are sort of operational issues, and less historical problems have come through, because these were all resolved. ... But let's put it this way, There's probably a better balance now to the audit committee because it's got another accountant on it' (Simon).

Nick explained how the audit committee operated:

'I will present the half year or the year-end accounts to the audit committee and I will go through whatever issues I believe are in those accounts. The auditors will make an independent report to that audit committee ... at the same meeting endorsing or not their views of the accounts and also bringing up whatever issues they think the audit committee should be aware of. So I think it actually works properly as it should at the moment and I don't have a problem with it' (Nick).

However, Nick did have a meeting with the audit committee chairman prior to the audit committee meeting to avoid surprises:

'I will have a meeting with the chairman of the audit committee before the meeting and will actually go through with him so that he's totally aware of anything and everything that might come up at the meeting. Again it's a no surprises situation. He's going to be embarrassed if he goes and sits in this committee meeting and learns things which he didn't know about' (Nick).

Nick also insisted on being present at the meeting following a previous misunderstanding with the auditors.

'There was some criticism of two of the people in my area from one of the audit committee meetings and that came back to me from the chairman who said,

'The auditors have said blah, blah, blah about X, Y and Z, and I said, "Well, that's not true". Anyway to cut a long story short it wasn't justified. It had been said off the cuff at a meeting ... and the whole thing got out of hand ... That sort of thing is very dangerous' (Nick).

Simon, who had not referred to this matter when we interviewed him, subsequently indicated his belief that it was a vital corporate governance practice for auditors to communicate with the audit committee without the executive directors being present. In his view this particular problem had arisen because the members of the audit committee had mishandled the way they had communicated his comments to Nick.

5.5 INTERACTION NS2: THE NEED FOR ACCOUNTING REFORM IN THE GROUP

Nick recognised soon after he joined the group that, apart from the urgent action necessary to keep it afloat, a change was needed in the group's overall approach to compliance with external reporting requirements. Nick had identified one particular problem about classification of certain leasing transaction between operating and finance leases.[5] A number of sale and leaseback transactions[6] had originally been taken out when the group was desperate for additional cash flow. But its subsequent need to obtain further finance coincided with changes in the regulatory framework, influenced by the ASB's new standards, which meant that the accounting treatment previously adopted in respect of some of the leases was no longer acceptable.

There was also a technical compliance issue which irritated Nick. He did not like Simon's firm's technical department coming up with last minute adjustments when he thought that all the technical issues arising from the audit had been settled.

---

[5] A finance lease is one which transfers substantially all the risks and rewards of ownership to the lessee, although the legal title to the asset remains with the lessor. It is accounted for as an asset and the capital element of the future rental payments is treated as a liability. Interest paid each year is charged to the profit and loss account. Any other lease is an operating lease. No asset or liability is set up and the lease payments are expensed annually through the profit and loss account. The effect of treating a lease relating to a long-term fixed asset as an operating lease is that long-term liabilities are not disclosed on the balance sheet.

[6] A sale and leaseback transaction is a form of financing where funds are raised on the security of an asset. No profit or loss arises on the sale and the leaseback is treated as a finance lease.

Nick had recognised the need for a change in the group's approach to accounting efficiency and compliance:

> 'Historically ... the auditors used to do a significant proportion of the accounting ... I don't believe that is the role of the auditors at all ... it's up to a company to present the accounts as they believe they ought to be presented ... they should know enough to be able to produce the accounts properly and effectively,' (Nick).

The board had also been scraping around for profits and Nick saw his arrival as an opportunity to be more prudent:

> 'Inevitably when somebody new comes in then they're in a much stronger position to provide for things and ignore as things were. Whereas management who had been there for a while ... especially when they are under pressure ... [*were*] using up any provisions there are and justifying why they shouldn't exist rather than why they should exist' (Nick).

He also realised that a more conservative approach would help the auditors:

> 'So to some extent the auditors had a much easier time when I arrived because ... I wanted to get the thing ... back into a sensible position, a sound financial position and that suited them, of course, as well and made their job a lot easier. So we were pushing water downhill really together rather than pushing it up hill' (Nick).

He was concerned that the board might have difficulty in adjusting to the changing culture and regulatory framework and decided to enlist Simon's help in bringing the changes about:

> 'Because of the history and state of affairs here when I arrived, which was pretty dire for a number of reasons, I actually went into partnership with the auditors and said "as far as I'm concerned I want to present true and fair accounts for this group and I'm not seeking to hide anything. Everything's going to be out on the table, but I want your help to do that ... because there are a lot of members of the board who are going to resist this approach, because it hasn't been the approach adopted historically"' (Nick).

Simon co-operated, because it was clear that the board had historically not been given sufficient information, except by the auditors. They therefore continued to prepare even more extensive memoranda on key issues which affected the audit in each year. These were targeted at the audit committee. Nick explained the objective:

'The auditors and I were working in the same road. We wanted the same thing really then and hence the long report by the auditors was partly to get the audit committee's attention to some of these things to go to the board' (Nick).

Simon considered that the primary cause of the accounting problems was the group's rapid expansion.

'Clearly even in the first year … we did a lot of work that we now don't do … but they relied on us much more than they do now. They hadn't got proper processes and procedures in place in terms of the consolidation … and that was very much a function, as I understand it, of the fact that they grew very quickly in the late 80s, and like a lot of fast growth companies they hadn't got the systems and procedures in place' (Simon).

Simon saw the long memoranda more as a function of the group's problems than as a part of a strategy to change boardroom attitudes:

'But primarily it was because the group had grown very quickly by way of acquisition, and it then diversified quickly by way of acquisition, so there were a lot of changes to the composition of the group and each one of those to some extent had to be explained – the accounting treatment had to be explained – there were errors of judgment. … It's a reflection of the past as to why [*the memoranda*] were so long' (Simon).

In the period immediately prior to Nick's arrival the board had been desperate for additional cash flow. One strategy to improve cash flow had been to engage in a number of leasing transactions, some of which had been classified as operating leases. Nick believed they should have been treated as finance leases.

'Before I arrived here, because of its shortage of funds, the group was leasing out everything that it could. Even the fresh air round the buildings was sort of leased out (*sic*) … There were operating leases which should have been finance leases' (Nick).

He expressed some disappointment that the original treatment of the leases had been accepted by the auditors, but recognised that it was now the auditors who were pushing for change:

'I mean there was tarmac on the car park, from office blocks, to chairs. … I mean literally huge amounts of the group had been subject to leases, some of which were finance leases quite genuinely, some of which were operating leases, some of which have been dressed up to be what they weren't. I think part of the problem was the auditors had actually accepted them once in one category and we ended up changing the category. ... That was the auditors' initiation ... so it wasn't a problem as far as I was concerned, because I wanted them in the way they should have been, but I was inevitably a little bit disappointed that they had been persuaded to allow them to be something they weren't' (Nick).

Nick understood that the ASB had brought about a change in attitudes to aggressive accounting and that some accounting treatments, which had previously been agreed to, were no longer acceptable:

'But I think it's easy to look back at a lot of things and say, "Well, why didn't people do it like that in the years gone by?" The requirements, the disciplines, all the ASB pronouncements are clarifying, in many areas, the way one does things, and I think it's easy to look back and criticise, with today's knowledge, what was done in the past. ... I suppose I'm defending them, but I mean, I think it is true with so many things in life' (Nick).

He also acknowledged that the auditors would have been put under considerable pressure by the previous board and the accounting areas were ill-defined:

'I think they were subjected to a lot more pressure ... from management. There was a lot of creative accounting here, and therefore they were ... in a much more difficult position ... because the clarity between what was right and wrong was much nearer the margin. Yes, I think with hindsight they were probably uncomfortable with some of it, but it wasn't absolutely wrong, necessarily the area was grey' (Nick).

Simon's view was not substantially different. He believed that the leases had been deliberately fashioned to keep them off the balance sheet:

'This in terms of the strategy and the structure again pre-dated me, but in summary what happened was, in the early nineties, [*the group*] had almost completed its expansion programme. ... It clearly was the start of the downturn in term of the operating profits, the recession etc. and it found itself short of cash. Now one way of realising cash is to enter into sale and leaseback operations ... they sold buildings, assets and then leased them back, and the way those were structured in the early nineties was with the intention to keep the leases ... off the balance sheet. ... The leases were structured in a way that they did not meet the then requirements of SSAP 21, of bringing those leases on to the balance sheet' (Simon).

Simon also acknowledged the culture change brought about by the ASB:

'But through the next two or three years and indeed up to now ... we have a different way of looking at these. I mean there's very much more substance over form ... and indeed specific rules about putting leases on balance sheets and the way one measures that has changed. ... When these changes were brought out, the leases were then treated as finance leases or capital leases and put on the balance sheet' (Simon).

The impact on profit was minimal and he did not believe that putting the liabilities on the balance sheet made any difference to the lenders:

'The different treatment again really only reflected a change in the accounting rules, because from the banks' perspective, they treated all the leases as finance leases from the word go, and the lessors were treated as lenders as indeed the banks were and any other creditors. So I mean the accounting classification didn't have any major impact ... It's purely the balance sheet presentation ... but the actual effect on profit and loss account tends to be minimal' (Simon).

Simon also believed that the company had entered the sale and leaseback transactions as a short-term bridge:

'They didn't anticipate that they would have the financial difficulties they eventually did have. I assume by this stage ... it was a short-term pick-up, that by generating cash in this way, by sale and leaseback, that that would see them through their immediate difficulties ... but that proved not to be so' (Simon).

The change of accounting policy on leasing was effected at about the same time as a revaluation of properties. Therefore it did not stand out in the accounts:

'We did all the calculations and we just sat down with Nick and said, "This is the way under current rules that they should be treated". Because all the properties were all being revalued anyway ... therefore it was nice and neat and easy, effectively to wrap it all up as part of the same exercise' (Simon).

The matter was explained to the audit committee, which had no accountant members at the time, as a necessary change:

'It was explained to them. They didn't do anything wrong before. I mean, just that the rules had changed. So it was merely reflecting a change' (Simon).

Although not directly related to the process of accounting reform, the technical department of Simon's firm carried out compliance reviews of the group's accounts. Nick found the timing of these reviews annoying. He did not like last-minute surprises:

> 'One of the things I do have a problem with is that ... there are faceless wonders who sit back in head office in the technical department and you can produce a set of accounts. ... You can go through the debate, you can agree a format, a presentation if you like of the P&L account ... and you think you're all there and these dratted draft accounts go off to the technical department and they say, "Well, wey hey, you can't do that! Oh no, no, no!" And then the audit partner comes back, "Oh the technical department says you can't do this!" We all have this fiasco and that's something I just don't like at the moment' (Nick).

5.6   INTERACTION NS3: NEGOTIATIONS OVER FEES

When Nick and Simon first became involved with the group the audit fees were high. The accounting function was not well organised and the auditors did a lot of basic work themselves. During the period when the group was struggling to stay in business, Simon's firm had done a great deal of work apart from providing audit services and the fees had continued to be high. The work for the financing arrangements had generated substantial extra fees. However, once the group had become more stable and the in-house accounting improved, Nick and Simon knew that the fees would be reduced. But the new chairman intervened and demanded an immediate and more drastic reduction in the fees, which Simon's firm felt obliged to concede for the sake of a good continuing relationship. Nick understood why the fees had originally been high:

> 'Audit fees used to be huge here and that was fairly understandable because of the nature of the work, and I said, "Yes, I understand why the fee level is where it is but what I would like is a breakdown of how you come to whatever. ... We could save the audit fee if they're spending 50 per cent of their time checking a debtors ledger, for example, and there's clearly an issue there where we should be providing information in a different way or a better way' (Nick).

Nick was critical of billing practices in the UK:

> 'In the UK we still have a bit of difficulty with this, a reluctance by professional firms to spell out the detail ... In the United States there are pages and pages and pages of telephone calls, an hour here an hour there, and all that to write down. You get it in the UK: to professional services – ten million pounds' (Nick).

Both parties accepted the high non-audit fee levels during the period when the financing arrangements were being renegotiated, but Simon had reduced some of his fees for this work:

'We did not recover 100 per cent of our costs and we did a number of deals with management ... you're now getting into [Simon's firm's] commerciality ... there's a lot of things one weighs up with taking those sorts of decisions. [*The group*] has been a client for a long time, and, you know, a good client from [*audit firm's*] perspective ... so we don't take the short-term view and say look we only got x recovery on that ... we can't do the work' (Simon).

The level of audit fees became a more difficult issue after the group was stabilised and the board changed. The new chairman had his own views about audit fees:

'He came on board and made it very clear, from day one, that the level of fees that had been paid in the past were paid because of all the problems, because of the long memos that had been written, and therefore he expected those fees to come down to a much reduced level and he charged Nick with the task' (Simon).

Nick and Simon both referred to the process of negotiating fees:

'The way the process worked was that each year we submit a proposal to the audit committee, and they – Nick makes a recommendation, and they agree or disagree' (Simon).

'It started off with the level and then you debate the use of individuals; inevitably there's a learning curve. I think, generally, we haven't had a huge problem. I mean the fees were coming down, inevitably with the size of the group coming down, ... auditing a group which has become easier and easier and ... we would expect the fees to be coming down at a more rapid rate than they were' (Nick).

Despite asking for a fee reduction, Nick still wanted to keep to the year-end reporting timetable. This had been speeded up, and the date of the preliminary announcement of the results,[7] which was audited by agreement,

---

[7] The preliminary announcement is required by the stock exchange to give information to the market as soon as the results for the period are known and in advance of the financial statements being available. Unlike the financial statements, the preliminary announcement is not required to be audited.

had been brought forward and was now shortly after the year-end. This put pressure on the auditors:

> 'One of the debates was about why the fee wasn't coming down when we are reducing the time it takes to produce the accounts. Last year we went out with audited accounts at the end of the year. I would not want to go back on that ... I don't want to go out with a preliminary statement which is unaudited' (Nick).

But he wasn't impressed by Simon's arguments about premium rates:

> 'And one of the things which was said is, "The fee hasn't come down quite so much because of the cost of auditing in our most busy period, which is January, February, March". Where we fell on our tighter time scale meant we had to pay premium rates ... that wound me up' (Nick).

Simon agreed to reduce the fees, but Nick believed it was the threat of a tender that brought it about:

> 'Seeing as they volunteered a 25 per cent reduction of the fees for this year I have no problem with them at all. ... We had a good meeting this year ... quite clearly what had changed was the prospective threat of a tender ... you go out for a tender and generally you come in with an audit fee which is 25 per cent or 30 per cent less' (Nick).

Simon agreed that the threat of a tender had a significant influence:

> 'They were reduced, one to reflect the fact that the audit is now significantly easier than it was ... but secondly there's a commerciality aspect ... the alternative is the audit goes out to tender ... that involves a lot of work on everybody's part, so there's a cost involved in that. So we took a view collectively here and said "Look, the chairman wants this" and we made a significant reduction which they accepted' (Simon).

Nick nevertheless wanted exactly the same service as he had before:

> 'I said, "that's OK but I still want an ... audited preliminary announcement"' (Nick).

Simon had already given this assurance:

> 'And we assured them there would be no loss of quality, no loss of service ... we do it because there's a commercial need to do it, not because there's a short-cut from a professional perspective' (Simon).

But Nick had doubts about the fee reduction, despite the pressure from the chairman, and mentioned alternative strategies:

'I'm just slightly nervous. I'd rather pay the old audit fee and make sure we get a quality job than the reduced fee and a reduced quality job. One or two audit firms are changing their philosophy ... They're saying, "We're not reducing the fee. What we're doing is giving the client what we think is a better service, by enhancing the service somehow" ... time will tell' (Nick).

Simon had strong views about the fee pressure that firms were facing from clients in general:

'As a generic issue, I can't bloody stand it to be honest. I think it's a hugely competitive market and if we're not careful we'll cut each other's throats. Because there's only so far you can keep on. Every time it goes out to tender you chop thirty-five, thirty per cent. You can't keep doing that, you know' (Simon).

Simon believed his client knew exactly what the situation was and expressed concern about the way things were going:

'They know exactly what the position is and ... they will take it for what it's worth. Hopefully they see it as a service. If they see it as a cost they'll get the cheapest price possible. I think we in the profession have got to make sure things don't go too far ... and say enough is enough' (Simon).

Simon also expressed his feelings about the pressure from the chairman:

'You feel frustration to some extent because you feel you've got a good relationship with the client, with the people you deal with day to day, and then, in this case, one individual changes, like the chairman, and he says "Forget all that. I want the cheapest one necessary." So all the investment has gone because he's changed the rules overnight. You'd have to be very thick-skinned if you ... just shrugged your shoulders and said, "Well, that doesn't have any impact on me or cause any problems", because clearly it does cause problems' (Simon).

He understood the pressure that Nick faced:

'He certainly would have wished the fee to come down. I think Nick would have accepted a slower reduction than the chairman ... he has the most contact with us ... I feel he gets more than a cost ... he does get added value and he sees it as more of a service. .... Nick wants the fee to come down because it reflects well on him. There's the macho thing as finance director ... the more you can demonstrate they do in-house, the less they have to pay externally, the better he is seen in his own light because this comes under his cost budget' (Simon).

5.7   ANALYSIS OF GENERAL CONTEXTUAL FACTORS

The relationship between Nick and Simon was very good, for a number of reasons:

- they had a common objective to keep the company going (to avoid loss of personal reputation and to protect their respective organisations);
- they had a common objective to adopt more prudent accounting policies to reassure potential lenders and comply with the increasing stringency of the regulatory framework;
- they were of similar age, with both being new to their role with the company;
- both had high integrity.

The contextual factors which influenced the outcomes of the interactions between Nick and Simon are set out diagramatically in Figure 5.1. These are drawn from the general circumstances of the group, the specific circumstances in which Nick and Simon found themselves, and the contextual influence NS(a). The influence of the contextual factors and the common goals of both Nick and Simon, as shown in the diagram, resulted in a very good working relationship between the two.

A larger listed company, NS plc had adopted an aggressive reporting style in the 1980s. The group now wished to moderate this style, in light of the current regulatory environment and the company's severe financial difficulties. The company's financial situation dominated the interactions in this case, and was instrumental to the boardroom reshuffle that brought in a new chairman and changed the audit committee. The new chairman was a grudging buyer of audit services.

5.8   THE SPECIFIC INTERACTIONS AND THEIR OUTCOMES

5.8.1   Interaction NS1: renegotiation of financing arrangements and year-end going concern problems

This financial reporting interaction concerned the group's future as a going concern, a fundamental accounting principle. It involved both judgement and compliance. At the end of year three, the extended borrowing facilities

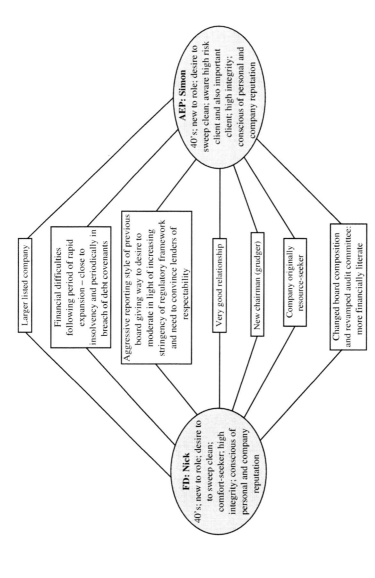

AEP: Simon
40's; new to role; desire to sweep clean; aware high risk client and also important client; high integrity; conscious of personal and company reputation

Larger listed company

Financial difficulties following period of rapid expansion – close to insolvency and periodically in breach of debt covenants

Aggressive reporting style of previous board giving way to desire to moderate in light of increasing stringency of regulatory framework and need to convince lenders of respectability

Very good relationship

New chairman (grudger)

Company originally resource-seeker

Changed board composition and revamped audit committee: more financially literate

FD: Nick
40's; new to role; desire to to sweep clean; comfort-seeker; high integrity; conscious of personal and company reputation

Figure 5.1 Nick and Simon: general context for interactions

were about to expire and new arrangements had been delayed by the lenders' insistence on changes to the board. Simon had made his position as auditor absolutely clear to Nick from the outset. Until the new finance was secured, the group was not a going concern and he would have to qualify the accounts.

The solution was to delay the preliminary announcement of the results for two months until the refinancing deal was in place, as Nick had not given a specific date for the announcement to the Stock Exchange. Thus, at the reporting date, the company could be classed as a going concern because the financing arrangements were secure for at least twelve months from the date the directors approved the accounts.

The specific contextual factors which influenced this outcome were the group's financial difficulties and both Nick and Simon's awareness of the consequences to the group, and to themselves personally, of a going concern qualification. A further factor which would have increased Simon's caution was that the group was in his firm's highest risk category. Nick may not have been aware of this at the time. Both parties were seeking a solution to avoid an undesirable outcome.

This interaction had a good outcome. By taking advantage of the flexibility within the reporting dates for preliminary announcements to the market, the group was able to comply with the regulatory framework and avoid disclosing its going concern problem. The consequence of this course of action was that the group was able to survive. However the smaller shareholders may not have been aware how close the group had been to collapse.

The outcome was easy to achieve. Simon's position in respect of the potential qualification was clear-cut from auditing standards. He took no risks and offered Nick no compromises. Nick respected his position.

5.8.2 Interaction NS2: the need for accounting reform in the group-accounting treatment of leases

This was a financial reporting interaction concerning recognition. It was a compliance issue. Nick and Simon wished to change the way in which certain existing leases were treated in the group accounts and so were agreed that the issue needed to be addressed. Simon stated his position quite clearly at the outset. The leases had intentionally been drawn up as operating leases to keep them off the balance sheet, although in substance they were finance leases and should have been on it. Figure 5.2 sets out the dimensions of this interaction, together with the parties involved, their specific objectives, and the strategies adopted.

77

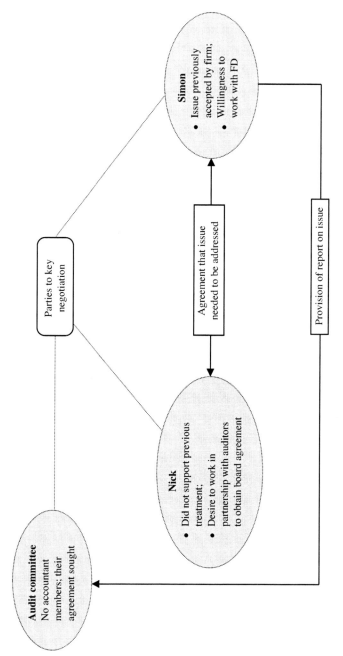

Figure 5.2   Treatment of leases (NS2)

Nick and Simon co-operated and devised a strategy of getting the audit committee on side. The audit committee had no accountant members and so the need for a change in policy had to be explained – a case for change had to be made and accepted. Simon prepared a detailed report on the issue, which was presented to the audit committee. The lack of accounting expertise on the committee meant that Simon was not questioned too hard. Having secured the agreement of the audit committee, it appears that board agreement did not prove to be problematic.

The contextual factor which influenced this interaction was the group's need to clean up its balance sheet in order to signal a strong compliance culture to future lenders, and to respond to the changing regulatory environment. This was not a problem for Nick, who disapproved of the original arrangements to which he had not been a party. It was more of a problem for the audit committee and the board, having to change what they had previously accepted. It was also potentially an embarrassment for Simon, who was proposing to change an accounting treatment which his predecessor had previously accepted. As the change of treatment coincided with a property revaluation, the impact did not stand out in the accounting numbers, although this does not appear to have been a strategy to minimise its visibility.

This financial reporting interaction had a good outcome. An existing aggressive accounting treatment was put right without acrimony.

The outcome was easy to achieve. Nick and Simon both wanted the change and the less expert audit committee and board were easily convinced by their combined case which emphasised the need to respond to the changing regulatory environment and played down the previous aggressive accounting.

5.8.3   Interaction NS3: negotiations over fees

This interaction was an audit issue and had no financial reporting outcome. Until Nick's appointment the group had been a resource seeker, particularly for accounting support, and had paid high fees to Simon's firm. It may also have been a status seeker during its earlier period of rapid growth. Nick, a comfort seeker, had improved the accounting, and after the refinancing was secured both he and Simon expected the fees to reduce over time.

Simon had only offered a small fee reduction on the grounds that the group required them to work at their busiest time of year. Nick did not accept this argument but it was the intervention of the new chairman that critically altered the path of this interaction. The new chairman wanted an immediate substantial fee reduction, and was prepared to put the audit out to tender to achieve it. Rather than incur the cost of a tender and risk losing the client, Simon's firm acceded to the chairman's wishes and reduced the fee.

The key contextual factor in this interaction was the newness of the chairman, who had no association with the group's recent history and had no relationship with Simon. He had not been involved in the efforts to refinance the group and had no loyalty either to Simon or Simon's firm. He was a fee grudger.

The outcome was good for the chairman, who achieved his objective in bringing the fee down. It was not good for Simon who had been threatened, and was upset, feeling that all his efforts to help the group through a very difficult period now counted for nothing. It was good for Nick in that he could demonstrate as finance director that the fees had come down, but being a comfort seeker, he was concerned in case the reduction in fees resulted in a reduced level of service and had to be reassured by Simon that this was not the case. One consequence of the outcome was the potential to undermine the very good relationship between Nick and Simon.

The outcome was easy to achieve because Simon was threatened with the loss of the client if he did not agree to reduce the fees.

5.9 CONCLUSION

Some key issues emerge from this case. Nick and Simon had a good working relationship and respected each other's judgements. Neither was prepared to compromise their personal integrity or the quality of the group's earnings. It was in both their interests for the group's accounts to be robust in order that the group could secure its future with potential lenders. Their mutual goals and personal standards of integrity resulted in good outcomes to their interactions in terms of financial reporting, which were easy to achieve. Where necessary they worked together to ensure that the rest of the board was persuaded to accept changes.

The group had adopted some very aggressive accounting practices, particularly in the way it accounted for leasing transactions, when it was in breach of its debt covenants. The group's financial problems and the existence of the covenants influenced the financial reporting policy and made it more aggressive. However, putting this right did not cause any serious difficulties, as both Nick and Simon were very clear as to their objectives. What could have been an embarrassment to Simon because his firm had historically gone along with the original accounting strategies was easily handled. It was facilitated by a change of audit partner, and the more robust accounting standards being introduced by the ASB.

Nick, as new finance director, produced a change of culture within this group and a much more conservative attitude to financial reporting. Although the group's accounts had always remained within the letter of the regulatory framework, Nick's arrival improved the quality of earnings. Such a shift in earnings quality would not be obvious to an external user of financial statements.

The going concern problem also raises some interesting issues. Simon as auditor, made his position absolutely clear to the group that he would qualify the accounts if the funding arrangements were not in place when their accounts were signed off. He took a firm line, offered no compromises and his position was accepted without question.

But it was not just at the year-end that the group had a going concern problem. There were doubts about its future viability throughout the period under discussion. What arose out of the year-end reporting cycle was the need to make a public statement about the position which put them all under pressure. The board was concerned that disclosure of the seriousness of the position until the funding was agreed would bring the group down. It is unlikely that investors or other users of the accounts would have been aware how serious the problems were. As it happened, delaying the announcement meant that the group was able to continue. But it is debatable whether further transparency would have made the situation any better. In the board's view it would have made it worse.

The influence wielded by city institutions is significant. The institutions with whom Nick was negotiating to provide further finance to the group insisted on a change to the composition of the board, which led to more effective corporate governance. The institutions were only prepared to lend money to people they could trust. The mere existence of an audit committee and compliance with the Cadbury code *per se* did not produce what the institutions wanted. It was the people that the institutions were interested in. As a result an audit committee which had previously been ineffective and had no accounting expertise was replaced by one which was much better.

The change of chairman brought about another attitude shift which was less to Simon's liking. The new chairman had not been involved in the efforts to save the group and had no loyalty or gratitude to Simon or his firm for his efforts in helping the group to stay afloat. Whereas Nick was a comfort seeker, the new chairman was a fee grudger and he wanted the audit doing as cheaply as possible. Threatened with a tender and the loss of his client, Simon reduced the fees. Personally he was upset because he had done so much for the group and Nick was left feeling uncomfortable because of the possibility of a reduced service. Thus a strong auditor/ finance director relationship can be undermined by other boardroom changes, particularly where the other board members do not fit the same buyer type profile as the finance director.

6 Thomas and James (TJ plc)

'You can't eat an elephant'

6.1 BACKGROUND TO THE CASE

This group had operations in the UK and overseas. It had been a private family owned company before its flotation and although it was listed the family still had a controlling interest in the group. There were no significant institutional shareholders. The group had performed well for several years since its flotation but trading had recently become more difficult. There were two underlying problems. First, quality defects in a key product line had undermined market share at a time when competitors were developing equivalent or better products. Second, a decision had been taken to develop a new product (henceforth Newpro), which required considerable investment. The development was progressing much more slowly than the board had expected. The reduction in profitability resulting from loss of market share had left the group with insufficient cash flow to continue to fund the development of Newpro at its existing level. Despite these setbacks, the group remained solvent, but further investment was needed to secure its long-term survival.

The board was dominated by the chairman, who was also the chief executive. He was the founder of the business and effectively controlled the group. He was approaching retirement age, and an obvious solution to the group's need for further investment was to seek a buyer while it remained a going concern. This solution was recognised by other members of the board, but it took some time for the chairman to agree. The chairman also was hostile to financial reporting regulations and resistant to regulatory change. The group did not have an audit committee, but before the Cadbury Code[1] was introduced there had been at least one non-executive director on the board. One of the non-executives was a chartered accountant.

Thomas, the finance director, was in his fifties and a chartered accountant. He had been with the group for some years, having previously been a partner in James's firm. James's firm had acted as auditors for the group for many years and also looked after the personal affairs of the chairman

---

[1] See footnote 4 in Chapter 5.

and other family members. Thomas had limited resources available to him. He was responsible for the accounts, which were initially put together by his assistant, and he also acted as company secretary. He regularly experienced difficulty in convincing the chairman of the need for the group to comply with the regulatory framework for financial reporting.

James, the engagement partner, was in his thirties. He had previously been the senior manager on the group's audit, so had some knowledge of the business. His predecessor engagement partner had of late paid little attention to the group as he had been preoccupied with another client which had major problems. The senior tax partner in James's office, who looked after the group's tax affairs, had known Thomas for many years and was an important client relationship link.

6.2   THE KEY ISSUES FOR THOMAS AND JAMES

Despite his problems with the chairman, Thomas knew that he was responsible for making sure that the group's accounts showed a true and fair view. He was less than enthusiastic about compliance with the Cadbury Code and the emerging new Financial Reporting Standards (FRSs), as he saw the changing and more rigorous regime as an extra burden on his limited resources, and a further source of friction with the chairman.

When James became involved with the group, he was a newly appointed partner. He recognised that the possibility of a change of ownership increased the client's risk profile for his firm. He wanted to make sure that the group's accounts would stand up to scrutiny from a potential buyer.

We interviewed Thomas and James separately and the interviews covered four accounting periods (designated as years one, two, three and four). Three key influences pervaded the interactions between them. These were: the dominant personality and the power of the chairman/chief executive, who did not like financial reporting regulation, and who had control not only of the board but also of the company through his family shareholdings; the declining profitability of the group; the poor relationship between Thomas and James.

We identified four interactions, set out below, which were of importance to Thomas and James. Other board members (particularly the chairman) and more senior partners in James's firm became involved at various stages.

- stock obsolescence provisions (*interaction TJ1*);

- treatment of product development costs under FRS 3[2] (*interaction TJ2*);
- accounting treatment of restructuring costs under FRS 3 (*interaction TJ3*);
- events surrounding the sale of the group (*interaction TJ4*).

Interactions TJ1, TJ2 and TJ3 had outcomes which affected the group financial statements. The outcome of interaction four did not affect the financial statements.

6.3   INTERACTION TJ1: STOCK OBSOLESCENCE PROVISIONS

Both Thomas and James believed that the stock was overvalued. It was not until a new computer system was installed that the problem was properly quantified. When it became apparent that the overvaluation was material, agreement had to be reached as to how it should be put right. An additional problem was the need to get the chairman to agree to the additional provisions. Thomas and James had different views about how the matter should be handled. Arising from this James commented on Thomas's lack of openness with him and Thomas expressed his opinion about the value of the audit service.

Thomas explained how the overvaluation had arisen. There had been three main causes. The first was historic:

> 'When it was a private company, going back rather a lot, there was a tendency for [*the company*] to overvalue its stock. ... We've been putting that right. I mean we've had several looks at it, including one when we went public. ... It's quite extraordinary for a private company to overvalue its stock really. It doesn't make sense, but anyway they did it' (Thomas).

The other reasons were more recent in origin:

> 'I think about [*year two*] the problem sort of re-emerged as our particular stock problem. ... The ... business which we're ... in became a maturer market. ... Obviously stock problems had a heightened importance and there was more to be written off than there had been previously ... The demand for our products has flattened out, partly because a lot of the industries in which they are used have de-manned ... The other thing of course is that the average unit price has dropped

---

[2] Financial Reporting Standard No. 3 (issued in October 1992 and amended in June 1993) introduced changes to the format of the profit and loss account; a note of historical cost profits and losses; a statement of total recognised gains and losses; and a reconciliation of movements in shareholders' funds.

quite dramatically ... older lines have gone out of production which gives you obsolete stock' (Thomas).

When James took over as the engagement partner he was seriously concerned about the over-valuation problem and was determined to get it put right:

'When I inherited [*the group*] there were problems in some of the balance sheet assets ... that needed addressing. ... So over a period of time my aim was to try and redress that balance and drive down some of the balance sheet carrying values of the assets. ... It was primarily the stock valuation' (James).

He had been surprised that some of the problems went back as far as the flotation:

'I'd like to think a finance director goes into a flotation ... having a few things hidden in the cupboard, shall we say, a few provisions here and there ... but not the other way round ... where it's short' (James).

But he also admitted that his predecessor engagement partner could have done more:

'The partner who dealt with it previously didn't even have a closing meeting with the finance director ... in the previous one or two years. ... I took him down to meet Thomas when I was the senior manager. ... We did have some concerns but we probably didn't have enough evidence to force the point, and the audit partner was prepared to live with what the position was and sign off. [*He*] spent quite a lot of time ... trying to save a plc up in [*northern city*] and he didn't spend a lot of his time on clients in [*James's office*]. Therefore we probably weren't addressing these issues as early as we should have been' (James).

It was not until the group installed a new computer system that the obsolescence problem could be quantified:

'We had a particular year where we thought we'd got more evidence to suggest that the stock was overvalued. There was ... almost no obsolescence provision there. They put in a new computer system and we were able to work out ... just how much slow moving stock we'd got ... But we did not have that sort of information available before' (James).

The extent of the overvaluation was material to the group:

'We just had the information from a stock obsolescence printout. But they couldn't deny it because they ... generated that information themselves and that came up with a big number' (James).

James and a more senior partner who had a long-standing relationship with the chairman tackled the problem.

> 'In this particular year we sat down with the chairman and Thomas and we said, "This cannot continue." I was determined we had to do something about it ... and we were able to reach agreement ... over a three-year period ... that we would drive down these stock values and build up the stock obsolescence [provision]' (James).

The three-year compromise was reached, as Thomas did not believe that there could be a big hit in one year:

> 'We knew about it and there would be ways and means ... you can't suddenly write several millions off your stock if you're a public company. You have to do it gradually' (Thomas).

James was prepared to accept a three-year period, but understood the risks:

> 'I'm afraid I take a pragmatic approach to auditing and you can't eat an elephant ... so I had to dissect the thing and ... get so much in one year and so much the next. My concern was that in the meantime if the company was sold there was a problem and ... if someone went to a bid, was to find that ... the balance sheet was overvalued that might give both the company and ourselves a problem' (James).

As it turned out, the sale took place after the third (and final) year of adjustments:

> 'We've now seen the company sold ... and there's no suggestion that the carrying value of stock is anything but about right. In fact the timing has been almost perfect' (James).

However the obsolescence provisions were not achieved without some friction:

> 'I think it caused some difficulty because the chairman didn't want to do it. I think Thomas recognised that there were problems ... [*the chairman's*] still running the business as the major shareholder. So it was ... a family company on the stock market ... Getting that initial agreement caused some friction but once it was in place we just got on and did it' (James).

James had a major concern that although Thomas had agreed to the adjustments, he was not keeping the chairman fully informed as things progressed:

'I think he was partly true to his word by not ... making the chairman aware of all the facts. He would just get on and do it. ... He would make the twenty thousand provision' (James).

But Thomas had developed his own ways of handling the chairman, and was not pleased when the auditors continued to draw the stock obsolescence provisions to the chairman's attention:

'Wretched thing the auditors will do though. I keep on telling them this. We in the accounts department do something. They then go and tell the chairman, "Oh, marvellous, you've done this and provided this on your stock", and he hits the roof. ... He tells me off for having provided something. ... You can't win on these things always' (Thomas).

But James wanted to be certain that the chairman and the rest of the board *did know* what was going on. He was not sure that Thomas was passing his concerns on:

'In the early days I was trying to deal with Thomas and I don't think I was getting anywhere. I was saying that we've got these difficulties on stock ... but I wasn't aware that Thomas was going back and telling the rest of his board about it. So as I became more experienced as partner I thought, "Right, got to tackle the rest of the board on this" as I became aware of more evidence to support my views' (James).

He felt that to some extent Thomas was not standing up to the chairman and was hiding behind the auditors:

'He should have been challenging his own chairman. He knew it wasn't right. ... If he didn't he shouldn't have been the finance director ... he should have been questioning these matters as well. And I feel that he allowed the auditors to do some of the dirty work. That's not meant with any personal criticism. I think that's what he should have done' (James).

Despite this, James did understand the problems Thomas faced in dealing with a difficult chairman who controlled the group:

'Thomas could be resistant because he knew that the chairman could be resistant. ... The chairman was resistant because the chairman, almost as a matter of pride rather than anything else, wants to report the best results for the group. ... In the chairman's eyes the best results meant a good profit, and obviously ... if you adjust the stock commensurate in line with profit ...' (James).

James expressed regret that Thomas had not been more willing to share the problems with him.

> 'Thomas had a fine line to tread because the chairman still ran the business and was a volatile character. Despite his outgoing personality to most people, he was still a difficult man to deal with so I can see that from Thomas's point of view. ... I would have liked Thomas to have almost sat down with me in the earlier days and said, "Can we work together on resolving some of these issues and how do we tackle them so we get the stock down?"' (James).

This was despite his belief that Thomas did not value the audit service:

> 'Thomas is an ex [*James's firm*] partner himself. He does not have a high view of auditors. He does not think they have value ... that may be the profession as a whole, that may be [*James's firm*] or me in particular' (James).

In this perception James was quite right:

> 'I don't find the audit itself much value, frankly. They rarely turn up anything that we don't already know about ... if ever. ... There are certain things that we do know about that they don't dig out. ... I don't think that we find within the accounts department that the audit actually helps us that much' (Thomas).

Furthermore, Thomas did not believe they understood the business:

> 'I think that goes for most auditors, you know, when you think about it. I don't think they do know [*the business*] particularly well' (Thomas).

6.4 INTERACTION TJ2: THE TREATMENT OF PRODUCT DEVELOPMENT COSTS UNDER FRS 3[3]

The development of Newpro had originally been undertaken in an attempt to add to the core business. However it was absorbing a lot of cash and by the end of year two was showing a substantial loss with no immediate prospect of matching income. The chairman did not want to comply with FRS 3 and show the loss above the line in the profit and loss account. The matter was not resolved until very late in year two.

---

[3] Under FRS 3, exceptional items are stated after operating profit or loss *only* if they relate to sale or termination of an operation; disposal of fixed assets; or a fundamental reorganisation or restructuring. In other cases they are included as part of operating profit or loss with an explanation in the notes to the accounts.

James and Thomas both describe how the matter progressed and also make telling observations on each other's behaviour and the behaviour of the chairman. James believed that Newpro was an attempt by the group to diversify from the core business which was losing ground:

> '[*Overseas market*] is a very difficult market for them now. And one of the ways they tried to move away from the core business was developing a new product ... but the problem was it was a start-up operation absorbing lots of cash and absorbing lots of profits' (James).

Thomas explained the problem for the year two accounts:

> 'By [*year two*] it was of such a size clearly we were losing money on it. Clearly we had to show it, somehow had to describe it in the accounts separately ... The principal argument that arose was that the chairman wanted it all below the line. I said to him "No, you can't do that under accounting standards these days"' (Thomas).

James explained the chairman's objectives further:

> 'The chairman wanted to treat certain things in certain ways which were almost what you call quasi extra-ordinary items under FRS 3. He wanted to identify it as non-on-going profits so it was clearly seen by everyone that that was the case. And there was a particular [*material amount*] that the chairman wanted to capitalise as some sort of marketing expense, and I said, "We cannot do this. I can't see any way", and I was continually telling Thomas and Thomas was agreeing with me' (James).

Thomas did not believe that the chairman's proposed accounting treatment of the marketing expenses would have been permitted before the introduction of FRS 3.

> 'I don't think actually ... one could ever have done it even going back some time' (Thomas).

James recognised that Thomas needed support against the chairman's ideas:

> 'Thomas was really needing our support to say that' (James).

Although the chairman eventually had to concede on the marketing expenses, he continued to push Thomas on the FRS 3 presentation and

Thomas asked James if a compromise could be reached:

> 'Thomas was then coming back and saying "There must be some way we can
> dress this up and what have you"' (James).

The chairman's persistence led to a meeting with a technical partner and
the involvement of the second partner[4] on the engagement to try and find a
solution:

> 'The chairman wanted to present it one way and I told him he couldn't do it that
> way and, well I mean, he went on and on and on and insisted on having his
> way. ... He wanted it right down the page rather than up the page, and you know
> it went on to the extent that in the Christmas break ... he had a meeting
> arranged ... with a technical partner to thrash this out' (Thomas).

The meeting was arranged at the last minute and James was on holiday but
a form of presentation was finally agreed:

> '[*Second partner*] and our technical partner had a meeting with the audit man-
> ager, the non-executive [*director*], Thomas and the chairman and we were able
> to come up with this form for presentation' (James).

James was not sure how the chairman felt about the final agreement on
presentation particularly as the issue had been resolved at a very late stage:

> 'I think that was quite amicable and was, was well received. ... That was dealt
> with pretty late ... I'm not sure how happy the chairman was about the way it
> was done, but that was the way it was. ... What might still have bugged him is
> [*he*] wanted to present the things he wanted to present. ... He didn't see why the
> rules had changed and he couldn't ... put so much into extra-ordinary items'
> (James).

However Thomas, although he agreed with the auditors' views on the
interpretation, thought they could have been more decisive and saved a lot
of trouble:

> 'Some auditors are always over-anxious to please all the time, and what irritated
> me personally was there was an over-anxiety to please instead of saying what

---

[4] It is usual for an additional partner to be involved with important (e.g., listed) audit clients,
in addition to the engagement partner, to act in a review and generally consultative capacity.

reality was perhaps as firmly, but that may be me. ... They dithered a bit ... to my mind it got blown out of all proportion ... if they had been a bit firmer earlier on, yes we might not have had some of the problems' (Thomas).

Although James acknowledged the problem was resolved very late, he felt that Thomas could have been more helpful and pro-active in the relationship:

'And with hindsight we maybe could have come up with that a little sooner. We could have been more instrumental in helping them and more creative in helping them do that. Again I think I would have found it helpful if Thomas would have come to me and talked about it that much earlier in the process than leave it towards the year-end' (James).

Finally Thomas made some comment on the behaviour of the chairman in this matter:

'I suspect he did lose his temper with me at some point ... but he does when he doesn't get his own way and when he knows he's wrong he loses his temper. ... I mean ... once he loses his temper it's usually a sign that he knows he's wrong' (Thomas).

After agreement had been reached, James felt that he had helped the group over a difficulty and was entitled to recover some of the extra costs which had been incurred in finding a solution:

'I went back to Thomas and said I wanted some fees for some of this. ... We had tried to be creative and helpful in saying what you can do within the rules and helping ... Thomas was reluctant to pay. ... It was a bit mixed in with ... Newpro because there was some overlap between us helping to finance it through our corporate finance department' (James).

Interestingly, it was the chairman who finally agreed to pay extra fees:

'The fees were a bit mixed up, but we finally, through talking the chairman, got some extra fees' (James).

This was important to James, as his firm did not recover the scale cost of the audit:

'We far from made a good scale recovery on the audit. We would write off time against our scale. ... We got pretty good scale recovery on the tax advice and the other work for them and ... let's face it ... audit ... is a difficult market anyway, isn't it. It's one thing to have our scale recovery, it's another thing to actually make it' (James).

6.5   INTERACTION TJ3: ACCOUNTING TREATMENT OF RESTRUCTURING COSTS UNDER FRS 3

In year three the group made a loss and an issue arose about the accounting treatment of material restructuring costs under FRS 3. The costs had arisen late in the year. Both the chairman and Thomas wanted to disclose these costs as exceptional under FRS 3. James, on the basis of preliminary technical advice had not dissented from this view, and it was not until a second technical review shortly before the board meeting to approve the accounts that it became apparent to him that the costs did not qualify for this treatment. As a result there was an acrimonious board meeting, including a conference call with the firm's national technical partner, but the auditor's view finally prevailed. However Thomas followed this up by insisting on a fee discount on the grounds of poor advice. Thomas and James both comment on each other's conduct throughout.

James described the overall position in respect of the year end audit:

'We didn't think we had too many issues on the audit side of things … they were abiding by the agreed stock policy. The rest of the balance sheet I don't think there were too many issues on it. … Clearly the results were hardening … and for the first time ever [*the group*], including Newpro, had made a loss' (James).

The restructuring costs arose very late in the year:

'There were some restructuring costs which occurred around the year end … I'll tell you what happened and I'll tell you what I think the mistakes I made were' (James).

Thomas described the sensitivity of the results for the year and his wish to clear the presentation of the restructuring costs with the auditors:

'On this particular point and presentation of it we had a fiasco in [*year three*] because the group accountant and myself, being aware that the presentation of [*the group*] numbers was an emotive point we discussed it with them … and they said to our surprise, "Yes, you can do it like this." … We thought they were wrong. We had another meeting with them and it was still OK and they passed it through their technical department, supposedly, who said the presentation was OK' (Thomas).

James gave his view of it:

'We had a meeting with Thomas just before Christmas in [*year three*] and we went through the draft accounts. ...We had these restructuring costs and we were showing them as exceptional under FRS 3. It was almost quasi-extraordinary under the old SSAP 6, and we'd already had a technical review.[5] But I did emphasise to Thomas that I needed to thoroughly understand what they were .... They needed to be fundamental to conform ... with FRS 3 in order to be shown in the way they were being shown, and they would have to be described as such in the operating and financial review' (James).

When the treatment has been apparently agreed, at a subsequent meeting the chairman decided he wanted to put more costs in and James and Thomas became more concerned:

'The chairman wanted to lump some more costs into these exceptional costs and Thomas was almost leading us, ... "Check out that you're happy the way these exceptional costs are being treated ... go back to your technical people" and I became increasingly concerned .... I didn't really think these did conform with FRS 3 the more I saw what they were' (James).

As a result James went back to his technical department who advised him on the basis of more information that the costs did not qualify as exceptional:

'Head of technical said "I don't believe these conform to fundamental ... all these costs are in making people redundant and rationalising the way the business is operated, not fundamentally changing the business." And it is that misunderstanding that we have got to get clear' (James).

The auditors' final interpretation of FRS 3 was not decided until the day before the board meeting at which the accounts were due to be approved. Thomas admitted to having doubted the original interpretation:

'Then on the day before we were having the meeting, the Board meeting to approve the accounts, which I describe as the Cadbury meeting, they rang up to say "Oh, you can't do it like this, you've got to do it like this." ...That's what I thought from the beginning you would have to do' (Thomas).

---

[5] This means that a draft of the accounts was referred to the firm's technical department for their review, to confirm compliance with the Companies Act and Accounting Standards.

James received dusty treatment from Thomas when he passed on the information about change of position:

> 'I phoned Thomas, faxed Thomas, and said, "I just don't believe we can present these as exceptional items. I just don't think we can go on with it, you know the Review Panel[6] will ... question it and I don't think you can get away with them as exceptional items", and Thomas said "Right, I just don't accept that", you know he virtually hung up on me, you know, which he's done in the past, you know, that's a bit the way he is really' (James).

James explained why he thought Thomas was angry:

> 'He was angry because I was telling him ... I couldn't, wouldn't go with what he was doing because I can't endorse it' (James).

He acknowledged that he had not communicated very well with Thomas over the issue:

> 'I think I probably left him with the impression that we ... found it acceptable and I'm sure Thomas has that impression. I intended to leave him with the impression that they had to be fundamental under FRS 3 ... I was aware of what he wanted to do. I don't think I'd explained it well enough to him and I think he'd gone away perhaps with that impression; however, I take the blame' (James).

Thomas did not like having to go the board with a proposed change to the accounts as presented:

> 'Well, we had to announce it was all different, they had changed their minds' (Thomas).

Being aware that the meeting was likely to be difficult James tried to bring in the second partner who had known Thomas for a long time. He also prepared an alternative presentation before he went:

> 'I went to the board meeting with my manager. [*Second partner*] was not contactable and they were trying to get hold of [*him*] because he'd known Thomas twenty, thirty years and known me two or three years .... I took [*the alternative presentation*] along to them at the time of that board meeting; it did not involve a massive redraft in the accounts. ... I did not go on with a complete problem with no solution' (James).

---

[6] The Financial Reporting Review Panel, whose remit is to enquire into the annual accounts of PLCs and large private companies which are brought to its attention. It has power to apply to the court for an order to amend the accounts, but has so far always reached agreement with the directors on remedial action to be taken.

When James went to the board meeting he found the board hostile and resistant to the change:

'I went to the board meeting and, you know, I had most of the board shouting at me saying, "You can't come along at this stage and say what you're saying"' (James).

Not surprisingly Thomas blamed James at the meeting for the lateness of the change:

'Thomas had a pre-prepared speech saying, "Look, over a period of time we've discussed these concerns, you are coming very late in the day and it's not acceptable"' (James).

James realised that he needed Thomas's support at the meeting. Despite feeling that Thomas could have been more helpful, he decided to take full responsibility for the problem himself:

'I could have gone along to that meeting and said, "Look, Thomas, you could have come along and talked to me earlier about this problem", because he talked to me very late. ... He's a finance director, he's a chartered accountant. ... It's his responsibility to prepare the accounts in accordance with the standards as much as it is ours to audit them. I went and took the full blame because I wanted Thomas's support in the board meeting to get it through. ... I do not believe it was all my fault. I think it was fifty-fifty, but I thought there's no point in having a big row and us all storming out of that board meeting and not coming to an agreement' (James).

James explained his strategy further:

'If I could get one or two people on my side when I'd constructively adopt this treatment ... and not end up with a qualification or a polarised position' (James).

The proceedings of the meeting were complicated by the behaviour of the non-executive director who took the side of the chairman.

'I mean the other amusing thing is actually the non-executive director who is a chartered accountant tends to side with chairman' (Thomas).

James also recognised the position of the non-executive director:

'I had to convince the non-executive who is himself a chartered accountant. He came along from various angles to try and say, "Why can't these be exceptional?" you know and was arguing it right the way through' (James).

He thought the non-executive director was concerned about his relationship with the chairman:

> '[*Non-executive director*] was trying to support the chairman by getting to what
> he wanted to substantiate, that we could all be comfortable with it as excep-
> tional. ... I think he wanted to stay close to the chairman, probably too close'
> (James).

During the meeting a decision was taken to hold a conference call with
the firm's senior technical partner:

> 'During the course of that meeting they wanted to speak to our technical partner
> because [*he*] had been helpful in the prior year on this. I don't think it was a
> "We don't respect your point of view James, but is this ultimately sanctioned by
> the technical partner ... who dealt with it?" They wanted to hear it from [*him*] as
> well, and just see whether there was another way' (James).

Thomas also referred to the discussion with the technical partner:

> 'There was a fairly lengthy conference call with the technical partner of the
> auditors' (Thomas).

James felt that the contribution of the technical partner was crucial to
the outcome of the issue:

> '[*Technical partner*] made a good contribution because he was able to cite some
> more varied examples of what were regarded as fundamental. ... It was that sort
> of argument which was able to stop the chairman and the non-executive talking
> late into the night' (James).

Eventually partly as a result of the discussion with the technical partner,
the chairman and the non-executive director agreed to the change:

> 'Eventually the chairman and the non-executive director gave in. ... They recog-
> nised ... the persuasiveness of the arguments that to comply with accounting
> standards you had to present it this way' (Thomas).

James remarked on non-executive director's change of position:

> 'He had to move his position when the arguments would convince him that ... we
> were right, and I think everyone left the meeting agreeing that we were right ... the
> treatment was right but it should have been addressed earlier and that's the mistake
> I made' (James).

Once the matter had been agreed, James felt he had achieved the right outcome but was then criticised by Thomas:

'It was late but it was better to get it done and Thomas then came out with all these things ... at the meeting saying "I didn't think it was right anyway", and "I think that's the true and fair view" ' (James).

James was also critical of Thomas's unwillingness to respond to his suggestions for mitigating the effects of the change of accounting treatment by liberal interpretation of the standards:

'I tried to say to Thomas there are other ways. You could do a headline. You could do different EPSs[7] on this. I don't want to manipulate the thing, but you could have a headline EPS and things, under whatever the various guidances are. Thomas didn't want to know about that. So I was trying to be creative in other ways and Thomas was unreceptive' (James).

Overall James felt that although he had decided to taken the blame for what had happened, Thomas had manipulated the situation such that he avoided blame himself:

'I felt let down by Thomas ... I think he ... had to save his face ... if I talked to Thomas it was all my fault. ... If he'd had more of a dialogue with his auditors it could have been avoided anyway. ... I almost felt Thomas had never been comfortable with the treatment but he led me on ... into a position that I was the one who had to tackle the problem to get the result that was right, and he knew was right, but I was the one taking the blame for it' (James).

Despite the ups and downs, James felt that his firm's audit procedures had worked and was relieved that he had got it right before the group was sold:

'I would have hated to be in some sort of sale where we'd got some accounting treatments that were dodgy. ... OK I got it right at the end of the day because I had a second partner, because I had a technical review, because of the processes that I adhere to as an auditor worked' (James).

---

[7] FRS 3 amended the definition of earnings per share (EPS), but it does permit additional EPS to be stated provided this is done on a consistent basis, is fully explained, and is reconciled to the amount required by the FRS.

He had doubts as to whether Thomas really wanted to play by the changed rules:

> 'I don't necessarily say whether I agree with FRS 3 but that's the rule and you have to play by the rules ... Thomas didn't want to play by the rules. He would say that he was up to date but he wasn't. It was too much trouble to change things and get them just right. He couldn't be bothered' (James).

Despite this criticism, James maintained that he respected Thomas's ability:

> 'I have a very good respect for Thomas. You'll play this tape back and sound as if I don't. I have a very good respect for him. I just wish we'd had more of a dialogue' (James).

However, James acknowledged that he had learned from the difficult experience at the board meeting:

> 'This sounds terribly pompous ... I felt it was character building. I felt I'd done the right thing and I could sleep at night. If I didn't do the right thing I wasn't doing my job as auditor and ok I'd left it later than I wanted but I got it right and I'd given them help in trying to get to another solution' (James).

James expressed his fear that after the meeting he might have lost the group as a client:

> 'If you want the honest truth, I felt that we may lose the audit because of it and I felt very responsible about that' (James).

Both Thomas and James expressed their views about the chairman's attitude to this particular problem and to compliance in general:

> 'The chairman came out feeling probably not very happy with his auditors. I think he felt his auditors ... who'd been through everything with him ... were letting him down, because he didn't get his own way. ... We weren't supporting what he wanted when times are not so good ... you know when times are good, it's easy' (James).

Thomas recognised that the chairman was difficult but felt that he could stand up to him:

> 'I feel I stand up to him. ... he's a very strong-minded individual and has his own views on some things, yes, and if he does he expects them to be. You have

to be very firm with him ... he accepts but never agrees if you like. I mean he'll go on saying he still thinks it's wrong for ever' (Thomas).

Thomas also confirmed that the Review Panel had been mentioned during the course of the discussions.

'I'd already told the chairman that there was the Review Panel ... but yes the Review Panel was mentioned, in passing of course, they might come on us and cause us to do something' (Thomas).

Thomas described the chairman's view of the Review Panel rather bluntly:

'Chairman, b***** them, you know' (Thomas).

After the AGM at which James's firm had been reappointed as auditors for a further year, Thomas wrote to James asking for a reduction in the fee:

'Because of the fiascoes ... I made them reduce their fee. I said if we supply our customers with a faulty product they return it and demand credit for it, and I think they were faulty in that and I made them knock something off the fee' (Thomas).

James was very upset by this:

'He waited until the AGM was over and then he wrote to me and asked for this credit note. ... I even wondered whether the chairman would even try and not re-appoint us ... I was obviously very upset. ... He wanted to, if you like almost in pounds, prove that it was our responsibility not his, and that's how I saw it' (James).

James discussed the problem with his partners and they decided to go along with Thomas's request:

'I took counsel with the most senior partners that have been partners much longer than I have and the end result was it was probably better to give the credit note than to make an issue of it' (James).

A lunch was arranged between the senior tax partner and Thomas (who had known each other for many years) to arrange things, but James was concerned whether, in view of Thomas's behaviour, he should continue as audit partner:

'[*Senior tax partner*] subsequently went out to lunch with Thomas, because I thought that was appropriate and I said to [*him*] "You must ask who they want to continue as audit partner. ... The firm's bigger than I am, do they want a change?" '(James).

Thomas did have some criticisms of James and the service they provided to the group:

'I must confess that at times I feel that they think that [*the group*] actually is under control and they don't actually have to pay it too much attention. ... I mean one of my comments would be that he leaves too much to his manager and doesn't pay enough attention to it himself' (Thomas).

However, despite the problems, Thomas wanted James to continue:

'The feedback was something like, "James is as good as we're going to get ... keep him ... keep him on the audit." So that's what we did ... anyway I would have to come off soon because I would be rotated ... I think I've got this year and next year' (James).

James acknowledged that he felt intimidated by Thomas:

'I should have been incisive and part of it is because Thomas, if he didn't like what he heard, would shout and bully and all the rest of it' (James).

6.6   INTERACTION TJ4: EVENTS SURROUNDING THE SALE OF THE GROUP

Both Thomas and James were aware that the group required further investment. As the chairman was approaching retirement age both believed he should be persuaded to seek a buyer before the financial position deteriorated further. Thomas made little comment on the events leading up to the sale. James had been embarrassed that the group had issued profit warnings to the Stock Exchange without telling him. He was also upset that after the final profit warning, a meeting was arranged with top partners in his firm to discuss the future of the group at which the chairman gave no indication that he was already well advanced in negotiations to sell.
     James was not consulted about the profit warnings:

'They issued profit warnings. On no occasion did the finance director or the chairman consult the auditors about any of those profit warnings' (James).

The final profit warning was a real problem for James who happened to be in another office of his firm on that day:

'I read it in the paper. I didn't have the *FT* that day. I had our managing partner of the firm. I had the head of audit e-mail me in our [*northern town*] office. E-mails to the effect ... of, "What the hell is going on at [*the group*]. Did you know about this? This is going to damage their credibility, our credibility. What the hell is happening and you must sort this out" ' (James).

James had to cancel his holiday and arrange a top-level meeting with the chairman, Thomas and senior partners of the firm:

'I was due to go away straight after that but we felt we should meet with them. ... Thomas intimated when I was fixing up that dinner, "Has the chairman not spoken to you yet?" They were talking to [*the purchasers*] but they didn't tell us' (James).

James did not know why the chairman kept it quiet but did not think the secrecy was connected to any audit related problems:

'I don't know why they didn't tell us about it ... one might draw down from this that the relationship was polarised and not good. I'm not sure it was the case. I'm not sure the chairman told anyone about it, and Thomas, I think, probably felt obliged not to tell us until he had specific permission to do so. I don't think it was a result of last time's audit or that sort of thing. I think, you know, I think it was just the chairman' (James).

He recognised that Thomas and the other directors had been trying to persuade the chairman to sell and at the dinner the auditors reiterated the same message:

'I think behind the scenes there was a lot of orchestration by his fellow directors over the last twelve months to get him to the point of saying he must sell or do something. I know Thomas had been encouraging him to sell. ... It was very sad the way the business was going and we were trying to get the chairman to the table to do something, to do a deal and sell it, to put a new chief executive in, do something because it couldn't carry on. ... The chairman probably realised from the share price. Maybe that's the way he was starting to look at it' (James).

But despite all the problems the deal went through, and James was relieved that he had succeeded in dealing with the accounting problems before the purchasers carried out their due diligence:[8]

'We had one meeting with [*the purchaser*]. He made it pretty clear that if there was anything untoward about it he may well follow up about the whole business.

---

[8] Due diligence – an American term for the investigation by, or on behalf of, the prospective purchaser into the affairs, and particularly the last few years' accounts, of the target company.

That made me feel a whole lot better that we'd got all these issues over the years resolved… I was pretty open in saying where we were and what the position was' (James).

James realised that his firm would lose the audit to the auditors of the new holding company but his closing comments reflected his overall feeling about the whole experience:

'All's well that ends well' (James).

6.7   ANALYSIS OF GENERAL CONTEXTUAL FACTORS

The relationship between Thomas and James was poor, being characterised by a lack of openness, a lack of trust and possibly respect, and particularly poor communication from Thomas to James. A number of factors seemed to have contributed to this unhappy state of affairs:

* there was an age gap – Thomas was significantly older and more experienced than James and may not have regarded James as an equal;
* James's firm was not well organised;
* Thomas was a former partner in James's firm and James was newly promoted to partner level and lacked experience; Thomas may have felt 'senior' to him; possibly as a result of his time with James's firm, Thomas made no secret of his grudging attitude to audit;
* Thomas viewed the regulatory regime as burdensome for small listed companies;
* the existence of a senior tax partner at James's firm with a close relationship with Thomas and the company chairman, resulting in James's willingness to rely on this relationship; James also felt threatened because Thomas and the chairman knew senior people in his firm and could go over his head;
* Thomas was in the habit of keeping information from the chairman to avoid confrontation; and
* the company had only one non-executive director and did not have an audit committee.

The small size of the company contributed to the company's 'resistant' reporting style. The financial circumstances of the company, which was experiencing declining profitability, were conditions that both gave rise to the specific interaction issues of the case and set the general context for them. Because of the company's trading difficulties, a buyer was being sought and so there was a need to report quality earnings. James in particular was sensitive to this and the risk to his firm if the company were sold and the accounts did not stand up to scrutiny.

Two individuals were influential in most of the major interactions between Thomas and James. On the company side, the chairman (also the CEO) was the founder of the company and his family still held a controlling interest. He was a dominant influence, prone to losses of temper, and was very resentful of the impact of the increasing stringency of the regulatory regime on 'his' company. Both the chairman and Thomas could be classed as grudgers in their attitude to the purchase of audit services. On the audit side, the senior tax partner who had advised the group for many years and, therefore, had a long-standing relationship with both Thomas and the chairman, was a significant influence.

These general contextual factors are set out in Figure 6.1.

6.8 THE SPECIFIC INTERACTIONS AND THEIR OUTCOMES

6.8.1 Interaction TJ1: stock obsolescence provisions

This was a financial reporting issue which concerned measurement and involved judgement and compliance. Both Thomas and James knew that the stock was over-valued. The records were poor and there was virtually no obsolescence provision. James's predecessor partner had neither qualified the audit report nor insisted that obsolescence provisions should be made. A newly installed computerised system with an ageing facility had revealed a material over-valuation. Both Thomas and James agreed that the issue needed to be addressed, although they did not immediately agree a strategy for implementing the necessary change. The chairman categorically did not want large provisions and, perhaps as a consequence, Thomas wanted to minimise the impact of the write-down on the annual accounts by spreading it over a number of years.

This interaction had two stages. Stage one resulted in the initial agreement to write off the over-valuation over three years. Stage two arose because, following the initial agreement, James was concerned that Thomas was not keeping the board fully informed about the provisions which were being made, and raised the matter with the board himself: that is, he felt obliged to escalate the interaction to protect his own position. Figure 6.2 shows the dimensions of the first stage of the interaction, together with the parties involved, their specific objectives and the strategies adopted.

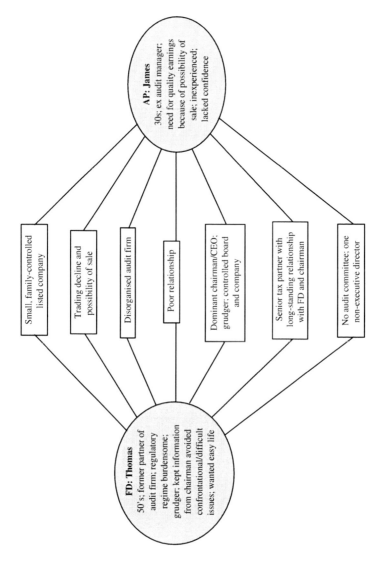

Figure 6.1 Thomas and James: general context for interactions

105

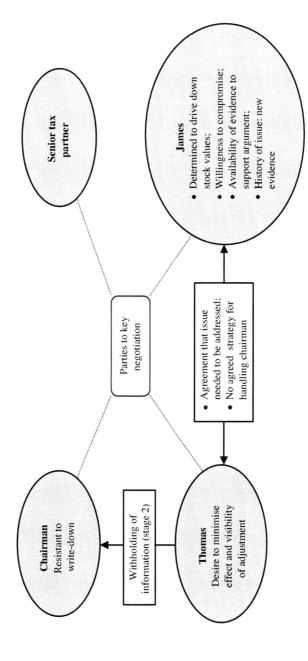

Figure 6.2   Stock obsolescence provisions interaction stages 1 and 2 (TJ1)

For stage one, anticipating the chairman's resistance to the write-downs, James involved the senior tax partner who had a long-standing relationship with the chairman, to add weight to the arguments. The specific contextual factors which influenced the outcome were: James's awareness that the group might be sold and the risk to him and his firm if the stock was overvalued at the time of sale; the difficulty of persuading the chairman to agree to the write-downs and reduce the declining profits even further; the problem for Thomas and James of having to put right an unsatisfactory standard of reporting which had been accepted by Thomas, and by James's predecessor in earlier years.

This stage of the interaction had a poor short-term outcome. Because the necessary adjustment was so large, it was spread over three years rather than being recognised and adjusted immediately. Thus, for two further years the stock in the balance sheet was not stated at the lower of cost or net realisable value as required by SSAP 9, and as shown in the group's accounting policies.

The outcome was slightly difficult to achieve because the chairman did not want to make the changes. It was made easier than it otherwise would have been because the evidence was convincing (having been produced by the company itself) and because both Thomas and James were prepared to compromise standards to get the chairman's agreement. Neither of them insisted that the total amount should be adjusted as soon as it was identified.

In the second stage of the interaction, which was an audit-related issue, James was concerned that Thomas was not keeping the board fully informed about the write-downs which were being made; i.e., he was withholding information from the board, and in particular the chairman. For this reason, this part of the interaction was escalated by James who, against Thomas's wishes, raised the matter with the board, to ensure they were fully aware of the provisions which were being made.

The key contextual factors which influenced the outcome of this interaction were the dominance of the chairman combined with his volatility, the poor relationship between Thomas and James and the absence of an audit committee (which would have been expected to deal with this issue). Thomas's strategy for avoiding problems with the chairman, and the rest of the board, was to withhold accounting information from them, but he was not open about this with James. James's preference would have been to work *with* Thomas, particularly in handling the chairman, but he was maturing as a partner and in the absence of Thomas's co-operation, he felt obliged to escalate the interaction to protect his own position and ensure that information was communicated properly.

This stage of the interaction had a good outcome in that the board was made aware of the provisions that were being made. It was a difficult interaction as James had made a unilateral decision to raise the issues with board. However, it further undermined the relationship between Thomas and James, because Thomas did not want the information to be passed on as it caused problems in his own relationship with the chairman.

6.8.2 Interaction TJ2: treatment of product development costs under FRS 3

This financial reporting issue related to classification in a primary statement and concerned compliance. In this case both Thomas and James knew from the outset that the chairman's preferred accounting treatment of the product development costs was not allowed under FRS 3. Figure 6.3 sets out the specific contextual factors in this interaction, together with the parties involved, their specific objectives, and the strategies adopted.

The key contextual factors which influenced this negotiation were the changing regulatory framework, the intransigence of the chairman and his initial refusal to accept what was required despite having the situation explained to him by Thomas, and James's lack of experience as a partner. He did not take a firm line with the chairman himself on this issue, but communicated his views through Thomas, who he knew disliked confrontation with the chairman. The poor relationship between Thomas and James meant that they did not take on the chairman together, and he therefore remained unconvinced of the need to comply with FRS 3.

The chairman escalated this interaction himself by insisting on a high-level meeting, at a very late stage in the reporting cycle, which included James's firm's national technical partner. Given that the situation was clear-cut from FRS 3, this meeting should not have been necessary. James was away at the time, but this clearly did not concern either side, and another partner attended in his place.

The final outcome was a poor one. It was creative compliance. Although James's firm, in the form of its senior technical partner, could not agree to the chairman's proposed treatment, which was blatant non-compliance with FRS 3, they did not want to upset him. This motivated them to be 'creative' and come up with a 'form for presentation' which highlighted the group's results without the loss-making activity, to accommodate the chairman. Both Thomas and James were critical of each other in not taking a firmer line earlier and leaving the chairman to escalate this.

The outcome was very difficult to achieve and more costly than it should have been. The position was, or should have been, clear-cut, but

108

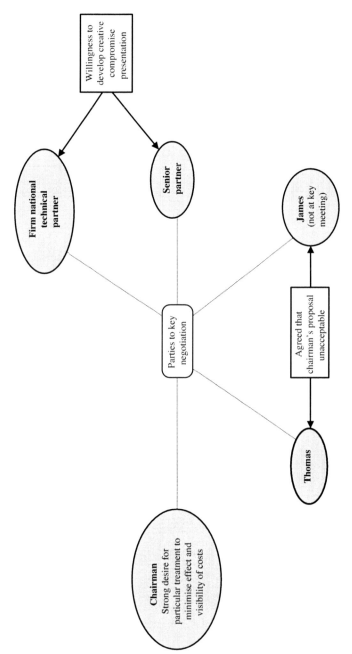

Figure 6.3   Product development costs interaction (TJ2)

neither Thomas nor James had initially taken a strong enough line with the chairman. This led to an unsatisfactory late compromise. It did not help the relationship between Thomas and James and Thomas resented being asked for extra fees for the meeting.

6.8.3   Interaction TJ3: treatment of restructuring costs under FRS 3

This financial reporting issue related to classification in a primary statement and concerned compliance. The negotiation had three stages. Table 6.1 sets out the key stages and intervening events of this interaction, while Figure 6.4 sets out the specific contextual factors in this interaction, together with the parties involved, their specific objectives, and the strategies adopted.

At stage one, the group was reporting a loss for the first time, and both Thomas and the chairman wanted to show the restructuring costs as exceptional items rather than as part of the operating profit. Having initially considered it and taken preliminary soundings, James had indicated to Thomas that this treatment was possible, with the caveat which was not much emphasised, that he needed fully to understand what the costs actually were. Thomas was not sure that James's interpretation was right, but took the advice offered and allowed the situation to develop, as it was what he and the chairman wanted.

After the accounts had been drafted, the chairman wanted to add more costs to the original amount, and Thomas, by this time convinced that James was wrong, asked him to reconfirm the position. A technical review of the draft accounts concluded that the costs did not qualify after all (a view that James had been coming to himself anyway, as he learnt more about them). Critically, the view of the technical department only became known the day before the scheduled board meeting to approve the accounts, placing the subsequent negotiation under time pressure.

Table 6.1   Restructuring costs interaction (TJ3): key stages and intervening events

Stage 1:	Thomas and James agree proposed treatment (provisionally on James's part) (Later technical review concludes proposed treatment is NOT acceptable)
Stage 2:	James communicates this to Thomas who does not accept change
Stage 3a:	No agreement forthcoming at board meeting next day
Stage 3b:	Decision to hold conference call with senior technical partner during meeting, resulting in capitulation by company

110

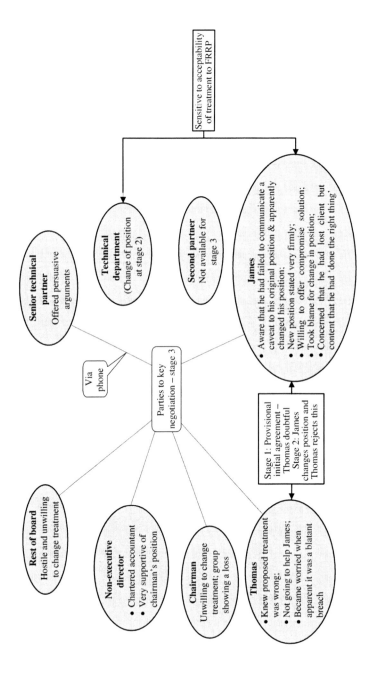

Figure 6.4 Restructuring costs interaction (TJ3)

In stage two, James informed Thomas of his change of position. This negotiation broke down, as James was now stating his position very firmly, and Thomas, although he knew that James was right, was refusing to accept James's shift of position at such a late stage. He effectively made James responsible for the mistake in front of the board.

Anticipating that the board meeting (stage three) was going to be difficult because of the unresolved issue and the lateness of the change in position, James adopted a three-part strategy to get the board's agreement. First, he tried (unsuccessfully) to arrange for a second partner who had known Thomas for many years to attend the meeting, believing this would improve the personal relationships among the parties to the negotiation. Second, he decided to offer a compromise solution in relation to the *presentation*, though not the *treatment*, of the costs (by suggesting the use of headline earnings). Third, he decided to take full blame himself for the late changes. Although he believed that Thomas had some responsibility for the problem, he wanted to offer him a face-saving outcome in front of the rest of the board, hoping thereby to gain his support.

Thomas was unreceptive both to the mitigating effect of the alternative presentation and to James's efforts to shield him from blame, preferring instead to go on the offensive, thereby protecting his own position in front of the chairman. The negotiation was made more difficult because the non-executive director, despite being a chartered accountant, initially supported the chairman.

The meeting reached a stalemate (stage three (a)). The board was not prepared to accept James's position and James was not prepared to shift. It was then decided to hold a conference call with the firm's senior technical partner (stage three (b)). The board was seeking to confirm James's stance by testing the authority of his position and seeking to confirm that no alternatives existed. This was confirmed by the senior technical partner and his arguments were persuasive, being based on fact, thus causing the board to shift its position. A compromise was reached on the presentation, which separated the results of Newpro with the reorganisation costs, which were loss-making, from the rest of the business which was profitable. The presentation was such that the reader's eye was drawn to the profitable rather than the loss-making aspects of the business.

A further outcome for James came when Thomas demanded a reduction in the current year's audit fees because of the original incorrect advice and the last minute aggravation and embarrassment which had been the consequence. (This was the reverse of the situation in interaction two where James had asked for extra fees.) James consulted with more senior partners and the credit was agreed, but he was very upset as he did not feel he was entirely to blame. As a consequence, James offered to stand down as audit partner, but Thomas, rather grudgingly, did not want to change.

In terms of financial reporting the outcome was poor. In the end the costs were not shown as exceptional, as this was clearly demonstrated to be contrary to the requirements of FRS 3. The presentation agreed highlighted the group results without the reorganisation costs. It was creative compliance. In terms of the fees, the outcome for Thomas was good as he got his fee reduction, but James was resentful that Thomas had demanded it.

This was a very difficult negotiation. The issue was clear-cut and should have been straightforward to resolve, but was confused by James's inexperience which led to a lack of clarity and firmness in his initial advice, which he later recognised himself. The developing problem was exacerbated by the poor underlying relationship between Thomas and James, the domineering chairman, and the very late stage at which the problem finally emerged. The events at the board meeting were influenced by the board's lack of confidence in James's advice and, in the absence of an audit committee, the weakness of the non-executive director as an independent voice.

6.8.4 Interaction TJ4: events surrounding the sale of the group

This was an audit issue. The events were a manifestation of the *lack* of interaction in the form of regular communication and continuing dialogue between the group and its auditors about key developments in the business. Although there is no obligation on directors to involve their auditors in the issuing of profit warnings and plans to sell their company, where the auditor is a respected advisor to a company, this information would normally be shared.

The chairman's lack of communication and his agreement to attend a meeting with senior partners in James's firm, when his plans to sell the group were well-advanced, demonstrated his lack of respect for James's firm and his unwillingness to involve them in his business decisions.

The outcome was neutral to Thomas and the chairman, who made their own decisions without consulting their auditors. It was highly embarrassing to James, who wanted to help his client but had been unable to establish an appropriate rapport with them, mainly through his inexperience, but who was then criticised by more senior partners for not being aware of what was happening in the group.

6.9 CONCLUSION

A number of fundamental issues relating to the interaction between an auditor and a company are illustrated by this case. The relationship between James and Thomas was unsatisfactory. The age and experience gap was too wide, and made worse because Thomas was a grudger and saw no value in the audit service. But Thomas's attitude was not surprising, as the group did not get a good service from James's firm. James's predecessor had spent little time with his client and, overall, the service was not co-ordinated. The firm appeared to rely on long-standing relationships to rescue problems rather than providing an effective co-ordinated service.

Thomas and James had little respect for each other and did not share problems or work together. James would have liked to do this but Thomas was not interested. James, probably because of his immaturity as partner, did not make his position absolutely clear from the outset on some issues. This lack of clarity, combined with the relationship problem, made the resolution of issues much more difficult than it needed to be. At times the relationship even became adversarial, where one undermined the other in the face of the company board and the chairman. Furthermore, as a former partner, Thomas knew many of James's seniors in the firm, had previously worked with James when he was the manager, not the partner on the job and was in a position to pull rank on him, as was the chairman. James's authority was also undermined when more senior people were brought in to rescue situations.

Apart from the lack of synergy between Thomas and James, other factors also undermined the relationship and potentially the integrity of the audit process. Although the group was publicly listed, the chairman, who was also the chief executive, effectively controlled the board and the company. There were no major institutional shareholders who could influence the group, and despite the listing, the chairman regarded the group as his own. He had absolute power to hire and fire both James and Thomas. There was no audit committee and the only non-executive director sided with the chairman when under pressure. The Cadbury code had little impact on corporate governance in this group and the chairman was uncontrollable. This may not have been a problem for other members of the chairman's family who had the opportunity to be close to events, but offered little protection to the external shareholders.

Being a young and inexperienced partner faced with a dominant chief executive and a much older and experienced finance director, both wanting to show the group in the most favourable light in declining circumstances, James tried to accommodate the board and offered to bend the rules to appease them. Although he was not willing to condone a blatant breach of an accounting standard on the face of the profit and loss account, and was ready to lose the client rather than allow this, he was prepared to mitigate the impact by adjusting the presentation of the information. He was also prepared to spread the stock adjustment over three years, when it should have been recognised as soon as it was quantified in spite of the risks that the company might be sold. He was in a difficult situation because the adjustment was so large and his predecessor partner had not faced up to it, which left him with a difficult historical situation. Putting it through in one year would have decimated the results and created a major confrontation with Thomas and the chairman. This particular compromise would not be visible to an outside user of the accounts.

Thomas would not go along with a blatant breach, but he had little respect for the changing regulatory framework and found it onerous. He also wanted to go as far as possible in accommodating the chairman. Thomas was therefore also prepared to bend the rules. What is more serious, given that he was the finance director, is that he had been willing to live for a long time with the knowledge that the group stock was overvalued without making much effort to put it right.

This case unfortunately produced three unsatisfactory outcomes in the area of financial reporting. What is most surprising about this situation is that James's firm were content to allow a newly appointed and therefore inexperienced partner to take responsibility for the audit of a listed company where it was known that the chairman controlled the company, the finance director was difficult to deal with, the corporate governance was weak and the circumstances were high risk because of the possibility that the company could be sold. James himself learned a lot from his baptism of fire but the judgement of the more senior partners in the firm and its risk management procedures in allowing this situation to develop is open to question.

7 Michael and Paul (MP plc)

'Paul's job is not to win friends, it's to protect our shareholders, and that's my job as well'

7.1 BACKGROUND TO THE CASE

This group was a very large international manufacturing company with substantial cash resources. The accounting function was well managed and there were a number of city luminaries on the board. The financial reporting culture within the group was conservative. Because of the group's status in the market, the board did not wish to attract criticism of any kind for its accounting policies. The group had an in-house treasury function to manage its funds and hedge its foreign currency transactions. Paul, the lead audit engagement partner, had in the past raised concerns about the organisation of the group's treasury activities. As the treasury function was growing it was becoming a more important issue and Paul raised the matter again. His concerns were supported by Michael, the group chief accountant, and the finance director, Joe. Michael was our interviewee. The matter was discussed by the audit committee and the main board and after some debate the treasury activities were restructured.

The group was steadily expanding through organic growth and acquisition. A number of acquisitions had been made by the group during the accounting periods referred to in our interviews. One acquisition had raised issues because its accounting policies were found to be less conservative than the group's and required substantial adjustments on consolidation. Paul indicated to Michael that the necessary adjustments were of such a size that he intended to issue a qualified audit report on the subsidiary's accounts which disclaimed on the opening position. The subsequent discussions involved the group's board, the directors of the newly acquired subsidiary and the previous auditors of the subsidiary, all of whom had different concerns and sensitivities. The interview material provides insights into the process of development of an audit qualification for a subsidiary in a major company which did not impact on the group opinion.

Michael, our company interviewee, was a chartered accountant in his forties and held the position of group chief accountant. He was responsible for the group's financial reporting activity and liaison with the auditors. The role of the finance director was of a somewhat broader nature. Michael considered that a key part of his role was to ensure that the group received no criticism relating to its financial reporting. He also needed to be on top of any emerging problem areas.

Paul, also in his forties, was the audit engagement partner. His firm had acted for the group for many years. The group was an important client to his firm and he was acutely aware of his responsibility to the shareholders and his firm. Because of the nature of the group's activities and its size, Paul considered he had a duty to use his position as external auditor to protect the interests of the shareholders and the board beyond his statutory responsibilities.

7.2   THE KEY ISSUES FOR MICHAEL AND PAUL

Integrity in the group's financial reporting process was important to Michael and Paul. Both were concerned to ensure that the group's accounts were above criticism. Both also felt they had a responsibility to look beyond the financial reporting process to ensure that there were no hidden problems which could have a material impact on the group or undermine confidence in it.

We interviewed Michael first (interview *a*). Our second interview was with Michael and Paul together (interview *b*). Michael gave us permission to interview Paul on condition that he was present. He, too, was very interested to hear what Paul had to say on matters we had previously discussed with him. We have indicated against Michael's comments which interview they formed part of.

Two contextual influences and two key interactions were identified from the interviews. The contextual influences are described first as they set the scene for the other interactions:

● the group's relationship with its auditors (*context MP(a)*);
● the role of the audit committee (*context MP(b)*);
● accounting treatment and disclosures relating to an acquisition (*interaction MP1*);
● control and accounting issues in the group's treasury function (*interaction MP2*).

7.3   CONTEXT MP(a): THE GROUP'S RELATIONSHIP
WITH ITS AUDITORS

Michael gave insights into three key aspects of the group's relationship with its auditors. He first commented on the group's conservatism and attitude to risk, the services which the group obtained from the auditors and the difficulty of distinguishing between audit and non-audit services. He first explained the culture of the board:

'The board has always had a high regard for the requirements of audit and the professional standards that imposes. I think the Board is equally mindful of the need to fulfill their statutory obligations. They don't want their reputations damaged in the city, so they are very supportive' (Michael, *a*).

He emphasised the group's attitude to compliance:

'We do try to adopt standards quickly and effectively ... I suspect there is a relationship between the level of prudence in a company's accounts and the level of discussion and negotiation. I would argue frankly that negotiations take place in companies that do not adopt best practice quickly ... that do not have an approach to completion of their accounts which is founded fundamentally in prudence' (Michael, *a*).

They were more likely to engage in discussion and negotiation with their auditors on judgemental rather than compliance issues:

'Where we have more negotiation is on areas which are not disclosure type items ... for example, fair values on acquisition is a very tricky area' (Michael, *a*).

Part of what the group paid the auditors for was their judgement:

'Fundamentally there is that judgment to be had which is why we pay [*Paul's firm*] so much money ... for the overall shape and picture of our accounts' (Michael, *a*).

Michael went on to comment on the way they worked in the face of increasing reporting burdens:

'We are getting flooded with demands. We do not have huge technical departments but we do have one guy who ... will say "Well, this is going to be an issue, Michael" and we will send our views to our external auditors for review to ensure that they are comfortable or not comfortable with what is being said ... four times a year we have regular dialogue with our auditors' (Michael, *a*).

It was the group's policy to use the external auditors as advisors on accounting matters rather than employ people in-house because of their wider experience.

'There are others who probably rely less on their auditors than we do ... which is why our non-audit fees are higher. We use external advice and support a lot

more than others, so we ask for accounting opinions more openly. We use them
on tax matters far more ... because we find that cheaper, actually than buying in
professionals who spend, say, fifty per cent of their time doing things we don't
want them to do' (Michael, *a*).

He also believed that having fewer staff provided less resource for creative
accounting:

'I always say when balancing prudence against commerciality, ... "Give me
another five accountants and I can fly more by the seat of my pants than I can at
the moment." With less people you tend to stick to the rules because to actually
be creative takes a lot of time, and a lot of energy, and a lot of people working
very hard' (Michael, *a*).

Another reason, in lean organisations, for relying on external advisors was
the complexity of the issues they had to deal with:

'You're seeing downsizing ... finance functions as well ... people are not there
and they have to call professionals in on specific tasks that require specific
detailed knowledge. Because the complexities are far greater, they are going to
take that advice and they'll implement it ... there will be fewer large accountancy functions within firms because the added value just isn't there for one-off
complex transactions' (Michael).

Michael provided his view on the distinction between audit and audit-
related advice:

'There's a huge amount of work which I would argue is very much audit-related
work, which is not audit but does not have the same ramifications for me as say
corporate finance or management consultancy work. A significant amount of
the non-audit would be taxation-related advice. It would also be things such as
accounting issues, statements of what is acceptable and unacceptable practice
which we ask for ... letters of ... an accounting nature' (Michael, *a*).

He felt that this distinction was not well understood by third parties and
could be communicated better:

'I don't think that is really picked up. One of the things I think big firms ought
to be thinking about is communicating a better description of this split ... if
there's a problem over the level that's non-audit-related. It doesn't necessarily
encompass the relationship we have with all the major firms. Currently we pay a
great deal more to the others for consultancy advice' (Michael, *a*).

However, they generally did not use their auditors for corporate finance work:

'If we want to buy a company we will go to an investment bank or use internal resources. It would be entirely unlikely that we would use [*Paul's firm*]. In fact they'd probably have a conflict with other clients' (Michael, *a*).

7.4 CONTEXT MP(b): THE ROLE OF THE AUDIT COMMITTEE

Michael then went on to describe the group's audit committee:

'Our audit committee members are senior members of our Board. Our audit committee chairman is actually our deputy chairman so he sees everything that goes on ... and we believe that [*Mr. XX*] will be joining, so overall I've got a very tough life over the next few years' (Michael, *a*).

He commented on a previous audit committee chairman:

'[*Mr. XY*] was an absolute terror. I don't think the finance director was allowed to attend audit committee meetings under [*Mr. XY*]. He was summoned to stand before the audit committee but it's slightly more relaxed now' (Michael, *b*).

Michael greatly respected the competence of the audit committee:

'They are serious players who will look you in the eye and drill your brains out because they know what you are doing. I don't hide anything because I know it's just not worth it' (Michael, *b*).

He gave an example:

'If I'm moving a provision from one place to another because really I just want to keep that provision around for a bit longer, then they are not going to be fooled by it. But as long as I'm erring on the side of caution, as long as I'm complying with all the rules and I'm not doing anything to damage the fabric of the company, or the relationship with the shareholders, or the government, the tax authorities in particular, then they're comfortable' (Michael, *b*).

The auditors were also accountable to the audit committee:

'Auditors have to be accountable to the audit committee, to be able to stand up and be able to say why they are suggesting something ... and whether they are happy with the response and the relationship they've had with me or with the management of the company and that is a very powerful tool as well' (Michael, *a*).

The auditors met regularly with the chairman and the chief executive:

'The auditors will, by matter of course, have separate discussions with the chairman and chief executive on the business on a number of occasions during the year. If there was a particular issue that came up the chairman with the chief executive will attend the audit committee and if he believes there is an issue there of concern he will then say, "Executive directors out, this is an audit committee matter that we want to discuss." Similarly they will have private consultations after the board if there is an issue' (Michael, *a*).

The current chairman of the audit committee was responsible only to the group chairman:

'His only responsibility is to the chairman. I think that is very powerful' (Michael, *a*).

However, the audit committee was not involved in determining audit fees:

'The negotiation of the audit fee is done by the finance director and the partners involved from the firm. We have a three-year rolling fee, a base case, and we work off exceptional costs above and below that. The audit fee is clearly outlined in our budget plan ... which is therefore picked up by the members of the audit committee. They do have access to the information to enable them to understand the basis of calculation' (Michael, *a*)

The audit committee was also not involved in the routine reappointment of the auditors:

'The reappointment process is pretty well automatic ... but if we chose to change our auditors the audit committee would have a paramount role to play in looking at other proposals' (Michael, *b*).

Michael then considered the group's dilemma in terms of Paul's firm's long-standing appointment:

'One of the issues that does come out there really is that our existing auditors have been in place for a significant amount of time. There may be an issue with that in terms of Cadbury, having auditors for that length of time. ... Directors have raised questions at previous audit committees to determine whether ... the time is right for a beauty parade.[1] ... That is something we bear in mind a lot' (Michael, *a*).

---

[1] *Beauty parade*: a colloquial term for putting the audit out to tender, usually by asking a small number of firms (perhaps four or so, including the incumbent) to make written submissions

However, Michael did not believe long-term audit appointments under-mined independence:

> 'I don't see there is a problem with having a longer-term relationship with a firm of auditors; in fact I'd argue that some of the risk environment elements only come out having had a lot of exposure to it' (Michael, *b*).

But he was concerned about the pushing of non-audit services:

> 'I think they are on a very difficult wicket balancing audit and non-audit issues. Audit partners are under pressure to put non-audit work into the firm, but yet, really, from an independence point of view, there's a limit to how far they can go. They're playing with a double-edged sword' (Michael, *a*).

7.5 INTERACTION MP1: ACCOUNTING TREATMENT AND DISCLOSURES RELATING TO AN ACQUISITION

During a recent accounting period the group had made an acquisition in order to strengthen its activity in one sector of its business. The deal was done quickly with only limited external due diligence[2] which was carried out by Paul's firm at the group's request. It was understood at the time of purchase that the target company (NS) was not financially robust. After the deal was done it was found that the accounting policies in NS were less conservative than those of its holding company and when adjustments were made to bring them into line, the fair values[3] of the assets acquired were much lower than expected. This created potential problems. The board was exposed to criticism from investors for paying too much for NS. The directors of NS, who had remained in post as part of the deal, faced a credibility problem from their new owner. Issues also arose about how the

---

how they would conduct the audit and what it would cost. This is followed by a meeting with each firm (the 'parade') and a decision about which firm to appoint. Changing auditors for a PLC requires approval from the Company's shareholders at the PLC's AGM.

[2] *Due diligence*: see footnote 8 in Chapter 6.

[3] *Fair values*: The Companies Act 1985, Sch.4A, paragraph 9 requires assets and liabilities of an acquired undertaking to be included in the consolidated balance sheet of the acquirer at their fair values at the date of acquisition – i.e., not necessarily at the amount they are included in the acquired company's accounting records. The differences must be disclosed in the accounts.

auditors of NS had reached their unqualified opinion on the previous year's accounts.

Paul insisted on qualifying NS's audit report because of uncertainty about the opening balance sheet.[4] However, as these opening figures would not form part of the group accounts, the qualification would not need to be carried through to the group audit report. Michael and Paul both described the sensitivities of all parties about this issue and their wish to reach an agreed position that was fair and properly reflected the position.

Michael described the acquisition and how the problem had emerged:

> 'NS's accounting policies were probably a little racier than ours … Their mind-set was based in the big-bath provisions of the late 80s and early 90s, "What can we physically get away with?" … Our auditors were doing the fair value work … they had a different firm of auditors … who did not qualify the accounts. We then buy NS. Within three months we're writing off £XXX million out of the balance sheet. We are qualifying the opening balance in essence. That has certain dynamics to it, because you are then very clearly taking a very different judgement, which you are allowed to do under FRS 5, of the value of what you have acquired and the judgement that NS's auditors necessarily took to sign off the closing balance sheet' (Michael, *a*).

Paul outlined when he became involved. This was followed by an interesting exchange between him and Michael:

> 'Basically what had happened was that NS themselves and one of Michael's team … had done the research into what possible fair values and ranges of issues there were and one of my partners and our detailed teams who had worked on it had equally looked at the facts' (Paul).

> 'Notice there were "facts" on his side and "thoughts" of where we were on our side' (Michael, *b*).

> 'Yes, that's always the case, Michael' (Paul).

> 'The power always lies with the auditor!' (Michael, *b*).

---

[4] *Opening balance sheet*: Where a subsidiary is acquired part way through the group's accounting year, the opening balance sheet for the consolidated accounts is at the date of acquisition, and assets and liabilities are to be stated at fair values. However, for the subsidiary its opening balance sheet is its previous closing balance sheet. Substantial fair value adjustments at the acquisition date call in question the validity of the values used in the opening balance sheet (in the absence of critical events between that date and the date of acquisition) – hence the auditor's uncertainty.

Paul's team had interviewed the management of NS and established that they had been close to breaching their debt covenants.[5] This had influenced the accounting:

'A number of them admitted fairly early on that they had had to present their accounts to comply with various lending covenants prior to their acquisition. ... They'd obviously been in a very tricky situation and. ... I wouldn't like to form a judgement on that. Clearly they had gone through a very difficult period prior to their acquisition by [*the group*] and they'd come to certain views and positions which they might not have done now. I suspect I wouldn't have felt comfortable as an auditor if I didn't go back and investigate' (Paul).

Michael recognised the trouble NS had been in but was more forthright about their previous auditors:

'I think that [*NS's auditors*] would have had an assessment of those accounts at that point in time with those market conditions, and my understanding is that they considered that a number of events within the balance sheet and profit and loss account were at the edge of prudence' (Michael, *a*).

He explained the group's view of the situation:

'We looked at what we could do to help them manage themselves out of the situation that they were in. ... We could have taken a more aggressive view of the realisable values within the assets and the time it would take to realise that value. If we took that aggressive view we would say we'll take all those hits and responsibilities now' (Michael, *a*).

He outlined why things were now different:

'They were no longer an independent company. They've got [*the group*] behind them and the group can afford to take a different view on their strategy. I didn't want to leave an impression that within that process there was heavy big-bathing[6] pre-FRS 5, because our auditors then come in and say, "Come on, you can have judgement over provisioning levels but you cannot charge the cost of any future deterioration ... as a pre-acquisition cost" ' (Michael, *a*).

---

[5] *Debt covenants*: see footnote 1 in Chapter 5.
[6] *Big-bathing*: Prior to FRSs 2, 5 and 6, some companies included in their fair value adjustments not only the provisions needed to reduce assets to their value at the date of acquisition but also provisions for costs to be incurred after acquisition. The result of this was that post-acquisition profits were not charged with these costs and were therefore maximised.

Michael also set out his own objectives for the group in sorting out the problem:

'I don't want to have a subsidiary where in three years' time there's another £xx million pounds of provision to make because we didn't sufficiently look at ... the fair value of the assets we were acquiring. ... Similarly I don't want any embarrassment of riches coming back over the next three years and superprofits made from a subsidiary because we've overcooked the level of provisions' (Michael, *a*).

The situation was complex with four parties involved:

'We actually had four interested parties. We had the old auditors of NS who were very concerned about preserving their professional integrity. ... We have the old management of NS who are now the new management, our own management who made the acquisition, and [*Paul's firm*]' (Michael, *a*).

He was aware of their preferences:

'[*NS's auditors*] would prefer not to have huge provisions ... the new organisation would prefer to have huge provisioning. I don't want the group to look as if it's overpaid for an acquisition ... and [*Paul's firm*], they've got no real axe to grind in fact. They're saying FRS 5. This is what it is. So those are the dynamics of a real life acquisition situation' (Michael, *a*).

Michael set out his opening position in the negotiation:

'You start off by saying "Look, management of NS, what do you believe the position really is?" We will then challenge that and say, "It cannot be at that level, at that level we bought an absolute dodo. You're not saying to me that you're managing a dodo ... and making it clear that we have bought a dodo." So we have a negotiation. We get to the level that we believe is reasonable.' (Michael, *a*).

He understood the embarrassment of the board of NS and their need to justify the change in provisioning:

'I think the trickiest position, to be frank, in all of this was the management of NS ... they are responsible for preparing their closing balance sheet. Within three months, there is a change of strategy, change of ownership, change of approach. That same management and that same board is now saying, "Actually the closing balance sheet should look like this." They are the people that had to move the most. ... They had a problem as a management team; the finance director and chief executive had just signed off their accounts so had to be satisfied that there was a requirement, based on a changing strategy, to take a different view' (Michael, *a*).

He also expressed his view on how he perceived the position of the two audit firms:

'[*NS auditors*'] get-out was, we prepared it on the basis of the financial records that were there and the representations from the management... [*Paul's firm*] didn't have to move at all ... but would be under pressure from NS management. Some of NS management would say, "Yes, there should be a big write-off." Others at NS would say, "No, it shouldn't be that high"' (Michael, *a*).

He envisaged a difficult negotiation between both audit firms:

'It's [*Paul's firm*] and [*NS's auditors*] between them are going to have a negotiation over what they both feel comfortable with. [*NS's auditors*] will have signed a set of accounts on a basis they're happy with them. [*Paul's firm*] also feel they're going to sign a set of accounts on a basis that they are happy with. But the trouble is the interplay between the two. ... They will need to square the circle' (Michael, *a*).

Michael then explained his own position on agreeing the actual numbers:

'I'm in the middle saying, "I want a straight line", and that's where we ended up really. It wasn't as big as it could have been, depending on your assumptions that you make. It wasn't as low as it could have been. It was somewhere in the middle which I believe was the reasonable route that [*Paul's firm*] felt comfortable with, and as I say, I think the management ultimately had to get comfortable with that and the previous auditors were happy' (Michael, *a*).

Paul described the process of assessing the fair values of the assets:

'I left it to Ann (the NS assignment partner) NS and Charles (Michael's assistant) to really try and agree on an item by item basis. Now there were a number of technical debates that went on which I kept abreast of. One was whether it was being consistent with a previous acquisition. ... I was particularly concerned from a group perspective, where they were doing one or two things which weren't consistent which we had to come to a view on, and secondly there was a specific issue on whether the tax affected anyone' (Paul).

The NS management were not entirely co-operative initially and Paul and Michael joined together to bring them into line over valuations that

Paul wanted:

> 'Yes, we did have to stand our ground firmly. I spoke to Michael and actually got some quite quick support on it. We actually forced them to do some external valuations that they weren't particularly keen to do. Again that was a matter of them saying no, coming to me and my speaking to Michael. ... My position was to tell Michael that I thought from both our points of view that this was something that we should get down and have done and that was done very quickly' (Paul).

Once this issue was resolved agreement could be reached:

> 'It was really down to Michael and me and Joe to look at it in the round to see if it made sense. We came to a view fairly quickly that actually NS were doing quite a sensible exercise, perhaps not providing as much as they could have done, but it was a matter of judgement and we reported to the group on that basis that they had certainly done what we would find acceptable' (Paul).

However, reaching agreement on the numbers did not resolve Paul's problem of deciding how the problem should be dealt with in the group's accounts. He described the process his firm went through in reaching their decision to qualify the opening position in NS's accounts:

> 'The first line was that Ann, who's the assignment partner for NS, came to an initial view that she thought this was going to have to be a qualification. ... We both agreed that some research be carried out to check our own professional standards and the relevant company law on qualification, the implications of doing so and knock on procedures' (Paul).

Obviously Michael was not at all enthusiastic about the possibility of a qualification. His initial tongue-in-cheek reaction to the proposed qualification, which produced loud laughter from Paul, was:

> 'I felt shocked and betrayed' (Michael, *b*).

In truth, Michael was very serious about the issue:

> '[Paul's firm] will play a very straight bat. Now in playing a straight bat [Paul's firm] are then in a difficult position ... because they have got to find a way of qualifying their accounts. Now we as a group, we don't want qualified accounts even if it is the opening balance sheet of a small subsidiary. I don't want any of my accounts qualified. So what is the form of words that you are going to be

able to use on a set of accounts ... which can actually say, "Hey, look guys, there's a £xxx million difference in the opening balance sheet." You know that's a pretty tough one' (Michael, *a*).

Paul and his partners went through a process of drawing up a draft qualification:

'Ann drew up an initial qualification which I looked at and we had it reviewed by ... the review partner we have on the job and also because [the group] ... is a major company, it was actually reviewed by our review panel who look at major qualifications. ... We treat [the group's] subsidiaries very importantly' (Paul).

They then discussed the initial wording with Michael and Joe:

'We all agreed that we were in this position and came round and talked to [the group] about the wording which did change as a result of the meeting. ... The company wanted it to be made clear that we couldn't form an opinion as opposed to hinting at any criticism of the opening position' (Paul).

Michael also did his homework on the requirements for a qualification and realised there was no choice about the qualification:

'We'd already done the work internally to determine ourselves ... where this stood in relation to the Companies Act and Paul's obligations and we were clear it was a disclaimer and we wanted wording that reflected that' (Michael, *b*).

He acknowledged Paul's firm's strong technical resources and the need to comply:

'The first thing we always do is say "Where is Paul coming from?" We go back to the same books ... we can't call on the same level of technical expertise but we can at least try and get an understanding of why he's formed that opinion' (Michael, *b*).

Michael further explained how he approached the negotiation with Paul over the qualification. He also commented more generally on his negotiating tactics with Paul:

'My first thought on this is always why on earth are we qualifying on a set of accounts that basically nobody has any interest in? ... There are no outside investors in NS. In whose interest is this? I will always start with that viewpoint and I will always start from a position that says, "Paul, you're being totally unreasonable." As he walks in the door that is the first thing I say so that we at least understand the opening position' (Michael, *b*).

He acknowledged Paul's skill as a negotiator and the underlying conservatism of the group:

> 'Paul will very quickly get me to the middle ground. He says, "Don't be ridiculous. This is the rationale and the reasons why." ... We are a very conservatively accounted for organisation. We will quickly move to that middle line. We have no interest in running up to the wire in issues like this. Paul ... has a lot of professional standards and other people looking at what he does and saying, " You cannot fall below this", and I equally have that pressure that says, "We do not want to be in front of the Financial Reporting Review Panel." We do not want to be hauled over for a Companies Act infringement' (Michael, *b*).

Michael also indicated his professional respect for Paul:

> 'He's worked with us a long time. He is professionally very, very competent and able ... and therefore we do rely on him. We rely on him to get us to that middle line quickly. ... We move very quickly from a "whose interest is this in?" to "there is going to be an impact. How do we manage that impact?" ' (Michael, *b*).

Paul explained the implications of the qualification and how it was explained to the group's management:

> 'It was a qualification that potentially could have been picked up by someone, the press, the City, and questions asked of course' (Paul).

It was therefore necessary to inform the main board:

> 'Not just the group finance director so that he's aware, but the chief executive would need to know so that he could pick that up. ... So it does get circulated certainly among the top team, and has to be done so that people understand the ramifications so that if they are, you know, questioned on those issues, they can respond' (Michael, *b*).

The group audit committee was the conduit to the main board:

> 'The group audit committee had reported our position ... and what we were going to do' (Paul).

Paul met with key executives to set out his position:

> 'There were three crucial discussions, but they weren't particularly lengthy ones. The chief executive asked me at one point, "Is this really necessary?" ... That was literally a five-minute discussion, and we said, "Yes" and he dropped it.

The chief executive of NS asked the same question, quizzed a bit more but equally dropped it fairly quickly and I know Ann did take the NS finance director through it in some detail, who was I think feeling not particularly happy. He wouldn't dispute the facts and therefore the facts led on to the qualification' (Paul).

Obviously the NS audit committee was also brought in:

'The NS audit committee looked at it in greater detail but I think by that stage people were reasonably comfortable with the facts and what we were going to say' (Paul).

Paul felt comfortable with how the qualification had worked out in terms of the group accounts:

'The qualification did refer to the uncertainty of the profit for the year in the subsidiary, but clearly, if we could make ourselves satisfied with the fair value opening position that went into [*the group*], our concerns about the opening position fell away in terms of the group accounts, as did the profit for that period' (Paul).

Despite all the problems both Paul and Michael felt that NS was a good acquisition for the group. NS's difficulties had arisen out of its non-core activities:

'The point of the acquisition was not an asset play. ... It was a cash flow play on the good bits ... which were hidden among [*other activities*] which that company should never have gone into. We believed that it was a little gem and it is proving to be that. ... You can of course argue the point as to how much you would have had to pay for the little gem' (Michael, *a*).

'I agree, you would probably have paid the same' (Paul).

They both agreed that it would have been better to know about the problem before the acquisition was announced:

'What would have been better for me would have been for everybody's eyes to have been open from day one ... to say this is going to be the likely scale and that would have been helpful' (Michael, *b*).

'Michael was always wary of some statements made on acquisition without full knowledge by [*the group's*] senior management team and you have to remember that this was announced ... with quite a lot of fanfare' (Paul).

A potential complication arose because Paul's firm had done the due diligence on the acquisition, but this had been a very limited exercise:

'It was a very short piece of work and caveated suitably as you'd have expected, tragically. ... They pointed out the areas but I think in our internal quantification of the potential exposure in those areas we had not done as much as perhaps we could have done' (Michael, *b*).

Paul explained further:

'The due diligence was literally a weekend ... which was to see the auditors' working papers ... you have to remember this was a public company' (Paul).

Michael teased him about his concerns on the due diligence:

'Was it when I said I'd sue your pants off?' (Michael, b).

'No' (Paul).

Paul was not unduly concerned about it:

'I wouldn't say of great concern ... I did during the process go back. I wanted to fully understand what we had done ... and I wanted to see what we had reported. I have to say having read it ... and also discussed what our verbal report was, which at the time I think was rather more important. I was quite content that there wasn't an issue, but I don't think that would have influenced me' (Paul).

Michael wasn't seriously worried either:

'We've always been clear in the due diligences that we've done that [*the board*] have been aware of the limitations of them and the scope of them. ... A lot of due diligences ... have been a joint effort which I think actually helps both parties. ... I think there is a danger of accountants doing all the due diligence work ... people who are used to [the business] can form a lot better judgements on the process and procedures than auditors can' (Michael, *b*).

Paul recognised the senior management's potential embarrassment at the disclosure of the events leading to the qualification and the need to understand their sensitivities:

'Auditing the group you need to be aware of the politics of the people involved. I think that's very important ... for instance I was at the ... announcement. It was useful to have sat in and heard what was said because I could equally anticipate [*the group's*] uncomfortableness in having to go back to the analysts ... with a slightly different story. ... Certainly some numbers that were potentially difficult to explain. So I was certainly mindful of that and the interrelationships between the management team here' (Paul).

He felt that it was more difficult to communicate his position to senior executives who were not accountants.

'It's not uncommon that we can ... agree reasonably readily with the group finance team and the group finance director, but then to have a secondary discussion or stand our ground against operational management ... it's as big a problem. Certainly getting the numbers right is the main problem. I am mindful of that ... if you look at the power scales, the ultimate sanction is to remove us as auditors and they may have an influence in that' (Paul).

Paul also wanted to be sure that management properly understood the issues:

'It's not only a matter of getting the numbers right and agreeing them with the finance team. ... It is a big communication exercise with senior management of the issues we've had, how we've dealt with them, why we've come to certain views. That is a big exercise and we think well worthwhile for us ... not least it helps them articulate that to the press and to the analysts in a sensible manner, which some of them find quite a tricky thing to do in accounting terms' (Paul).

Paul did not think that this particular issue threatened his firm's appointment but gave insights into the importance of being right:

'They are not trying to push the boundaries out and they are not a client where we have a reputational problem with the management team ... with clients like that I don't think you can be removed over a technical issue ... that can be debated at a technical level. ... It is much more about confidence ... from the senior management as to whether on a whole range of issues you have tended to be right ... that you are coming to the right level of when to stand your ground, when not to stand your ground and handling ... the personalities in the right way' (Paul).

Michael agreed that there was little point in removing an auditor on a technical issue:

'There's very little mileage gained from taking on a new auditor on a technical point. They normally have the edge in terms of technical expertise, so you lose on that one anyway. If you are a public company, you do not want to be going against your auditors in any event, certainly not in front of the Financial Reporting Review Panel, because that undermines the credibility that the City sees in the management of that company, not the auditor' (Michael, *b*).

Michael felt at the end of the day that a very satisfactory outcome had been reached:

> 'I think ultimately, at the end, everybody took away from this what he or she felt they needed to. Professional pride was salvaged. Management responsibility, and accountability was effectively met. I got what I wanted and we didn't look as if we'd overpaid for an acquisition. But it was a very, very hard process' (Michael, *a*).

Paul had his own view:

> 'On this type of situation ... there are certain professional standards and situations that have to be dealt with, and I have a line below which I will not go, and usually [*the group*] have another line and we have to come to a happy position in between where we both win. ... I think that is by and large where we both got to' (Paul).

7.6   INTERACTION MP2: CONTROL AND ACCOUNTING PROBLEMS IN THE GROUP'S TREASURY FUNCTION

Paul had expressed concerns to Michael about certain elements of control over the trading activities in the group's treasury department. He was also uncomfortable with the group's accounting policy in respect of the timing of income recognition for some treasury activities and was aware that changes to the income recognition policy would have an impact on short-term profits. These concerns convinced Paul that this had become an important issue which needed to be raised at board level. Michael and Joe supported Paul's position before the board. Paul was aware that he was taking a major stance on what was fundamentally a matter of judgement and was conscious of the risk to the client relationship and his own position as engagement partner if he got it wrong. However after some very difficult discussions, particularly with the senior management responsible for treasury activities, the board accepted Paul's criticisms and implemented changes.

7.6.1   Interview evidence

Most of the discussion about this issue came out of the interview where both Michael and Paul were present. Michael had initially been reluctant to mention the subject because of the sensitivities surrounding it. Paul opened the discussion:

> 'The half-year review led us to a view that we had concerns about controls in a particular area of the treasury department which we felt needed bringing to the

attention of senior management within [*the group*]. That clearly caused concern, caused antagonism because some of the facts were certainly not agreed and from our point of view quite a lot of pressure was put on us in terms of what we were saying' (Paul).

Michael explained the complexity of the treasury activities and the sensitivities at the time:

'There is always pressure for profits growth. Our treasury department has moved into complex transactions and this requires even greater vigilance' (Michael, *b*).

He explained what the key accounting issue was about:

'Without going into the fine detail of it, there was potential within an accounting issue for a review of our profits. The accounting issue boiled down to the timing of profit recognition and the matching of assets and liabilities' (Michael, *b*).

Paul explained how his concerns had developed from the half-year review:

'We do quite a thorough half year review ... and it feeds into our audit ... over a period of about ten days ... the team were bringing to me more and more ... this big issue we had on matching, but also we had a number of other control issues, both hard and weak. Some where we thought there had been some breakdowns but also some of these more softy, feely things. Attitude in management and attitude in individuals had been fed into us' (Paul).

In the end, Paul decided to take the matter further:

'I came to the view that I was uncomfortable with the level of controls, the amount of attention it was getting from the senior management team within the treasury department and felt that part of our secondary role with them ... of giving advice and feedback, was that we had to make a fairly strong statement that we were seriously concerned about the control climate' (Paul).

He then took advice from colleagues:

'I talked it over with the specialist treasury review partner. ... We'd also brought in a specialist to get a second opinion on the accounting issue because it was significant. ... I wanted to make sure my ground was solid' (Paul).

Then he agreed the next steps and how to proceed initially:

'We agreed a position on sorting out the accounting issue, but more importantly we agreed a position that we had to report our concerns ... to a number of the directors and the senior team in the treasury department' (Paul).

Paul first informed the senior accountants:

'I have to say I tipped Michael and Joe that there was an issue brewing' (Paul).

Michael explained his view of the accounting adjustments:

'I don't sweat on £xx million. I'd sweat on £xxx million at the end of the day, but don't tell [*Paul*] that because I'll fight for every million pounds that I can possibly get at the end of the year' (Michael, *b*).

He explained his concerns regarding the possible impact on the business of the problem and the difficulty of managing the uncertainty:

'Forty percent of my concern was a numbers issue, but it's the sixty percent that bothers me; I'd classify this as endemic risk ... and if you don't have endemic risk factored in to your pricing then any financial issue can get bigger. My concern was not the timing issue nor that we might have to find ... £xx million of profit elsewhere. What worried me more, frankly, was concern over endemic risk ... you don't know what necessarily you're going to find, and the sense of the unknown for an accountant is ... sort of an abhorrence really, because you can't manage the unknowns, you can only manage what you can quantify' (Michael, *b*).

Paul then raised the matter formally, firstly with the treasury department:

'It was somewhat unfortunate that some of the senior treasury people were actually away at the time but certainly those that we had there were aware of the concern in giving us ... a sort of explanation, but not one I bought into. We showed both [*Michael and Joe*] and treasury the words that were going into our audit committee report and actually that was a fairly open debate' (Paul).

Paul felt that Joe was supportive but worried about the implications:

'Joe, particularly, had some other things to add to the story. ... My perception was that he didn't disagree with what we were saying but he was certainly, sort of nervous as to the implications of it. Equally ... this was going to cause friction at various levels ... I think we were all fairly clear at that point that there was going to be a bit of a bust-up over it' (Paul).

Matters then moved on quickly to reporting to the chairman:

'Joe was so concerned about the sort of comments we were making that I then saw the chief executive, I think that evening, to explain to him what we were going to say ... the day before we were due to see him and the chairman anyway.

I thought it fairer to give it to him overnight. So we saw him and the chairman the following day as part of our clearance of the half year, but this was clearly the most major point being made' (Paul).

By this stage the numbers were less of an issue than the controls:

'We broadly came to a view on ... handling the numbers ... that was a secondary issue at this stage' (Paul).

The matter was next referred to the audit committee:

'We reported it to the audit committee a few days later, who heard a short explanation from the treasury department, not a great deal ... the audit committee was attended by the chief executive and the chairman which is unusual. We felt they wished to be there to handle the issue from the chief executive's point of view, but equally they wanted to share their thoughts with the non-executives who make up the audit committee, and also the audit committee met without any of the executives present with us to discuss it' (Paul).

The next stop was the full board meeting to approve the half-year figures:

'We then reported the issue to the main board, two or three days later as they were approving the half year numbers, at which point we got comfortable with the numbers surrounding the control issue' (Paul).

Paul did not attend these meetings on his own:

'I would never go to the audit committee on my own. We always go two or three of us. Equally the board, there were three of us who went to the board ... I have to say though the audit committee did ask to see me individually, partly because we were talking about individuals at the time and I think they wanted to keep that within a small circle' (Paul).

After the half year was cleared, further discussions took place with management in the treasury department who were, understandably, not happy with events:

'We had a much fuller debate with the senior treasury management who didn't like at all the comments that we had made, didn't agree with a lot of the facts and were generally trying to repair the issue. ... Although there was one accounting issue, I didn't see that as any different from a number of control issues, attitudinal issues ... they weren't clear-cut. ... One of the approaches they tried was to try and debate every one of them and knock us down on everything' (Paul).

Michael had been concerned that some of the responses given to Paul were inconsistent and this had led him to support Paul's position:

> 'On the accounting issue, I wasn't satisfied that we gave three different versions of events to our external auditors, none of which were consistent with what appeared to me to be going on. ... That worried me and I was wholly behind Paul on that one ... so whilst I was under pressure, my line was very clear' (Michael, *b*).

Michael knew he had to take an unambivalent position:

> 'When you get a big issue like that you have to decide pretty early on where you're going to vote and you either stand up behind your auditor or you stand up behind your management team' (Michael, *b*).

He respected Paul for his stand:

> 'I think, whilst it's to Paul's credit that he took this issue on, he took it on knowing, or I hope he knew at the time, that he'd got the support of the finance director and the group chief accountant' (Michael, *b*).

Paul acknowledged that the discussions had been difficult and at times he had felt under a lot of pressure to drop the issue:

> 'The treasury team, I have to say, and other people who got involved did throw a number of issues at us ... we did have some fairly violent discussions. I was concerned that they might try to influence our reappointment as auditors' (Paul).

The treasury management's spirited defence of their position led to further discussion at boardroom level, which was followed by main board action to deal with problems:

> 'They were being criticised so, I suppose, like all of us they tried to put a different spin on it. That led to a further meeting with the chief executive and the chairman, at which we re-iterated our concerns and explained further ... how I'd come to this view. ... Various actions were taken by the board who discussed it at their following board meeting' (Paul).

Michael fully supported the action which changed reporting lines:

> 'The fact that subsequently there has been change indicates that ... there was no smoke without fire. We've done things to address the issues that Paul has raised' (Michael, *b*).

'There have been a number of redefinitions of responsibility' (Paul).

'And much clearer lines' (Michael, *b*).

Having described the events which led up to the issue being raised at board level and the outcomes, both Paul and Michael reflected on what had taken place. Paul began by describing how he saw his responsibilities as auditor of the group, and why he had raised the issue:

'A firm like ours auditing a company like [*the group*], I think has a much wider responsibility, is employed by the shareholders ultimately for a different role, clearly to form a view on the accounts, but an equally important secondary view is to ... challenge management, give them recommendations, give them feed-back on the business and risks they are running. ... It wasn't really my statutory responsibility ... we felt it was our obligation to [*the group*] in its broadest sense' (Paul).

He admitted to doubts about what he was doing as it was at the edge of his statutory responsibility and was fundamentally judgemental:

'It was a judgement. ... Frankly I came back a number of times to question myself whether I'd made the right judgement call on the grounds that I didn't need to make it, but felt obliged to do so. ... A lot of it was cultural. It wasn't a black and white statutory issue' (Paul).

The support of his partners with whom he consulted was a great comfort to Paul:

'I had consulted fairly widely and that's the great strength of a partnership ... so I felt strong in that regard' (Paul).

Paul appreciated that by taking the issue to the highest level in the group he risked reputation damage for his firm if he got it wrong:

'If you look at the board of [the group] we'd also made some fairly strong com-ments which, if proved wrong, would have damaged our reputation amongst a range of people who are directors of a very large range of ... companies. ... There was a major reputational issue for us if I'd made the wrong call' (Paul).

However, one or two of Paul's partners were not as supportive:

'A very natural inclination is to say we don't want to fight, you know, we much prefer to have a very happy client who thinks that every moment in time everything is wonderful. Some people don't like conflict. I have to say that that they were in the minority and I wouldn't like it to get blown out of any proportion that this was an issue' (Paul).

Michael was also aware that support for Paul from his partners was not unanimous and was disappointed by this:

'I'm not convinced that all the partners of [*Paul's firm*] were necessarily of the same opinion and that is slightly disappointing, because I believe, if you're going to get the management of a company behind you on an issue, you ought to have your own firm behind you on an issue as well. ... Fair do's to Paul ... other than knowing he'd got our support at a group level he'd not got a lot else. He's the one that took all of that' (Michael, *b*).

Michael understood that once the issue was raised it had to be followed through:

'You can't drop an important issue on the table and then say, "Well, I've raised it. They've shouted at me. I'm going to walk away", because that actually, I believe damages the relationship and your reputation, because, when the next one comes up I'd blow that issue away' (Michael, *b*).

If he had failed to carry his point, Paul knew that his personal credibility would be so damaged that he would not be able to continue with the client:

'I was very well aware that if I couldn't stand my ground and couldn't argue the issue then at the very least I would have to step down as the partner responsible for [*the group*], (Paul).

Michael understood the risk Paul was running:

'It could have gone horribly wrong ... the exposure across the entire board. I mean you're talking about people who sit on the boards of ... major companies ... the reputational risk would have been very high for [*Paul's firm*], but I think he did the right thing' (Michael, *b*).

A further issue for Paul was the possibility that his firm might lose the audit as a result of his actions:

'There was a body of opinion building up which could lead to us losing a major client. You could easily see something like that happening which clearly would be an issue that I would have to deal with within the firm ... no partner ... would want to lose something like [*the group*]' (Paul).

Michael did not believe the group would change auditors over such an issue:

> 'If we were ever considering changing auditors, it would not be based on techni-
> cal competence, fees, or the debate we have about technical issues, it would be
> about the corporate governance issues of … a long-term relationship with one
> auditor. Every now and again for corporate governance issues … you ought to
> have a look around' (Michael, *b*).

Paul believed that his stance had not overall changed his relationship
with the client, although some individuals were put out by it:

> 'It varies among people, but even those that could see it as being a direct criticism
> of them … I think there is a grudging acceptance … that it was right. … [*The
> group*] tends to read more into the personalities than we do. … They would prob-
> ably be very critical of the way we handled it on the grounds that they would have
> much preferred us to … sort it with them and not escalate it as we did' (Paul).

He then explained why he had not taken that approach:

> 'I wasn't convinced that the team would necessarily have handled it comprehen-
> sively and, given the risk, I thought it had to be addressed at a non-executive
> level of the board' (Paul).

Michael agreed with Paul's assessment, but felt that the people who had
been criticised would not get over it:

> 'I don't think we will ever repair the wound, but I think there is a grudging
> acceptance … we have made significant progress in terms of the issues that Paul
> was raising, so I think there was an acknowledgment that things could have
> been improved' (Michael, *b*).

Paul anticipated short and medium-term difficulties with the relationship but thought it would come right in the end:

> 'I believed it would actually enhance our view in the long term, but I accepted
> that I was going to have a pretty rough ride in the medium term, and I still think
> we haven't quite got to the medium term yet. There is still the odd ramification,
> but I don't think it has harmed us long term as a firm' (Paul).

In Michael's view Paul had enhanced his reputation:

> 'In my opinion he's enhanced his reputation considerably. If our management
> didn't want to hear these things then, frankly we're not doing the right thing by

our shareholder base. ... Paul's job is not to win friends, it is to protect our shareholders and that's ... my job as well ... and it's the finance director's job. That is what we are here to do' (Michael, *b*).

Both agreed that their co-operation over the issue had been a success:

> 'I think it's a good example of where, we had a mutual view of having to win, certainly with the finance team here and [Paul's firm] in terms of an organisation' (Paul).

> 'I think it's probably one of the best mutual wins you can talk about in this process of negotiation' (Michael, *b*).

7.7   ANALYSIS OF GENERAL CONTEXTUAL FACTORS

The relationship between Michael and Paul was very good, for a variety of reasons:

- they had mutual objectives – both were very sensitive to the need for the group to be beyond reproach because of its profile in the market-place and both were concerned to protect the shareholders;
- both had a very high level of professional integrity;
- they were of similar age;
- they had compatible personalities, the relationship being characterised by humour; and
- mutual trust and respect existed between them.

Because of the group's profile the board had a highly compliant and conservative reporting style. Not surprisingly, therefore, the group was, by consensus, an extreme comfort-seeker in terms of audit services. It was also a resource-seeker in relation to technical accounting advice. Also, not surprisingly, the corporate governance was strong and the role of the audit committee was taken very seriously. The committee comprised senior board members with a high level of accounting and business expertise. The contextual influences on the outcomes of the interactions between Michael and Paul are set out diagrammatically in Figure 7.1. These are drawn from the general circumstances of the group, the specific circumstances in which Michael and Paul found themselves and the two contextual issues referred to in sections 7.3 and 7.4. The combination of all the contextual factors relating to the group itself (particularly the conservatism, the strong corporate governance culture and highly competent audit committee)

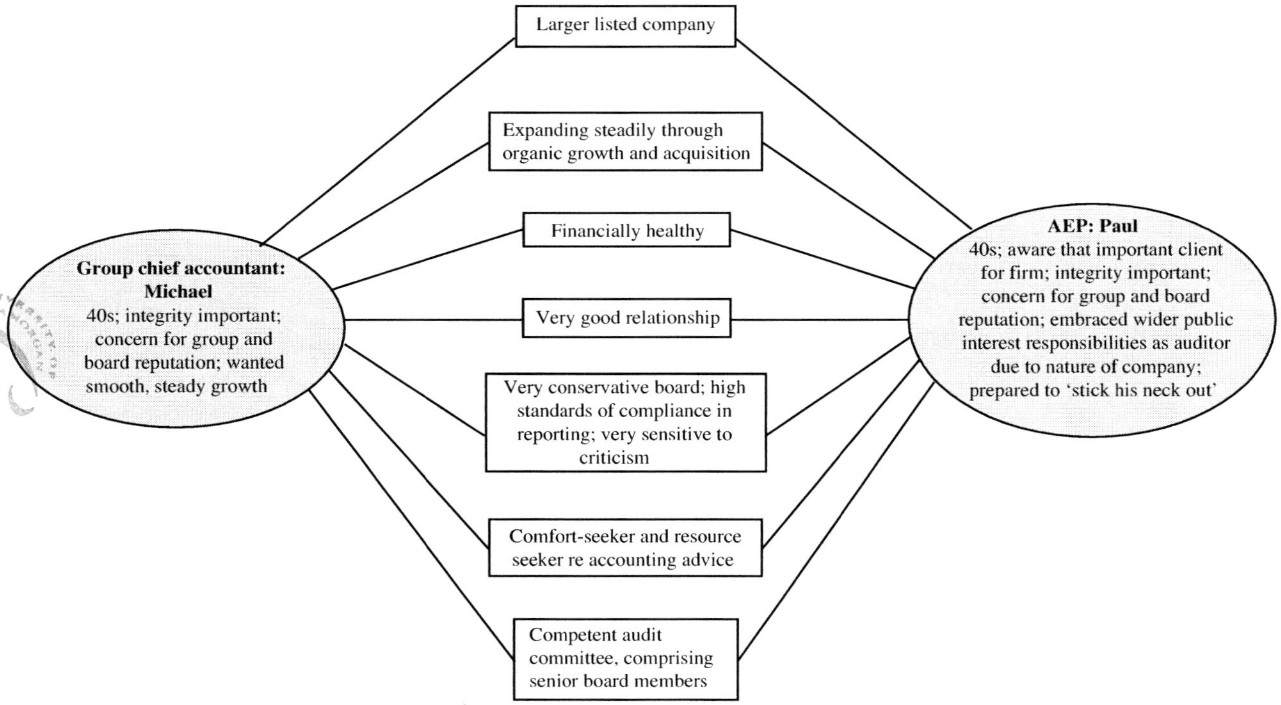
Group chief accountant: Michael
40s; integrity important; concern for group and board reputation; wanted smooth, steady growth
Larger listed company
Expanding steadily through organic growth and acquisition
Financially healthy
Very good relationship
Very conservative board; high standards of compliance in reporting; very sensitive to criticism
Comfort-seeker and resource seeker re accounting advice
Competent audit committee, comprising senior board members
AEP: Paul
40s; aware that important client for firm; integrity important; concern for group and board reputation; embraced wider public interest responsibilities as auditor due to nature of company; prepared to 'stick his neck out'

Figure 7.1 Michael and Paul: general context for interactions

together with the high integrity of both Michael and Paul resulted in a very good working relationship between them, as they both sought to preserve the group's public respectability.

7.8   THE SPECIFIC INTERACTIONS AND THEIR OUTCOMES

7.8.1   Interaction MP1: accounting issues relating to an acquisition

This accounting issue concerned measurement. It was about the agreement of fair values on an acquisition (NS). This was a judgement issue and the amounts involved were material. The problem arose after the acquisition had been completed when it became apparent to Michael that the newly acquired subsidiary had adopted a more aggressive approach to the valuation of its assets than would be acceptable to the group. Before the acquisition NS had been close to breaching its debt covenants and the need to stay within them had driven the board to minimise NS's loss provisions. Michael and Paul agreed that substantial write-downs would be required to align the subsidiary's accounting policies with those of the group. This was potentially embarrassing to the main board, as substantial post-acquisition write-downs could imply that they had overpaid for the acquisition. It was a potential embarrassment to the management of NS who had remained with their company after the acquisition and who would have to agree to shift their position on provisioning policy. NS's auditors also faced being challenged about the level of provisions which they had been prepared to accept.

The interactions were complicated because of the various parties involved whose positions had to be considered in agreeing the final outcomes. There were three distinct stages to the negotiation which are summarised in Table 7.1. The first stage was for Michael and Paul, with Joe the finance director in the background, to reach agreement on the fair values which would be brought into the accounts. Figure 7.2(a) sets out the dimensions and specific contextual factors in this stage of the interaction, together with

Table 7.1   Acquisition accounting interaction (MP1): key stages

Stage 1: Negotiation of numbers by Michael and Paul with NS management and NS auditors.

Stage 2: Negotiation of audit qualification between Michael, Joe and Paul.

Stage 3: Communication of outcome to all affected parties to explain the position on the audit report. Final communication to the main board.

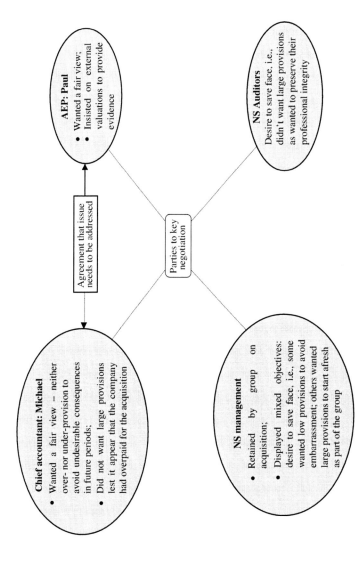

AEP: Paul
- Wanted a fair view;
- Insisted on external valuations to provide evidence

NS Auditors
Desire to save face, i.e., didn't want large provisions as wanted to preserve their professional integrity

Agreement that issue needs to be addressed

Parties to key negotiation

Chief accountant: Michael
- Wanted a fair view – neither over- nor under-provision to avoid undesirable consequences in future periods;
- Did not want large provisions lest it appear that the company had overpaid for the acquisition

NS management
- Retained by group on acquisition;
- Displayed mixed objectives: desire to save face, i.e., some wanted low provisions to avoid embarrassment; others wanted large provisions to start afresh as part of the group

Figure 7.2(a) Acquisition accounting interaction (MP1) – stage 1: negotiation of numbers

the parties involved, their specific objectives, and the strategies adopted. This stage involved negotiation with NS's management and auditors. Michael and Paul were quite clear that they wanted the fair values of NS's assets in the group's accounts to be a proper reflection of the true position and this was the predominant influence. But they were sensitive to the situation that NS management and auditors were facing, which required them to accept a material change to numbers that they had previously approved, albeit in a different and more financially strained corporate environment.

NS's management added to the complexity by taking differing positions. Some managers wanted large provisions to put the past behind them. Others, and the NS auditors, wanted to avoid the embarrassment of a substantial shift of position by restricting the provisions. Michael, Paul and Joe desired provisions that fairly reflected asset values because they did not want future profits to be distorted as a result of under- or over-provisioning on the acquisition. Michael and Paul stood together on this, and when NS's management were reluctant to provide external valuations for Paul, Michael was quick to support him. In the end, supported by the external valuations, agreement was reached with which Michael and Paul were comfortable and which was also accepted by the other parties. The balance of power in this negotiation lay with Michael and Paul, rather than NS and its auditors who had to move their position considerably. They were assisted in this by justifying the shift in terms of the change of ownership and which brought different corporate cultures and strategies. A key difference was that their new owner was financially healthy and therefore had no need to squeeze provisions.

The next stage in the negotiation concerned the need for, and wording of, an audit qualification in NS's own accounts in relation to the opening position for the year. This arose because of the material differences between asset values held by NS and the fair values of the assets brought into the group accounts, which Paul considered carried back to NS's opening position for the year, which was prior to the acquisition. (The results of the subsidiary would only be consolidated into the group from the date of acquisition to the group's year-end.) Having carefully researched the need for a qualification, Paul immediately informed Joe and Michael, stating his position very firmly. Paul then consulted his review partner on the proposed wording of the qualification, and because of the group's importance it was also referred to a high-level internal review panel in the firm. He then discussed the proposed wording with Joe and Michael. They had by then satisfied themselves that a qualification was unavoidable, as the problem was fundamental to NS's accounts. The issue then became one of whether the qualification should take the form of an adverse opinion, i.e., a disagreement over the opening position as stated, or a disclaimer of opinion, i.e., an inability, through limitation of the scope of the audit, to form an opinion on the opening position. Michael and Joe preferred the disclaimer to an adverse opinion. Paul was comfortable with this, as under the circumstances either position could have been justified. Figure 7.2(b) sets out the parties involved in this stage of the interaction and the strategies adopted.

The final stage in the negotiation involved the communication of the solution agreed between the primary parties upward to the main board via the audit committee and downward to the NS board and audit committee. Although the need for the qualification was clearly established, it was a sensitive issue. Paul and Ann therefore held separate meetings to set out the position to key players before taking it to the audit committees and the boards of NS and group. Paul met separately with the two chief executives and Ann with the finance director of NS. The NS directors were uncomfortable but the evidence was convincing and not seriously challenged. The group main board, being conservative and wanting the group accounts to be of high quality, readily accepted the qualification.

This interaction involved tough negotiation for both Michael and Paul in the first stage where they operated together to try to achieve an outcome which was acceptable primarily to them but also to the main parties involved. Once this had been achieved, the second and third stages of the negotiation were more straightforward as the case for the qualification was supported by very strong evidence. Overall, the outcome of the interaction was achieved as easily as it could be, given the number of parties involved and the complexity of the issues.

The negotiation had a good outcome as the fair values brought into the group accounts were reached by a rigorous process including independent valuation, and the concerns about NS's opening position were properly disclosed in that company's accounts.

7.8.2 Interaction MP2: control and accounting problems in the group's treasury function

This interaction involved one measurement and one corporate governance issue. Both were matters of judgement which were of significance to the group. The interaction was complex, passing through three distinct stages and involving a number of parties. The three stages are shown in Table 7.2, while Figure 7.3 sets out the specific contextual factors in this interaction, together with the parties involved, their specific objectives, and the strategies adopted.

Paul became concerned about an accounting problem and internal controls following the half-year review. He came to the view that he had a

146

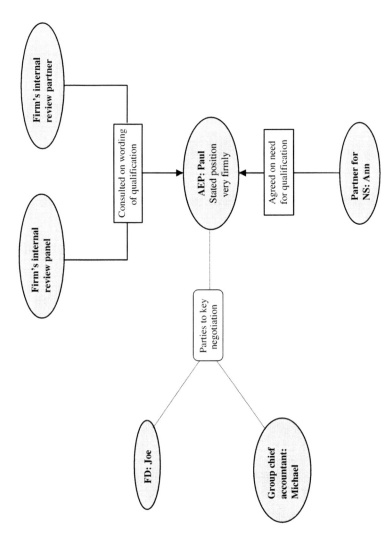

Figure 7.2(b)   Acquisition accounting interaction (MP1) – stage 2: wording of audit qualification

Table 7.2   Control and accounting issues re treasury function interaction (MP2): key stages and intervening events

---

Stage 1: Paul identified the issue and consulted with his firm. He agreed his position on the numbers and the need to raise the control issue with the group board.

Stage 2: Paul reported the concern to:
1. The group chief accountant and the group finance director (informally).
2. The treasury department management (formally).
3. The CEO (informally).
4. The chairman and the CEO (formally).
5. The group audit committee, which was attended by Paul and two other partners. The chairman and the CEO were also present. A short explanation was also given by the treasury management.
6. The full board with the half-year results. The accounting adjustment was approved and the control issue noted.

Stage 3: 1. Further discussions were held between Paul, Joe, Michael and the treasury management, who were pressing for the control issue to be dropped. Michael supported Paul against the treasury management.
2. The issue then returned to the main board who agreed to make changes to the areas of responsibility and reporting lines.

---

responsibility to take his concerns further. In taking this decision, he was acting in tune with the main board's conservatism. Because of the group's status the board did not wish to attract any criticism. He adopted a cautious approach to raising the issues, as the implications, particularly for the control issue, were serious and far-reaching. His use of the terms 'friction' and 'bust-up' are indicative of his expectations regarding the consequences of his action. Paul was well aware that he was putting both his own and his firm's credibility at risk if he was wrong or if he mishandled the situation.

Stage one in this interaction involved Paul consulting within his firm to seek confirmation and authority for the position he was about to take. He consulted first with the specialist treasury review partner on both issues and then sought a specialist second opinion on the accounting problem. A position was agreed on the accounting issue. Agreement was also reached that there was a need to raise the concerns about controls. As both issues would eventually reach the main board, it was recognised that this would escalate the control issue, which was more sensitive.

The second stage in this interaction was to take the issues through varying levels of group management and eventually to the main board. Paul managed this very carefully. He first warned Joe and Michael that a problem had

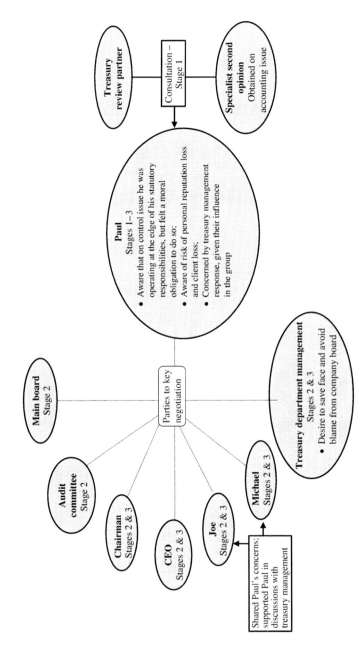

Figure 7.3 Control and accounting issues re treasury function interaction (MP2)

arisen. Then a more formal meeting was held with Joe and Michael and members of the treasury management team who were available at the time, so that Paul could tell them that both matters would be referred to in his report to the audit committee. Paul then gave the group CEO notice of the problems before he met with the CEO and the chairman to discuss the half-year results. This was followed by an audit committee meeting, at which Paul was supported by two of his partners. The audit committee was also attended by the group chairman and CEO. The treasury management executives were invited to comment on what was being raised. It was recognised that the control issues were a greater cause for concern than the changes to the accounting numbers, which could reasonably be quantified. Finally, having paved the way very carefully, Paul, again supported by two of his partners, reported formally to the main board at the meeting where the half-year results were approved. The board agreed the proposed accounting adjustment and recognised the control problem. Final resolution of the control problem was not reached at this stage, where the primary concern was to clear the half-year results.

The third stage developed after the half-year results had been cleared. The treasury management challenged in detail the matters raised by Paul as they were a criticism of the manner in which they operated. But Paul did not back down, even though he was aware that he did not have the unanimous support of his partners and it could undermine his relationship with the group and even lead to losing the audit. He knew there were serious implications for his personal reputation and the reputation of his firm if he were proved wrong. At worst he could lose the client. What he did have, however, was the support of Michael and Joe. Having fended off the treasury management criticisms, Paul then had another meeting with the chairman and the CEO to suggest a way forward. The board then agreed a course of action at its next meeting to address Paul's concerns.

This interaction had one good financial reporting outcome and one good corporate governance outcome. The adjustments to the accounting numbers which Paul had recommended were accepted by the group board, and the board also agreed to make changes to the internal control structure within the treasury department in response to Paul's concerns.

The first outcome was relatively easy to achieve as there was numeric evidence to support Paul's proposals and the board's inherent conservatism facilitated his recommendations for a more prudent approach. The second outcome was very difficult because the senior management in the group treasury department saw Paul's concerns as a direct criticism of them, and fought a hard battle against him. Paul stuck to his guns despite the risks to his own position.

7.9   CONCLUSION

Some very interesting issues emerge from this case. Both interactions involved reconciling differing cultural attitudes within an organisation whose board and senior finance officers were conservative and comfort-seeking. Interestingly, although it was a large organisation the group also relied heavily on its auditors for a lot of technical accounting advice, preferring this route to employing more people itself.

The culture clashes arose first from the acquisition of NS, where, faced with breaching its debt covenants, the level of provisioning in the accounts before the acquisition had been light. It was described by Michael as being *'at the edge of prudence'* and was not acceptable to the group's more conservative culture, but being a judgement issue there was no right answer. Although the previous auditors had signed off the NS accounts as true and fair, Paul had not shared their view of true and fair. This illustrates how the views of auditors vary on judgement issues. However, as NS had been taken over by a group which had adequate resources, there was no longer any need for light provisioning. The issue for the group and its auditors was how to deal with an inherited problem in a way which everyone who was remaining with the organisation could accept. The case also illustrates the difficulty of agreeing fair values on acquisitions when different parties have differing motivations for how they want the numbers to look.

Paul and Michael, who had common objectives in ensuring that the board's conservatism was reflected in its accounting practices, co-operated in bringing about a solution which was acceptable to all parties. Paul was very explicit about his position throughout, both on the need for independent valuations and on the necessity for a qualified audit report, something Michael certainly did not want. Paul left no scope for argument and was respected by Michael for the unambiguity of his position.

The second culture clash arose within the treasury department where the highly capable management challenged the matters raised by Paul and aggressively defended their position against him. The numbers issue was easier to resolve because of the existence of evidence. The price of failure for Paul in this case was very high but he managed the process very carefully. He took it through various levels in the organisation and persisted. Michael, who had also been put under pressure by the treasury management stood behind Paul against them, as he believed he needed to take an unambiguous position himself. However, Michael acknowledged it was Paul who had risked his reputation by escalating the issue and in the end the group was better for it. Paul knew that it did not necessarily end there and, in taking his responsibilities beyond his strict statutory duty, was aware that he could have destabilised his relationship with the group in the medium term.

8 Colin, Richard and Andrew (CRA plc)

'Cushions and pillows'

8.1 BACKGROUND TO THE CASE

This group's core business was building materials and quarrying. It was also developing a waste disposal business. There was a desire to present the group to its investors in a good light but within the bounds of respectability.

Shortly before our interviews, two major acquisitions had been made. One, Neweng, was in its core business activity; the other, Cleanup, was in waste disposal. Inevitably, there were fair values to be agreed on the acquisitions.[1] In an earlier year there had also been a major restructuring in the core business for which provisions had been established,[2] the claw-back of which had to be agreed year on year with the auditors. A further substantive accounting issue arose from the construction of some large fixed plant which was financed through long-term finance leasing arrangements. The calculation of the annual interest charge to the profit and loss account was complicated by changing interest rates.[3]

At the time of our interview, there was a possibility that the group could be the target of a hostile bid, although no firm positions had been taken.

We had arranged to interview Colin, the group finance director. He felt that a more comprehensive view of the group's accounting issues would be obtained if Richard, the group accountant, were also present. He had therefore invited Richard to the meeting as well. Colin was in his fifties and

---

[1] See footnote 3 in Chapter 7.

[2] Provisions set up in a previous year for the cost of major restructuring are available to be used as the costs are actually incurred – a process described as 'clawback' which may take several years to use up the provision. The auditors are concerned that only amounts relating to the original purpose of the provision are set against it instead of being charged against profits. Such provisions are no longer permitted under FRS 12, which was issued in September 1998.

[3] See footnote 5 in Chapter 5 for a general description of the effect of SSAP 21. This provides that 'The total finance charge under a finance lease' (here described as the annual interest charge) 'should be allocated to accounting periods during the lease term so as to produce a constant periodic rate of charge on the remaining balance of the obligation for each accounting period, or a reasonable approximation thereto'.

very experienced in the industry. Richard was much younger. Both had been with the group for some years and were qualified accountants.

Andrew, the senior engagement partner, was also a senior partner in his firm. Because of the group's size other partners were involved as well. Andrew was also in his fifties. His firm had been auditors to the group for some years. Andrew asked us not to record the interview with him, so extensive notes were taken and dictated directly after the meeting took place. Verbatim quotes from Andrew's interview are therefore limited.

8.2   THE KEY ISSUES FOR COLIN, RICHARD AND ANDREW

There had been a number of changes within the group during the period under discussion, which had required accounting effort to sort out. Although they wanted to stay well within the regulatory framework, Colin and Richard were prepared to take a fairly aggressive approach to accounting treatments. Andrew, a mature and experienced audit partner, was well aware of this. At the time of our interview, he was mindful of the possibility of a hostile bid, which he knew could provide an incentive to the board to show the group's financial position in the strongest possible light, as this would add to the shareholder value and serve to make the bid more costly. As the potential bidder was in the same industry sector, Andrew was aware that the board's accounting policies would come under close scrutiny. He did not believe it was wise for their accounting policies to appear less prudent than those of the predator company. He understood the need for the accounts to be strong but only within the limits which were acceptable.

Five interactions and two contextual influences emerged from the interviews.

- accounting for two acquisitions (*interactions CRA1, CRA2 and CRA3*);
- accounting for long-term leases on fixed plant (*interaction CRA4*);
- restructuring provisions (*interaction CRA5*);
- the working relationship between the group and its auditors (*context CRA(a)*);
- the procedure for clearing the year-end accounts and the role of the audit committee (*context CRA (b)*).

8.3   INTERACTIONS CRA1, CRA2 AND CRA3: ACCOUNTING FOR TWO ACQUISITIONS

During the latest accounting period the group had made two acquisitions, both of which had been substantial. One was an overseas acquisition in their core area of business and the other was an additional waste disposal business. The overseas acquisition, Neweng, was relatively trouble free and Colin and Richard acquiesced to Andrew's views on the fair values to be brought into the group accounts. Agreement of the fair values for the waste disposal acquisition, Cleanup, was less straightforward, particularly in respect of valuations and depreciation rates for the landfill sites.

Before discussing details of the acquisitions, Richard set out the group's view on acquisition accounting. He recognised that fair values were a major issue in many companies:

'There's no question about it … fair value on acquisition accounting is … the higher level of judgement in determining the numbers you're going to give individually and in the group financial statements. … It's obviously an area where risks can be taken with post-acquisition profit performance' (Richard).

Although it had been the subject of interaction with the auditors, he believed that the group was reasonably prudent in this area:

'Acquisition accounting has been … one of the greatest focuses of tension as far as auditors are concerned, understandably so. Some companies, and we are not among them, would take a very, very aggressive stance in dealing with acquisition accounting. … [*The group*] has taken a reasonably prudent approach in the scale of things. … Discussions with auditors are probably not quite so tiresome as they might be in another organisation but nevertheless there are fairly lengthy conversations in this particular area' (Richard).

The two major acquisitions Neweng and Cleanup had led to discussions with the auditors:

'There was a fair degree of discussion during the course of the year over the final goodwill number, obviously it's got to be resolved' (Richard).

Colin and Richard had been helped by an internal auditor with experience in acquisition accounting:

'One of our auditors, who came from a financial house, has got particular experience in fair value acquisition accounting and he was involved in managing acquisition profits from an accounting point of view, so as the expert he was included in dealing with these acquisitions' (Richard).

Colin and Richard then described the two acquisitions.

8.3.1   Interaction CRA1: the Neweng acquisition

Colin first set out the background to the acquisition:

> 'We were looking for a company that was strong in [*country X*], hadn't got a
> worldwide distribution network but the products were a complementary fit. ...
> We found one after a two year search' (Colin).

Andrew's firm had limited involvement in the due diligence:[4]

> 'We did involve [*Andrew's firm*] in working with us to a price, and in fact the
> partner, Tim, spent a fair bit of time helping us to understand the ... acquisition
> in terms of the value, the accounting issues that would arise and a number of
> other important matters' (Colin).

The group did not always use its auditors for due diligence. There were
also conflicts of interest to consider:

> 'We do some ourselves. They helped us with some of the due diligence.
> Wherever they have a conflict ... and they're auditors to certain targets, then
> we wouldn't use them' (Colin).

The main issue in this acquisition related to property values, but it was
not material in terms of the total acquisition:

> 'The issue there was fundamentally one of valuing the buildings, which were a
> relatively small part of the value and then effectively the goodwill' (Colin).

Andrew had also found 'little to worry about' in this acquisition other
than the fair value of the property which he believed was overstated. The
property was recently constructed and had been revalued shortly before the
acquisition. Concerns about the value attached to the building had emerged
from the due diligence work. Andrew thought that the valuation, which had
been put in place by the vendors, 'was daft'. He was nevertheless keen to
ensure that the group should not make adjustments with the objective of
taking a 'big bath'.[5]

---

[4] See footnote 8 in Chapter 6.
[5] See footnote 6 in Chapter 7.

Overall, Richard felt that the process of reaching agreement was straightforward and left little scope for manoeuvre, although they had tried:

'I mean, the balance sheet of that company that we were acquiring was totally
clean. So the opportunities for creative accounting on that particular acquisition
were fairly limited. We did try and push the horizons out within the areas that
are allowed by accounting standards' (Richard).

There had been one or two minor disagreements with the auditors:

'We had one or two minor disagreements with the auditors over ... issues relating to costs that that they thought probably should be charged against post-
acquisition. We're talking about very small sums, perhaps £XXX thousand in an
acquisition of £YY million ... the area of dispute was relatively small. ... We
very quickly came to an agreement over what was the proper opening balance
sheet and what were the proper fair value adjustments' (Richard).

In this case, because the adjustments were small, Richard and Colin
decided to go along with the auditors' wishes:

'In fairness, at the end of the day we gracefully gave up on that one. We could
have stuck our heels in and taken a slightly more aggressive approach, but we
didn't and it's all about relationships. ... I think it was appropriate to consider
their view again' (Richard).

8.3.2 Interaction CRA2: agreeing the fair values in the Cleanup acquisition

Colin provided the background to this acquisition:

'We already had a waste management business ... We had been looking at further acquisitions and we particularly wanted the Cleanup business. We ended up
agreeing the price' (Colin).

He then explained the key issues in a waste management acquisition:

'The issues with a waste business are holes in the ground and contracts to fill
those holes ... or gas generation facilities. So you're fundamentally looking at
the value of a cubic metre of void space and that's where one starts from with
the acquisition of a waste company' (Colin).

Richard set out the issue of future liabilities on landfill sites:

'We've got two issues ... putting a value on holes and then assessing what the
liabilities are at the balance sheet date for the key area ... the environmental

costs and restoration costs, and it's highly judgemental. I don't know, how do you put a value on a landfill site?' (Richard).

Andrew explained that the valuation was particularly difficult in this case. Cleanup was a subsidiary of a much larger group, Scrubbit. The sites had been owned by Cleanup for many years and, prior to the disposal of Cleanup, Scrubbit had used the sites for its own purposes. The value of the sites as recorded in Cleanup's own accounting records was very low as all that had been charged to them were costs associated with work that had been carried out to make them safe. This was a comparable situation to sites which could come from the group's own quarrying activities, which were not being bought from third parties for a very considerable price.

At the time of acquisition, the net book value of Cleanup's assets represented less than 15 per cent of the purchase consideration. This was a different situation for Colin and Richard from that of an earlier acquisition where the landfill sites had been bought by the acquirer at arm's length shortly before the group had bought the company.

Andrew also recognised the difficulty of trying to estimate and make appropriate provision for the 'potential environmental liabilities'. In this area there was 'very little in accounting standards' which was of assistance, but there was recent legislation which required the licensed holders of landfill sites to retain responsibility for the sites for thirty years after they ceased to be in use.

Colin explained what the potential problems were:

'It's where you get a badly engineered site and the waste actually seeps into a watercourse. That's where it gets potentially very difficult' (Colin).

They calculated the liabilities based on probability theory:

'The issue is restoration costs and potential liabilities if something did go wrong ... it's not just a general issue. There's actually a calculation of the probability of something not going according to plan' (Colin).

The group took advice from different sources on key issues such as this:

'We would listen to what the auditors have to say, certainly as part of due diligence, and the regulatory director who's in the operational area. We've got people who totally understand ... that sort of issue ... We take advantage of their expertise and consult them' (Colin).

They also sought second opinions where they believed the issue was potentially very serious:

> 'On the key sites ... where there's a potential problem we employ a specialist to do just that' (Colin).

In this particular case they had decided what their position would be before the auditors were heavily involved:

> 'In essence they weren't involved in the process until we'd taken a particular position ourselves, well in advance of the end of the year' (Colin).

When he became aware of the issues, Andrew consulted within his firm. As the thirty-year legislation was relatively new, the issue of estimating liabilities was common to all his firm's clients who had landfill sites. Andrew described 'lengthy debates with the technical people' over the issue.

There were some areas of disagreement but Richard saw the input from Andrew's firm as a positive contribution to the resolution of the problem:

> 'It would be wrong to say they came back with a fundamentally different posi- tion. They came back with some ideas and concepts about how we could view it from their angle, and perhaps ideas we can consider ourselves, without compro- mising the position overall. So they came back in a positive way and with areas to assist us and quantify more properly ... the liabilities aspect, for example, and also their own particular point of view. So it wasn't a confrontation sort of dialogue. It was in some ways helpful' (Colin).

Richard agreed with Colin's interpretation and also pointed out that the differences in the actual numbers between the group and the auditors was relatively small:

> 'I don't think in terms of overall total numbers ... we were very far away ... but in honesty their alternative view wasn't dissimilar to ours in quantum. We had some areas where we thought they could be more aggressive than what was in the books. ... I don't think overall there was a major disagreement. It wasn't confrontational' (Richard).

Andrew agreed that there was 'no real difference of opinion' between the auditor and the company over this issue. He saw the process as a 'dynamic model for seeking a solution' and a means of 'getting a good dialogue going to seek the right answer'. He felt that there had been enough time to sort the problem out and eventually they agreed on a substantial increase to the underlying asset value which brought it closer to the purchase consideration. Andrew did not think that this was too aggressive even bearing in mind the group's position in respect of a possible bid.

8.3.3   Interaction CRA3: accounting for depreciation on the Cleanup landfill sites

A further issue emerged about how the sites should be depreciated and how the provision for restoration and monitoring, which they were required to make, should be accounted for. Andrew was concerned more about the depreciation issue than about the valuation of the sites. The group had adopted a policy of increasing the annual depreciation charge over the lives of the sites and of spreading the restoration provision over the lives of the sites in proportion to the income flow from them. Andrew understood the judgemental nature of the policy because 'assumptions are being made about future pricings and judgements, which can change extremely quickly'. His view of such complex assumptions was that 'the answer lies within the business'. Each case was unique and dependent on the soundness of the approach adopted by the company. However he did not like the depreciation policy.

He therefore informed the board that he was not 'overly happy' with their depreciation policy. He did not believe that the method was appropriate, but 'as it was not prohibited by standards', he did not feel that he could 'insist that they should change it'.

Colin was rather more circumspect about both the fair values in interaction two, and the depreciation policy. He speculated about how Andrew would have reacted if they had suggested the fair values should be much lower:

> 'This is in the area of provisions and provision releases … if we had gone down the road … of the virtual write-off of the whole value of an acquisition to goodwill … which clearly we haven't done … that clearly colours [*Andrew's firm's*] reasoning. We'd have had confrontations with them. … This in a sense is the sort of culture that an organisation builds up and the auditor knows what sort of culture that is' (Colin).

Andrew understood the culture issue very well. He felt that the depreciation policy particularly was more aggressive than 'their normal style' and suspected that that it was linked to their concerns about the possible bid. He warned the board that if they became too aggressive in their accounting policies it would be spotted by the analysts and could lead to criticism which they would not want. Furthermore 'in a bid scenario it could be used to discredit other areas of the company's accounting, if doubts were expressed about any parts of it'. It could therefore be counter-productive to what they wanted to achieve.

Overall, Andrew viewed the Cleanup acquisition as 'a premium strategic acquisition which suited them geographically'. As site licences were difficult to obtain, he believed the right way to expand this part of the group's business was to 'buy into it'.

8.4   INTERACTION CRA4: ACCOUNTING FOR LONG-TERM LEASES ON FIXED PLANT

The group had found it necessary to replace some major items of fixed plant, the cost of which was substantial. The plant was assembled on site and construction work was also required. It was financed by long-term lease contracts. Because of the length and complexity of the contracts and changing interest rates, difficulty was experienced in calculating the amount of interest which should be charged annually to the profit and loss account. Andrew initially felt that the charge was too low. It took some time to reach agreement.

Richard began by explaining what the issue was about:

'The specific issue is on finance leases ... and down to the approach that the company decided to take in accounting for the leases, which are fairly complex and fairly material as well. ... We're talking about £XXX million pounds worth of assets' (Richard).

The assets had taken some time to construct:

'Originally the assets were constructed over a period from 19XX to 19XY, a three-year draw down. ... Obviously the sums involved are quite material ... just the odd decimal point' (Richard).

The problem arose from how the interest charge was to be allocated throughout the period of the lease.

'It wasn't, in essence, accounting based. ... It was more of a method of calculation, determining the charge against profits from a variety of different alternatives, and we were perhaps taking an approach that was less prudent than [*Andrew's firm*] may have wished us to take' (Richard).

They were aware that they needed to get agreement from the auditors for the accounting treatment they were proposing:

> 'Because of its size and because of the particular stance we took, it was necessary to get some sort of agreement with the auditors' (Richard).

This agreement was not initially forthcoming:

> 'They took, initially, a different view' (Richard).

Colin explained that there was no argument over the total interest to be charged, only the spread:

> 'We had agreement on the interest … that was going to be expensed over the life of the asset. It was just a question of which portion was in appropriate periods, and we just had a different view on the appropriate treatment in compliance with recommended accounting practice' (Colin).

The auditors felt that they were not charging enough to the profit and loss account:

> 'In their view we were charging an inappropriately low amount to profit and loss account' (Colin).

Richard did not believe the numbers were material:

> 'We're not talking about material numbers here, in the context of [*the group*]. We've got a profit of £XXX million' (Richard).

Andrew was more explicit in describing the problem. It arose because the original facility with the lenders had been set up when interest rates were higher. As the equipment was coming into use, the group was drawing down the funds at a lower rate of interest. Andrew referred to the need to 'understand the dynamics' of the leases and believed it was 'less a question of what the standards said than whether what the company was doing made sense'. The original rate had been implicit in all the calculations but this was now too high, and they were receiving rebates based on the changes in the interest rates. He felt that the revised calculations at a lower rate of interest looked low and felt that the rebates could be coming in too quickly. Although the company 'appeared to have done what they were supposed to do, the figures did not look sensible'. As a result he felt, 'There was a need to move away from a precise application of the standard'.

Andrew acknowledged that, in the context of the group profits at the time, the matter was not material, but he wanted to understand it fully because he 'did not want to run up against a materiality buffer in subsequent years'. He was concerned because he 'could not understand why the numbers were coming out looking the way they were'. He therefore discussed the matter with his firm's technical department and asked one of the firm's leasing specialists 'to look very hard at the impact of SSAP 21'.

Richard and Colin were aware that Andrew had consulted his firm's technical department. Nevertheless it had taken a long time to sort it out:

'They had specific technical advice from their technical department. It actually took them twelve months before they agreed with it' (Richard).

Richard believed that the engagement team had a good understanding of leasing issues:

'They have quite a bit of experience in large leasing deals, so they weren't coming to us with a naïve approach. They had a clear understanding of what they consider as appropriate' (Richard).

In line with Andrew's view, Richard believed that the problem was one of interpretation rather than compliance:

'At the end of the day it was just a judgement issue. It wasn't saying you're not complying with the recommended accounting practice. It was just interpretation' (Richard).

Colin agreed with Richard:

'It is quite a complex issue to be fair … We could spend as long as we did with them and maybe record many discussions going on for literally hours about how the calculation of interest should be undertaken, but actually there is no fundamentally correct or incorrect way of doing it. There is an approach. There are areas around the edge where you can go in one direction or the other' (Colin).

The timing of the recognition of the problem had also caused some difficulty as it had spanned two accounting periods:

'The problems were not identified during the construction period, it was more towards the end of it' (Richard).

When it arose it was raised at one of the regular pre-year-end meetings:

> 'Having identified the problem it was part of this pre-year-end process, and
> included in the discussions after this' (Richard).

The matter was not completely settled by the time the accounts were
signed off and Richard felt uncomfortable about the unresolved issues:

> 'We were very uncomfortable saying something with which the auditors were
> not materially happy … the discussions that were at a technical level were car-
> ried on to the end of the [*next*] twelve months' (Richard).

Because of the uncertainty about the calculations, and the fact that
his firm was coming up with different numbers, Andrew had asked the
company to bring in an extra provision 'over and above the interest that
had been calculated by the company'. In the meantime he continued to re-
examine the leasing models and rerun them to see what the results were.
The extra provision was agreed on the understanding that it would be
released in subsequent years if it was not needed.
  Colin and Richard were happy with the final outcome:

> 'It was resolved to our total satisfaction' (Richard).

Colin emphasised that the solution agreed did not constitute a change of
accounting policy:

> 'We haven't changed the accounting policy. It was the application of the calcu-
> lation of the interest charge, so it didn't affect the accounting policy' (Colin).

Andrew recognised that sorting out this adjustment was difficult
because, 'There was not much in the standard to help them' and putting in
the additional provision 'seemed the best answer at the time'. He was sure
that there was 'no … unreasonableness going on' and the matter had not
been a 'big issue'. However, when they came to the following year, the
company's view had proved to be right and they had reverted to the
original calculations'.
  Despite having been proved right in the first place, Colin recognised
that they would continue to monitor the position:

> 'We'll certainly come back to it this year to say, "Where's the charge that we made
> for the interest on these leases. Are we still happy with the calculation?" … Leasing

is … quite dynamic in our view and new techniques and things will emerge, and we'll certainly be looking at those in the future' (Colin).

8.5   INTERACTION CRA5: RESTRUCTURING PROVISIONS

In an earlier year, the group had restructured its core business and reduced the workforce by approximately 20 per cent. As all the costs of this restructuring were not immediate, provisions were set up against which the costs would be charged as they arose. In the year under discussion, Andrew was concerned that the group was charging some costs against the provision that may have been more appropriately charged direct to the profit and loss account in the year. This did not breach any accounting standards and in the context of the group's results was not material. However, as he did not agree with the treatment, he voiced his disapproval at a main board meeting.

Colin described the costs associated with the restructuring:

'We had plans to shed about XXX hundred people. Prior to commencing the reorganisation, we included a restructuring provision in the accounts for that year, which was £XX million. About half the costs related to employees, man-power costs really, redundancy, pension costs, retraining … the rest related to implications from buildings, offices, whatever' (Colin).

He then explained how they had agreed the provision with Andrew's firm:

'We constructed, pretty carefully, the basis for that restructuring provision and spent a fair amount of time with [*Andrew's firm*] agreeing precisely what we couldn't do and how much we'd justified' (Colin).

As an illustration Colin described the difficulty of assessing the level of the provision for redundancy costs:

'One of the issues for example was that we didn't know who the XXX hundred would be. There's an enormous difference between somebody who's been with us for twelve months and somebody who's been with us a long time. So we had to calculate on average what the unit cost of each redundancy would be. We didn't have one. We had several. [*Andrew's firm*] came back with alternatives and at the end of the day the numbers were not far different and we agreed the unit charge that we would include. It was just an illustration but in some areas they totally signed off to this restructuring provision' (Colin).

Richard indicated that there had been compromise in reaching the final figure:

> 'There was give and take in getting to the final number. We may have adjusted numbers is some areas and [*Andrew's firm*] may have suggested some adjustments that we could make in certain areas. It is part of the process of getting to the best number at the end of the day' (Richard).

Agreement over the amounts written off against the provisions in subsequent years had proved more troublesome. Colin indicated that there had been an area of disagreement:

> 'There have been occasions, and there was one this year, where we just disagree' (Colin).

He explained that the issue arose from an unused part of the provision:

> 'It was the release from the restructuring provision. ... We had £X million which we could have regarded as the result of earlier calculations. We couldn't actually use it in the period we expected to use it, so the question was, 'what do you do with that £X million?' (Colin).

They decided to charge some continuing costs to the provision which they believed were attributable to the restructuring, but the auditors disagreed with this treatment:

> 'We took the view that we could justify some of our ongoing costs, like training and those sort of things, and release the provision to cover those costs. They just said, "Well, we don't agree". We then explained that we intended these people who worked on the restructuring issues to be included in the restructuring provision' (Colin).

Andrew was not happy that some salary costs and overheads had been written off against the restructuring provision, when it appeared to him that these costs were more properly a current year expense. He felt that the restructuring provision was 'being utilised for expenses for which it was not intended'.

However Colin and Richard were not going to back down:

> 'On some issues we would change and on other issues we would explain to them that we take an alternative view. This was one area where we just failed to get a compromise' (Richard).

Andrew disagreed with this accounting treatment but was conscious that the effect amounted to less than 1 per cent of the group's annual profit and there was no breach of an accounting standard. He recognised that the figure was 'just not big enough' to justify a major confrontation because it was 'not material to the opinion'. It was therefore not a matter on which he would qualify his audit report.

Colin was also aware of the materiality issue:

'It was not material enough for them to qualify the accounts. Andrew had a view and I wasn't prepared to take his view and he disagreed with what we were doing' (Colin).

Andrew realised that Colin was not prepared to shift his position. As he believed the accounting treatment was wrong he raised it with the audit committee and the board personally and referred to it in the following terms in his written report:

'Whilst there is not an accounting standard which prohibits utilisation of provisions in this way, the impact is to keep out of operating costs an element of the normal establishment overhead. Operating profits are consequently flattered and we do not support this practice' (Andrew).

Colin had also put his point of view to the board:

'They did state very clearly to the board that this is their view, and the board had to understand that this is my view. These are the reasons ... then they had to take a decision' (Colin).

He recognised that the position would have been very different if the effects had been material:

'If it was material we would have reflected very hard on whether we wanted our accounts qualified and that would have been a serious issue. I'm speculating because it was regarded by [*Andrew's firm*] as not material and we felt strongly that what we were doing was totally justified. There was nothing that was contravening any accounting standards, we didn't really see why we should change our approach' (Colin).

Colin emphasised that there was no acrimony between him and Andrew over this issue, and there was no hostility when Andrew put his case to the board meeting:

'In no shape or form was it ever heated. It was operated in a leisured and calculated way. Andrew went through his arguments and we listened to that and he did the same at the board. He ... stated his position. He'd done his job. The board had a view to take' (Colin).

In the event, the board supported Colin:

'Well, they took the view that what we were doing was justified. They understood Andrew's points ... we were not contravening any standards' (Colin).

Colin acknowledged that this accounting treatment was a bit aggressive but suggested that the board accepted that there were other areas in the accounts where they had been very prudent:

'To take the whole thing into account, had we been aggressive in every single area of our results ... I think we would have taken a different view. Indeed I would have, but in other areas we had been very prudent when you take the whole thing together' (Colin).

According to Andrew, one or two of the directors had questioned the accounting treatment but their reaction was not to make the changes. 'Because it was not material' he did not want to fall out with the group. He acknowledged that he too was aware of the 'cushions and pillows' in other parts of the accounts. He did, however, feel that the possibility of a bid could be influencing behaviour in this particular matter.

Without referring to the bid, Colin had hinted that at times the group might want the accounts to look good:

'There are occasions where we would clearly like to present the accounts in the best light, but only within the limits of how other companies might behave' (Colin).

The bid did not materialise.

8.6   CONTEXT CRA(a): THE WORKING RELATIONSHIP BETWEEN THE GROUP AND ITS AUDITORS

Andrew, Colin and Richard all referred to the working relationship and to the group's image as a listed company. Neither side wanted to attract any criticism for the group's accounting policies, and Andrew at times reminded Colin and Richard of the reputation risks if they adopted accounting policies that were too aggressive. They held regular meetings and kept in touch throughout the year. A key objective was to identify accounting issues in good time and work together to avoid any kind of confrontation.

Andrew considered the group accounting function was strong and that they 'did not need to be educated into providing information in the accounts'. They took their listed company status very seriously and were 'very keen to get things right'. He had two or three formally scheduled meetings throughout the year and there was also regular communication by telephone. He felt that the group wanted to 'consider the ramifications of all the things they do as they go along'. He had never felt that there was a culture of 'withholding information'. Issues were always raised with him when there was 'something to consider'.

Colin also perceived the relationship to be open and interactive:

> 'We have an ongoing relationship during the year. It isn't just when we get to the final accounts when they descend on us. It isn't like that at all ... We would hide nothing' (Colin).

There had been changes in personnel but he did not feel that this had undermined the relationship:

> 'Very professional ... We've been with [*Andrew's firm*] for some years now. ... They changed the senior partner so it hasn't always been the same people. The partner that deals with us wasn't a partner originally. He was sort of the team leader ... the people that Richard deals with directly below that level have changed quite significantly' (Colin).

Colin clearly valued the interaction with Andrew:

> 'I think we have a relationship where, apart from being professional, Andrew feels able to ring me and the chairman to say, "I am concerned about this" and we discuss it, and equally I will flag up for Andrew when we are thinking of doing something, "If we were to do this, Andrew, can you give us an indication of what your stance would be?" So we are not in a situation of being, "We've done this and you can take a view, but we don't care what your view is" '.

He felt that the group's interests and Andrew's firm's interests converged:

> 'What we both want is to produce ... fair accounts so people can see the true position and that's [*Andrew's firm's*] interests and ours as well' (Colin).

Andrew did not think he would reach a situation with the group where there were 'fundamental unresolved disagreements' which could lead to him qualifying the group's accounts. He did not believe that the group would wish to 'go beyond what was acceptable'. Most of the items he dealt with had a technical content and, in the event of a dispute, he would draw on the opinion of his firm's technical experts. His client would not want to 'push me further than I am prepared to go, and our technical panel is prepared to go'. He firmly believed that his own reputation, his firm's reputation and the group's reputation were worth 'more than the price of signing off a duff set of accounts'.

Colin could not envisage the group's accounts being qualified either:

> 'The last thing we would want is a qualified set of accounts ... I think we would try to avoid it, but with due respect though ... I can hardly imagine what would cause us to say, "Well, go ahead, qualify them if you wish". I don't think we would get to that stage' (Colin).

Andrew thought it unlikely that the group would ever justifiably find itself in front of the Financial Reporting Review Panel. Richard made his views on the Panel quite clear:

> 'The thought of the company being referred to the Review Panel is not something that would be welcome. ... It concerns me to that extra degree on a particular issue to want to get it right' (Richard).

He said that Andrew had mentioned that the Review Panel was looking rather hard at acquisition provisions but did not believe that there was an implied threat for the group:

> 'They don't threaten us. They just use the benefit of their advice from networking' (Richard).

Richard did not want any problems with the accounts:

> 'That's just not the image of the company ... but how can any event be where we don't look good?' (Richard).

8.7   CONTEXT CRA(b): THE PROCEDURE FOR CLEARING THE YEAR-END ACCOUNTS AND THE ROLE OF THE AUDIT COMMITTEE

The group had a clearly defined procedure for producing and approving the year-end accounts. The process started in the subsidiary companies and eventually fed through to the board via other committees, including the audit committee. A prime objective for Colin and Richard was to try to ensure that no unresolved issues were put before the main board.

Before describing the year-end process, Colin explained how the audit committee operated:

> 'The audit committee meets, probably four times a year. ... The chairman and I are required to attend, though we are not members of it. The group [*internal*] auditor on the finance side will report to the audit committee independently and we will have to answer questions in essence that relate to us' (Colin).

The internal auditors attended all the audit committee meetings. The external auditors always attended the audit committee which approved the year-end accounts and were invited to others:

> 'It's just the year-end one usually. We sometimes bring them into the audit committee that's looking at the audit plan. We present an audit plan to the audit committee which is probably halfway through one of the cycles for the following year. If we feel ... and Andrew feels that they should be present because there's an issue they want to address they can attend. As far as I recall they've never attended that. Part of the terms of reference of the audit committee is that it can call [*Andrew's firm*] to attend at any time, either to a regular meeting or a special one' (Colin).

Before the year-end a pre-audit meeting was held where potential issues about the accounts were raised and discussed:

> 'We have a meeting before the end of the year where we flag up to [*Andrew's firm*] the issues that we feel should be discussed between us at the end of the year. We ... say to them, "These are the issues that we feel we need to discuss" and similarly they will have questions about, "We understand that during the year you've done this and that", so well before the end of the year we will have identified the issues that need to be considered' (Colin).

Colin also liked to have the draft accounts out quickly to give them time:

> 'We do try to get the accounts finished fairly quickly so we've got a period of discussion of what might be considered major issues. Then we know if we've got differences, what those differences are and what the discussions will be on ... and concluded or not concluded as part of the final audit' (Colin).

Andrew described the year-end procedures. The group had a number of subsidiaries and operating divisions and his team would initially discuss accounting issues arising from them with the divisional directors and accountants. He would then have a 'final round up' with Colin and Richard or, if necessary, hold further discussions with them. They would then meet with the chairman.

Colin went through the meeting process in more detail:

> 'The first information will be with Richard ... Richard meets the [*junior*] partner and the audit manager, and the next session, maybe more than one, is Richard and myself and the senior partner ... the [*junior*] partner and the audit manager ... the same three meet with the chairman and myself and Richard subsequently. There may be more than one meeting but there are three successive meetings from which the more important issues will be discussed with the chairman before they get to the audit committee' (Colin).

There was also a process in the subsidiaries:

> 'And that's at group level. Each of the individual subsidiaries of the group has its own audit committee, which we may be involved in but normally aren't' (Richard).

The first meeting, run by Richard, was to give the auditors an opportunity to go away and consider the issues before the meetings with Colin and Andrew and the subsequent meeting with the chairman:

> 'I would float the issues with them, present our position with the facts so that they can obviously go away and take a judgement and take a view, before the next two formal meetings take place' (Richard).

Colin commented on the formality of the process:

> 'The meeting Richard has is, to a degree, formal because it's the start of the ... formal audit. They are all formal but I think we are sensible enough not to, as it were, sit on opposite sides of the table and demand things of each other. It works pretty well in terms of these are the issues. Are we agreed on ... what the issue is and what options we've got to deal with that issue and then are we really going to propose a solution to it? Sometimes we're not, and if we're not we go through what Richard has just described' (Colin).

The meeting with the chairman was followed by a meeting with the executive directors before the accounts and reports were taken to the audit committee. Both Andrew and Colin presented reports to the audit committee. Andrew said that Colin's report comprised 'a financial analysis of the business and a report of the highlights of the judgemental areas where they had made decisions'. Andrew himself produced a paper on 'audit issues and judgemental areas' because he 'wanted to be sure that the audit committee were aware of all the judgemental areas'. The chairman always attended the audit committee:

> 'When it comes to the final accounts the external auditors present their own report to the audit committee when the chairman himself is there' (Colin).

Following the audit committee meeting, the accounts would go to the main board for approval, accompanied by both Colin and Andrew's papers. Colin described the auditors' role at the audit committee and the board meeting:

> 'They go to the audit committee … on issues that affect the financial statements. They do a formal, full presentation to the audit committee and then to the board. The chairman of the audit committee will make a statement. The auditors usually say to the board something like, "We've audited the accounts" (hopefully they will say with good co-operation) "and we are not qualifying the accounts in any way, but these two or three items are not what we think they should be." So it is a formal presentation' (Colin).

The board presentation would normally take the auditors about half an hour but in the audit committee:

> 'They can go on as long as they want' (Colin).

The auditors' letters to management followed up the year-end audit meetings. As the group was complex, letters were sent not only to the main board but also to the boards of the subsidiaries. This was not a subject on which Andrew commented but Colin did. He first described how the letters were presented:

> 'They produce a management letter and report to each subsidiary … and they'll produce one predominantly for me and one for the audit committee, which is not that dissimilar'(Colin).

The issues raised in the letters were presented in a structured format:

> 'It's stratified … they focus on areas that have been brought forward from last year that have been properly dealt with, areas brought forward from last year,

which, at this stage, they feel we haven't dealt with, and then the other things they wish to raise. They usually quantify those on the basis of importance' (Colin).

Colin had a few doubts about the value of the management letters:

'I wouldn't overplay the management letters because I think that by the time we get the management letters we know what the issues are. There's nothing new in the management letters that we are not already aware of' (Colin).

Sometimes Colin felt that issues which had not appeared to be of significance during the audit took greater prominence in the management letters:

'There is an issue which is not a major problem by any means ... We do find the auditor, in the management letter, wishes to stress something which, when we've had prior discussions, didn't seem to be important at all' (Colin).

This sometimes caused problems with the audit committee:

'We've had one or two problems with the audit committee. I've been surprised at the way in which the auditor has presented the point. Instead of it being almost a passing comment, they say the committee should be aware of this and they get quite excited' (Colin).

He felt the auditors relied heavily on the group's own internal audit findings for the management letter material:

'The internal audit reports are extensively used ... and what we often find is that [*Andrew's firm*] will feed back to us something the internal auditor already said to us' (Colin).

Colin saw some value in the formal recording process but not much else:

'I don't think the management letter's unduly helpful to be honest. It does record things for posterity and it helps us next year to see what were the issues' (Colin).

8.8   ANALYSIS OF GENERAL CONTEXTUAL FACTORS

The general contextual influences on the interactions between Colin, Richard and Andrew and identified in sections 8.6 and 8.7 are shown diagrammatically in Figure 8.1. The relationship between the three individuals

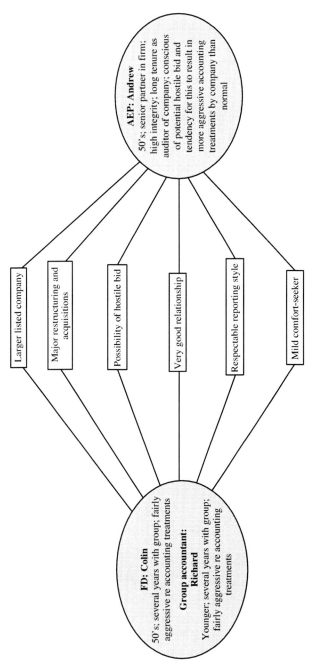

AEP: Andrew

50's; senior partner in firm; high integrity; long tenure as auditor of company; conscious of potential hostile bid and tendency for this to result in more aggressive accounting treatments by company than normal

Larger listed company

Major restructuring and acquisitions

Possibility of hostile bid

Very good relationship

Respectable reporting style

Mild comfort-seeker

FD: Colin

50's; several years with group; fairly aggressive re accounting treatments

Group accountant: Richard

Younger; several years with group; fairly aggressive re accounting treatments

Figure 8.1   Colin, Richard and Andrew: general context for interactions

was very good, for a number of reasons:

- Colin and Richard had worked together for some years and there were no differences of opinion between them;
- Andrew had been the engagement partner for some years and mutual trust and respect existed between him and Colin and Richard;
- the relationship was pro-active on both sides with problems being raised by either side as they arose and resolved by reasoned debate;
- Andrew was a senior partner in his firm and had very high integrity; he was not prepared to risk his own or firm's reputation by supporting overly aggressive accounting practices; Colin and Richard were aware that he would object to any such proposals; and
- they had a common objective to ensure that the group did not damage its reputation by adopting inappropriate accounting policies.

At this point in the group's history, the possibility of a hostile takeover bid was a significant factor and those within the group were anxious to show the group's results in the best possible light. Andrew, however, was alert to the dangers of the group going too far and damaging its reputation, thereby giving the bidder the opportunity to criticise the accounts.

8.9   THE SPECIFIC INTERACTIONS AND THEIR OUTCOMES

8.9.1   Interaction CRA1: the Neweng acquisition

The financial reporting issue arising here related to recognition and measurement and was a matter of judgement. It was about the valuation of a property which was to be brought into the fair value calculation on the acquisition. Andrew believed this property was overvalued by the vendor. The recognition issue related to the allocation of certain costs to pre- or post-acquisition profits.

Although both Colin's and Richard's natural inclination was to adopt a more aggressive treatment than Andrew recommended, they chose not to escalate this particular issue into a major negotiation but gave in 'gracefully'. This was because the amounts concerned were not material and they were conscious of other, more material, ongoing interactions where they might have to resolve a more serious difference of opinion with Andrew. In essence, they decided to engage in strategic give and take across the whole series of issues which they knew were coming up.

This interaction had a good outcome and was easy to achieve. This was because, as part of an overall strategy, Colin and Richard had already decided to comply with Andrew's wishes. This, and the fact that the matter was not material, were the key influences in this case.

8.9.2 Interaction CRA2: agreeing the fair values in the Cleanup acquisition

Two financial reporting issues arose out of this acquisition. The first (CRA2) related to the fair values of the landfill sites acquired and the provisions that needed to be made in the fair value calculation for future environmental and restoration costs. The second (CRA3) related to the post-acquisition depreciation policy for the sites.

Figure 8.2 sets out the specific contextual factors which influenced the fair values, together with the parties involved, their specific objectives, and the strategies adopted. This interaction involved recognition and measurement. The amounts involved in agreeing the fair values were material and highly judgemental, and were complicated by the fact of the sites having, for historical reasons, a very low value in Cleanup's own records. Both sides agreed there was an issue which needed to be addressed but, as it was a specialist area, there was little guidance available from accounting standards. Both sides independently sought advice on possible methods to use in the valuation process and on the provisions. Andrew consulted within his firm. Meanwhile, Colin and Richard consulted the group's regulatory director and external specialists. They came to initial views and then exchanged ideas. A good dialogue ensued and agreement to bring in an appropriate fair value was reached smoothly, based largely on the evidence and arguments available. There was no serious difference between them. The interaction did not escalate and no other parties became involved in reaching the final outcome.

Andrew was of the view that Colin and Richard may have adopted a slightly more aggressive position than was normal, due to the potential hostile takeover bid. Nevertheless, his view was that they were clearly within the bounds of acceptability.

This was a good outcome which was achieved easily and was an judgement issue. The key influences in this interaction were the need of both sides to resolve the problem and the expert opinions were obtained.

8.9.3 Interaction CRA3: accounting for depreciation on the landfill sites

A more difficult financial reporting interaction arose in respect of the post-acquisition depreciation policy for the sites acquired and the allocation of

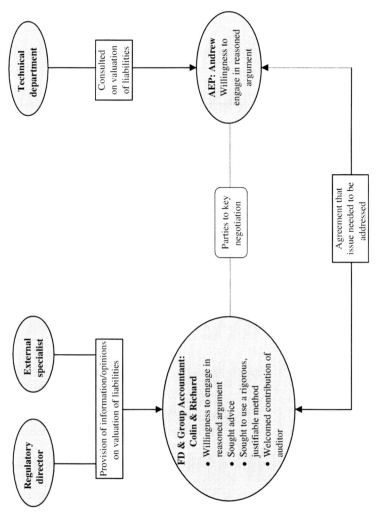

Figure 8.2   Cleanup acquisition interaction (CRA2)

the restoration provision. This was a measurement issue and a matter of judgement. The accounting policy that the group planned to adopt was to increase the annual depreciation charge over the lives of the sites and to spread the restoration provision in proportion to the income flow. Andrew was uncomfortable with the depreciation policy, which he felt was inappropriate and more aggressive than usual, and stated his view very firmly at the outset. However, he was unable to insist on the policy being changed because it was not incorrect and was not prohibited in the standards. However he was not prepared to accept what was being proposed by Colin and Richard without expressing his concerns to the main board about the risks in adopting unusually aggressive accounting policies in the face of a hostile bid. He was concerned that the potential bidder could use it as an opportunity to undermine the board. He therefore escalated the interaction. This action by Andrew was in keeping with the US Blue Ribbon Committee's recommendations that auditors comment to the board on the quality of a company's financial reporting.[6]

The key influences in this outcome were the lack of clear guidance in the framework and the determination of Colin and Richard to stick with the accounting policy even though Andrew believed it was aggressive. The potential bid could also have influenced their decision to adopt the policy. Figure 8.3 sets out the specific contextual factors in this interaction, together with the parties involved, their specific objectives, and the strategies adopted.

This was as good an outcome as could be achieved under the circumstances, and was slightly difficult to achieve. Andrew was not happy with the policy being adopted by the group but did not have a strong enough case to insist it be changed. However he did ensure that the main board was aware of his concerns and also went beyond his statutory responsibilities to warn them of the risks to their reputation.

8.9.4 Interaction CRA4: accounting for long-term leases on fixed plant

This financial reporting issue involved measurement and concerned the allocation of interest charges over the lives of long-term finance leases. It had been complicated because interest rates had fallen since the leases had been set up and the group was receiving rebates from the lessor.

---

[6] The Blue Ribbon Committee was set up by the New York Stock Exchange and the National Association of Securities Dealers to consider the ways of improving the effectiveness of audit committees in the US. Among the recommendations in its influential report which was issued in 1999 was that auditors should report to the company board on the quality of financial reporting.

178

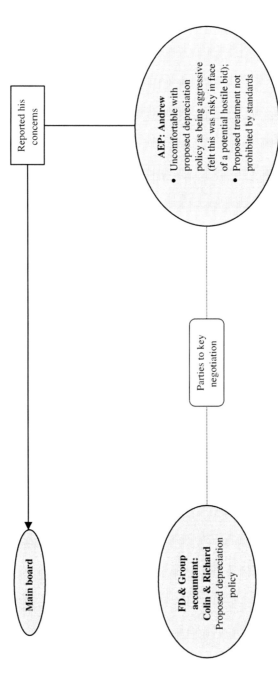

Figure 8.3   Depreciation policy interaction (CRA3)

The amounts involved were not material and the correct treatment was a matter of judgement as the accounting standards were silent on the issue. However, Andrew was conscious of the possibility that the issue could become material to profits in subsequent years, and so he was anxious to get the principles right from the beginning. Andrew obtained advice from his firm's technical department and one of the firm's leasing specialists. Meanwhile, Colin and Richard had also been developing independently a method for calculating the interest charges.

The issue was identified close to a year-end and hence the interaction was conducted under a degree of time pressure. The numbers produced initially by both parties were significantly different and, with the time available, it was not possible to agree on the best procedure to use. The interest charge amounts that Andrew's model was producing for the current period were higher than those produced using the company's model. To reach agreement, a compromise solution was suggested by Andrew and agreed to, which was to bring in an extra provision which could be released later if it was not needed. By the following year all parties had taken the opportunity to examine the issue further and Andrew's extra provision was released as being unnecessary.

Figure 8.4 sets out the specific contextual factors in this interaction, together with the parties involved, their specific objectives, and the strategies adopted. The key influences in this outcome were the highly complex nature of the problem, the lack of clear guidance and time pressure. Both parties had the common goal of trying to find the best answer to the problem.

This interaction had a good outcome. It was obtained easily due to the quality of the primary relationship and the type of approach taken by both parties to the negotiation.

8.9.5 Interaction CRA5: restructuring provisions

This financial reporting interaction concerned recognition of certain costs – either as a set-off against the restructuring provision, which was the preferred company treatment, or as a charge against profits which was the auditor's preferred treatment. It was a matter of judgement. The amount involved was not material (< 1 per cent of profit) and there was no breach of an accounting standard. However, Andrew was firmly of the belief that the proposed accounting treatment was wrong. Figure 8.5 sets out the specific contextual factors in this interaction, together with the parties involved, their specific objectives, and the strategies adopted.

Both parties stated their position very firmly at the outset. Because of the nature of the issue, it was not possible to resolve the disagreement

180

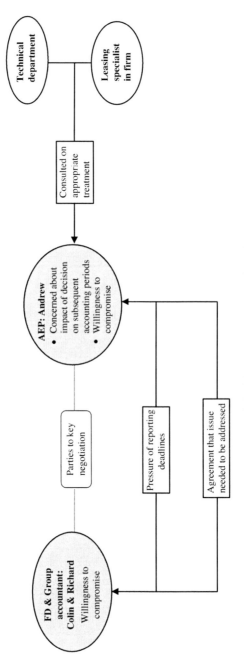

Figure 8.4   Finance leases interaction (CRA4)

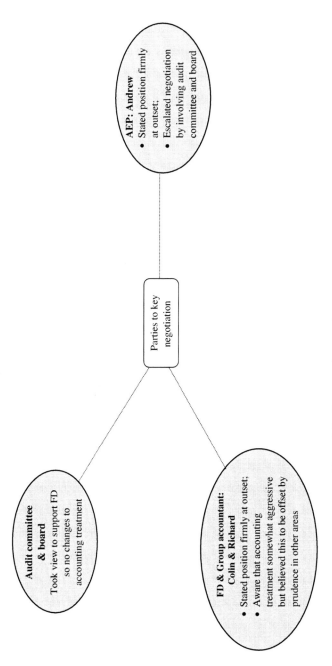

Figure 8.5 Restructuring provisions interaction (CRA5)

using reason or compromise (the normal procedure adopted by the primary parties given the co-operative nature of their relationship). Consequently, Andrew sought to apply a sanction. As it was not a matter upon which it was appropriate to qualify the audit report because it was not material, Andrew instead escalated the interaction by involving the audit committee and the board. Both primary parties presented their cases to the audit committee and board in a calm atmosphere and the board decided to support Colin's proposed treatment. The possible hostile bid and the knowledge that the company had been prudent in other areas of its financial reporting may have influenced this decision. However, Colin did acknowledge that if the matter had been material and a qualified audit report was a possibility they would have 'reflected very hard'.

The key influences in this interaction were the determination of Colin and Richard to proceed with their chosen course of action regardless of Andrew's advice that it was wrong, and their knowledge that the issue was not sufficiently material to justify a qualified audit report.

The outcome was as good as it could be under the current regulations, as Andrew did force the board to take a view on the accounting treatment. He could do no more. His action was again in line with the Blue Ribbon Committee's recommendation that auditors comment to the board on the quality of their financial reporting.

The outcome had the potential to be acrimonious but was only slightly difficult to achieve because of the respect both parties had for each other's position. Colin commented specifically on the calm and measured way in which Andrew had handled the interaction with the board and the audit committee and the fact that although there was a serious difference of opinion the interaction never became heated.

8.10   CONCLUSION

Some interesting issues emerge from this case. There was a very good relationship between Andrew and Colin and Richard. They were completely open with each other but their goals were not entirely in accord. In resolving the highly technical complex issues in interactions two and four, where there was no predetermined answer, both parties worked entirely in harmony to find the optimal solution. In other areas, Colin and Richard showed themselves prepared to adopt quite aggressive accounting policies to present the group's results in the best possible light. This was particularly apparent at the time of our interviews when there was a strong possibility of a hostile bid and the group board was motivated to present strong results to deter the predator. Colin and Richard were mild comfort-seekers, but this did not stop them trying to get aggressive accounting practices past Andrew.

Andrew, however, had very high personal integrity. He was equally concerned to protect the reputation of his firm and the reputation of the group from any criticism that could result from overly aggressive accounting practices, of which he openly disapproved. In this respect, he could be perceived as being the accounting conscience of the group. Colin and Richard understood Andrew's position and were able to anticipate what his reaction to some of their proposed accounting treatments would be.

The interactions described in this case all related to areas of judgement where the regulatory framework provided no clear-cut solution. There are good examples in interactions two and four of how both sides took expert advice in the highly complex and difficult technical areas (valuation of landfill sites and determination of leasing revenues) and then worked together to find the most appropriate accounting treatment for the issues. A key problem area emerged in this case on the determination of fair values on acquisitions.

It is interesting to observe how Colin and Richard chose their battlegrounds in their interactions with Andrew. They were prepared to give in to him on some issues but not on others. On the two issues where Andrew did not get his way, interactions three and five, he was sufficiently concerned to ensure that the group board was fully aware of his reservations and the implications for the group's reputation, a practice recently recommended by the Blue Ribbon Committee in the US. In both cases, he could not enforce his view because they were judgement calls and he could not cite a specific regulatory breach. Colin and Richard were well aware of this. They were also aware that Andrew would not qualify their accounts on the issues because they were not sufficiently material. As a result, Andrew was obliged to accept their proposed accounting practices.

Although the group had a strong and well-defined procedure for taking accounts through various subsidiaries and audit committees to the main board, it did not stop some aggressive accounting practices being accepted by the main board.

9 Robert and Charles (RC plc)

'They don't challenge me enough'

9.1 BACKGROUND TO THE CASE

This group was a manufacturer and had established a reputation for high quality. In keeping with the group's reputation, the board wished to maintain a respectable image with its financial reporting and avoid criticism. There were a number of accountants on the board and the audit committee. The composition of the audit committee had changed following the Cadbury[1] corporate governance recommendations and the committee now contained a high level of accounting expertise.

The group was financially sound and was expanding through acquisition. It was operating in a very competitive market internationally. The board had experienced problems with one particular acquisition which was in the same line of business, which we refer to as Coreco. The main issue concerned the level of provisions to be applied to Coreco's assets in order to bring their fair values into the group accounts, and how the adjustments should be made and disclosed. Agreement also had to be reached under the provisions of FRS 7[2] about the accounting treatment of some Coreco businesses which the group had acquired but intended to dispose of as soon as possible. All these issues involved negotiation with the auditors.

The board sought to obtain value for money in the purchase of all its professional services and regularly communicated with alternative service providers.

Robert, our company interviewee, had recently been appointed group finance director, after his predecessor, Lawrence, left the group. He was previously group financial controller and therefore was familiar with the group's accounting function. Robert was in his early forties.

Charles, the audit engagement partner, was younger than Robert. Robert had previously worked for Charles's firm where Charles had been his

---

[1] See footnote 4 in Chapter 5.
[2] Financial Reporting Standard (FRS) 7 sets out the principles of accounting for an acquisition in the books and consolidated financial statements of the acquirer. Where a discrete part of an acquired entity is sold within approximately one year of acquisition it is to be treated as a single asset for the purpose of determining fair values, and valued on the basis of the actual or estimated net proceeds of sale.

junior. Charles had established a good working relationship with Robert's predecessor, Lawrence, but had yet to build a similar relationship with Robert. Some of the issues which Charles referred to had been discussed with Lawrence before he left the group. Charles had been the engagement partner for the group for some time and was due to be rotated off [3] within two years. He was also in the process of changing his own career path. He was planning to move to a firm of consultants. A more senior partner in the firm acted as review partner for the group.

9.2 THE KEY ISSUES FOR ROBERT AND CHARLES

The board's wish to avoid criticism in its financial reporting activities was particularly important to Robert as the newly appointed finance director. Nevertheless, Robert wished to show the group's results in the best possible light, as the market was very competitive. In this respect he looked to Charles's firm to ensure that the group did not go too far and damage its reputation. He nevertheless put Charles under pressure in respect of fee negotiations, and non-audit services were intentionally given to other competitor firms. Charles was aware of the group's need to protect its reputation, and was aware of his responsibility to protect his firm's reputation.

We interviewed Robert and Charles separately. We identified three interactions which were connected with the Coreco acquisition, and two contextual issues:

- accounting for businesses which were to be sold on after the Coreco acquisition (*interaction RC1*);
- agreeing the accounting treatment and the level of provisions for stock and defective products to be brought into the group accounts on the Coreco acquisition (*interaction RC2*);
- accounting for and disclosure of post-acquisition reorganisation costs (*interactions RC3 and RC4*);
- the composition of the audit committee and its role in accounting and auditing issues (*context RC(a)*); and
- the working relationships between the parties and the effect on fee negotiation (*context (RC(b)*).

---

[3] The ethical rules of ICAEW note that, where the same engagement partner acts for a client for a prolonged period, a familiarity threat will arise – e.g., of no longer being able to be independent. For listed companies it is provided that no audit engagement partner remains in charge of such an audit for longer than seven years, and should not return to that role for a further five years.

9.3   INTERACTION RC1: ACCOUNTING FOR BUSINESSES
   WHICH WERE TO BE SOLD ON AFTER THE CORECO
   ACQUISITION

During Lawrence's last year as finance director the group had made a large acquisition. Coreco was a listed company and therefore no due diligence could be carried out.[4] The Board's intention was to retain the core business of Coreco and dispose of the rest. This led to complex accounting under FRS 7 where the businesses earmarked for sale were brought in at the present value of their estimated future selling price. The original estimates required downward revision following the receipt of offers for the businesses. Agreement of this valuation had been reached mainly through discussions between Charles and Lawrence, Robert's predecessor. At first Lawrence was reluctant to make the adjustment, but he was convinced once he realised that if he did not, there was a possibility that the losses could go through a future profit and loss account. During the interviews it was Charles who focused on this issue.

Charles described the impact of FRS 7 on the accounting for the Coreco acquisition, and his discussions with Lawrence. The Board had never intended to retain all the businesses:

> 'They bought a bunch of businesses at Coreco, some of which were then to be resold within a ten-month time span' (Charles).

The decision to dispose of some parts of the business had been part of the board's strategy in acquiring it:

> 'It was part of the strategy paper when they bought Coreco. ... There was debate about which ones would be realised when, but ... there was no dispute about what they were putting into the sale' (Charles).

Charles and Lawrence realised that applying FRS 7 in these circumstances would be helpful. As the companies to be sold would only be retained for a short time, it would be better for their earnings to be excluded from the group profit and loss account to avoid short-term distortion:

> '[*Lawrence*] was very keen to exclude the earnings of these subsidiaries which were to be sold from the profit and loss account ... because it was going to be a

---

[4] It is normal to investigate the affairs of a prospective purchase in such detail as is possible – to ensure that there is adequate value for the price to be paid. This is called 'due diligence'. In the case of a listed company being acquired, this investigation has to be restricted to information publicly available.

distortion over a two-year period. They were going to be in and out again and this seemed the right solution, and it was very convenient to meet our objective' (Charles).

Resolving the values to be attached to the businesses was difficult and time consuming:

'Inevitably there was an awful lot of discussion because FRS 7 was new to everybody involved. It was as new to me as it was to them .... That was the big issue because we held those businesses with a net present value of their estimated sale prices and that was really ground-breaking stuff' (Charles).

To obtain the present values, the group had relied on estimates of sales proceeds provided by a merchant bank, which proved to be overstated:

'You can get an estimate of your future sale proceeds and when you expect to sell. What in the event happened was that those sale prices were over-optimistic. They got a merchant bank to provide an estimate of the proceeds. As a result at the next year-end we had to adjust the goodwill with the difference' (Charles).

The overvaluation came to light very quickly as the acquisition had taken place close to the year-end. By the time the accounts were being completed, offers were coming in for some of the businesses. Charles and Lawrence agreed to write the estimates down:

'I was uncomfortable with some of the estimates ... the sale process was taking place as we were closing off the accounts ... we could see the bits coming into it. I think Lawrence was uncomfortable and so we agreed to mark down the merchant bank estimates by £xx million' (Charles).

Lawrence had originally not wished to make changes. He had advised the board that he fully supported the valuations both before and after the acquisitions and was embarrassed by the reduction. But the need for change was overwhelming. If the estimates were overstated, the loss after one further year would hit the profit and loss account rather than goodwill:

'He didn't want to do that but ... we just persuaded him with the facts. ... The bids were coming in lower than the estimates ... and also under FRS 7 you have a full year to get your estimates right and make the adjustments through the goodwill' (Charles).

Lawrence was persuaded that it was better to keep the estimates low to avoid losses eventually going through the profit and loss account:

> 'If subsequently you haven't sold the business you need to make a further adjustment through profit and loss account. ... In those circumstances we agreed to push the estimates down ... because if you're wrong you avoid loss and you might even make a profit' (Charles).

Some difficulty had been experienced in explaining what was happening to the audit committee. FRS 7 was complex and relatively new, and the committee had not been privy to the process of reaching the original estimates:

> 'They weren't involved in the formulation of the figures. We simply had to explain to them why this was being done. ... It wasn't difficult once you understood the principle but it was certainly difficult to explain it ... to the audit committee because it was fresh to them' (Charles).

It also had to be explained to the group's analysts because of the impact on earnings:

> 'The company had to explain all this to their analysts, because if you're net present valuing something, obviously that present value unwinds as you get closer and closer to the realisation date and that's an implicit interest. It features quite a lot in earnings per share. This is novel stuff because we don't do much net present value accounting in this country. We had to apply the right discount rate and things like that' (Charles).

Robert explained that the auditors had not been involved in the discussions on the acquisition, and therefore they weren't aware of the valuation issues which had been considered at that stage:

> 'It was a quoted company so there was virtually no due diligence. ... There was some but it was all sitting around a table with our corporate finance advisors and the auditors weren't at that table. ... Those specific problems they did not know about ... right at the start, but we were quite open as soon as they came up' (Robert).

Charles also explained the position as he saw it:

> 'It was a public takeover, you see, and they didn't have access to due diligence and we didn't get the chance to do it' (Charles).

9.4 INTERACTION RC2: AGREEING THE ACCOUNTING TREATMENT AND THE LEVEL OF PROVISIONS FOR STOCK AND DEFECTIVE PRODUCTS

Prior to its acquisition Coreco had not been performing well, and had been under pressure to produce profits. It was felt that the provisions which had been made by the Coreco management against stocks and the supply of defective products in last audited accounts were too low for the group's more conservative accounting policies. Discussions took place about additional provisions[5] needed to bring the fair values of Coreco's assets into the group accounts and how they should be accounted for.

Robert explained how he approached the accounting issues arising from the acquisition with the auditors:

'Around the acquisition which was [*two months before the year end*] I would have said "Right, let's now start thinking how we're going to account ... we will work with you", so that we would all address the issues. There were two or three items which I think were debatable on how we should treat them. One ... was for some provisions on [*stock and defective products*]' (Robert).

As the date of acquisition was not the year-end, the books of Coreco had not been closed off. Consideration was given to making adjustments in Coreco's own books before the fair values on consolidation were worked out. Charles summed the position up from his point of view:

'Basically you inherit a set of books that have never been closed off, adjust those to get them straight, then bring your accounting policies in line and then work out your goodwill' (Charles).

---

[5] If there are differences between the accounting policies of the acquiring and the acquired entities, adjustments have to be made to the assets and liabilities at the date of acquisition, to ensure that all are consolidated by the acquirer on a basis consistent with its existing accounting policies. This may require judgemental decisions to be taken, for example in respect of depreciation, bad debts and stocks. FRS 6 requires that the accounting records of the acquired company should not be changed before consolidation, and all adjustments made for consolidation purposes to establish fair values should be charged to the goodwill on acquisition account and disclosed in the group financial statements. Subsequent adjustments which are found to be necessary to the fair values should be made through the goodwill account, not the profit and loss account in the first full financial year following the acquisition. Any further adjustments should be recognised as profits or losses when identified, or in the case of correction of fundamental errors, as prior year adjustments.

The key issues related to the defective supplies provision and the stock provision. Robert first of all described the discussions with Coreco's management:

> 'We went to talk to all of Coreco's management and said, " What about your [*stock*] provision?" and they said, "Phoar, well, we haven't got nearly enough". ... This is the managers. ... "Yes", we said, "Why didn't you put it in the books?", and they said, "That's a good idea". There was also another provision to do with defective [*supplies*]' (Robert).

Robert explained his beliefs about the reasons for the light provisions:

> 'One of the reasons is that Coreco was under pressure to report good profits because everybody knew we were looking at them ... I suspect there might have been a tendency to ... be a bit light on some of those provisions' (Robert).

He did not believe that Coreco's accounts were mis-stated but he emphasised the subjectivity of some accounting issues:

> 'It was all within the boundaries of materiality ... I'm not in any way suggesting that either Coreco or [*Coreco's auditors*] were mis-stating the accounts. ... The key point was that the local management felt that they were unhappy with the level of provision in their books. ... When you produce a set of accounts there is always subjectivity ... you take a view on where you want to be in that range' (Robert).

Robert explained that he had only become involved in this issue, which had arisen in a subsidiary, because it was potentially material to the group accounts:

> 'It happened locally at the site ... where the provision actually is ... then because it is material, I mean, only just material ... it became a group issue' (Robert).

A decision was taken to treat these additional provisions as having been made by the Coreco management before the acquisition, based on the argument that the provisions should have been made by them at that time. The impact of this was that the additional provisions would not have to be disclosed in the accounts as fair value adjustments, as required by FRS 6. Robert acknowledged that they were in a grey area:

> 'This is where it gets grey doesn't it? Because we felt that that the provision was totally understated and needed to be reinstated. ... You always need to have a provision because you never know when one of your customers is going to

come back to you. ... So you have a pot you can dig into if you have an error or some problem with the stock. ... The issue was whether or not it was going to be an accounting policy alignment or whether it would be less visible' (Robert).

Robert recognised that Charles was not comfortable with the group's intentions. He first commented on the relationship with the auditors:

'This is where the relationship with the auditors is so interesting, because they said, "Well, we're not very happy with it", so you say, "Why not?" ' (Robert).

However, he fully understood what Charles' concern was if the provision was not disclosed as an accounting policy alignment. It could less visibly be brought back to profit in future years:

'This [stock] provision. They were not entirely happy with our thinking. I think they felt we might have been trying to ... put in an acquisition provision through the back door. They wanted to satisfy themselves, and we wanted to satisfy ourselves, that our arguments ... were justified and that we weren't just trying to put it through. ... I know what they're worried about. They are worried that we are going to release that provision to profit at some stage and therefore overstate our profits' (Robert).

Robert viewed the non-recording of the provisions at the acquisition date as an omission by the Coreco management to process the journal entries at a date other than the year-end:

'According to the standards you should rule off exactly as you found the books as you arrived ... but we felt that ... simply because somebody hadn't got a bit of paper out and written a journal voucher was a purely mechanical thing, and if you like, the books, if properly written up, would have included these provisions' (Robert).

Robert further reinforced his arguments by suggesting that the under-provision on the stock could have been accumulating for fourteen months:

'If the [year end] provision was light then there could have been twelve months lightness of provision plus two' (Robert).

Charles accepted that as Coreco's records had not been audited at the date of acquisition some flexibility was possible:

'Because we hadn't bought Coreco at the financial auditing year end ... their books had never been closed off. So there was some flexibility ... to adjust their

books to get them right as if they had been audited at the acquisition date'
(Charles).

He accepted Robert's arguments about the accounting treatment in
respect of the stock and defective supplies provisions:

'We backed that into the opening balance sheet because it was a pre-existing
condition of the Coreco business … so that stuff went through the acquisition
originally' (Charles).

Interestingly Charles had not consulted his second partner on this issue
but he had referred it to his firm's technical department, who appeared to
concur with his view:

'No, just put it through the technical department' (Charles).

He described the second partner's role:

'He attends the audit committee, gets a briefing shortly before that. He doesn't
get involved in the day-to-day relationship with the finance director' (Charles).

However, Charles made it clear to Robert that any overprovision should
be written back to the goodwill account, not to profit and loss. Robert was
unconvinced of the practicality of this:

'The only point they put up was that they said, "Look, if that provision does
prove to be surplus, then you must write it back to goodwill rather than writing
it back through the profit and loss account." It's an interesting one … because if
in another year's time we … are a little bit over-provided on this … provision,
frankly it would have lost its identity because meanwhile things will have been
going in and out' (Robert).

Robert was not sure what his auditors would be able to do:

'They raised it just last week in the context of audit planning for [*the next year-
end*]. … We must have a look at this provision. What they haven't addressed is
what will happen if it's surplus. Incidentally, I don't think it will be surplus, but
if they viewed it was, I'm not quite sure what their proposal would be' (Robert).

He explained why he would resist a write-back of the provision:

'Let's just say, for the sake of argument, we keep a two per cent provision [*of
turnover*] for [*defective products*] … and after five years we find that actually

our [*defective product*] isn't two per cent it's one and a half per cent. So we think "Well, actually, we should only have one and a half per cent provision." So the question is then, that £xxx hundred thousand pounds, where will that go? ... It doesn't relate to anything specific' (Robert).

Although he had pushed for this accounting treatment, of making the provisions in Coreco's own accounts rather than as disclosed fair value adjustments, on reflection Robert felt uncomfortable with what had happened:

'I think I would have respected them more if they'd gone to the audit committee and said, "Non-execs, we disagree with your finance director on this one ... We think this treatment ... is not in the spirit of FRS 6 and we disagree with it." But what they tend to say is, "We note this treatment which is permissible under the standard and anyway it isn't material ... which I think it is too wishy washy"' (Robert).

The second, more senior partner did not behave differently:

'No, he doesn't. You can see why I'm ambivalent about it' (Robert).

Robert's underlying concern was that the group could damage its reputation by sailing too close to the wind without being warned by the auditors:

'It makes life easy. On the other hand ... the worst thing that could happen is for us to get away with something ... then find that we shouldn't have done it and whatever happens I don't want to be in that position ... integrity is the key ... which is why I work conservatively with the accounts' (Robert).

9.5 INTERACTION RC3: ACCOUNTING FOR POST-ACQUISITION REORGANISATION COSTS

A further issue arose because Lawrence had wanted to bring a provision for post-acquisition reorganisation costs into the acquisition accounting and treat it as part of the goodwill calculation.[6] Charles explained Lawrence's view:

'Lawrence was very uncomfortable. He couldn't see why, when you buy a business you couldn't provide for what you were going to do with it. ... He tried to

---

[6] FRS 7 does not permit provision for reorganisation costs expected to be incurred as a result of the acquisition to be included as liabilities acquired, since they are not liabilities of the acquired entity at the date of acquisition.

persuade me that his way of thinking was right and we had a robust discussion with him … at the end of the day it wasn't material' (Charles).

Although the amount was not material to the accounts, this treatment is specifically forbidden by FRS 7 and Charles was having none of it. In the face of a robust stance from Charles the matter was dropped:

'They pride themselves at [*the group*] on getting their accounting correct … and this does have an impact on the profit and loss account. So I said "If you want to put it through as an acquisition adjustment I can't stop you because it is not material, and my reaction is to qualify the audit report … as technically its wrong", and they changed it' (Charles).

9.6 INTERACTION RC4: DISCLOSURE OF REORGANISATION COSTS

One issue had arisen on which Robert had on his own initiative consulted the audit committee. The fact of the auditors being present at the meeting seemed to be of secondary importance to him. The issue related to the disclosure of reorganisation costs under FRS 3. The decision as to how to present the information was left to the audit committee:

'FRS 3[7] you know is quite clear about earnings per share. We have used, as an alternative measure, headline earnings per share as defined by IIMR[8]. We had some reorganisation costs which show up on the profit and loss account. … Now the issue was how should we treat that in earnings per share, and we presented the audit committee with two alternatives. One which we just stopped at headline earnings per share and the other was that we introduced yet a third measure of earnings which would be headline earnings per ordinary share before the reorganisation costs' (Robert).

---

[7] FRS 3 requires earnings per share to be calculated on profit attributable to equity shareholders. Those wishing to highlight any other version of earnings per share are required to provide an explanation of the particular significance they attach to that version and to itemise and quantify the adjustments they are making to the earnings per share required by FRS 3.

[8] The Institute of Investment Management and Research 'Statement of Investment Practice No. 1 – The Definition of IIMR Headline Earnings' seeks to find an earnings figure that will reflect trading performance but will also limit the need to exercise judgement in its calculation, so that it can be used as an unambiguous reference point between user, the press and statistical companies.

Robert was concerned how a third earnings measure would be viewed:

'Would we be clouding the issue yet further? On the other hand, I think readers of the accounts, in particular the analysts would want that number straight away and it would be useful to give it to them' (Robert).

He understood that this would not please the standard setters:

'We also recognised that the writer of FRS 3 might not be entirely happy about it because we've now got three measures of earnings per share. ... It's trying to help not hinder. All we're doing is a bit of arithmetic for the analysts' (Robert).

Robert also described the auditors' and the non-executive directors' involvement in the discussion:

'They [*the auditors*] joined in the discussion because they attend the audit committee ... they certainly weren't leading it ... the discussion was among the non-execs and the execs as to what would have been the most helpful. [*Charles's firm*] would have been asked "Is that acceptable and do you think it would be helpful?" and they said "Yes"' (Robert).

9.7 CONTEXT RC(a): THE COMPOSITION OF THE AUDIT COMMITTEE AND ITS INVOLVEMENT IN ACCOUNTING AND AUDITING ISSUES

The audit committee had changed its composition since the Cadbury recommendations had been implemented. A number of senior accountants had joined the board and the audit committee as non-executive directors and this had influenced the way in which the audit committee operated. Both Robert and Charles commented on this. They also explained how they set out to resolve problems between them rather than take unresolved issues to the audit committee.

Robert explained how he saw the role of the audit committee in respect of accounting and auditing issues:

'The audit committee will only get involved at the audit committee meeting ... when the accounts are presented by management, by myself and my team. [*Charles's firm*] will also produce a report for the audit committee ... at that stage there will be some issues flagged up ... and then the audit committee will look to management and that basically means the financial controller and the finance director and say, "What are your views on these issues that [*Charles's firm*] has raised?"' (Robert).

As the group had a number of operating subsidiaries, Robert explained how issues came through for the audit committee's attention:

> 'Well, the process would be that they would be raised locally. They would then come up through the organisation to the financial controller … who sits two doors from here … our doors are normally open. … Last year-end, for example, he said, "These are the issues that the auditors will be bringing forward to the formal document that will actually go to the audit committee" ' (Robert).

Robert did not see the role of the audit committee as one of opining on accounting issues:

> Now there is a possibility that we would welcome the audit committee's advice on a particular issue. It's pretty rare' (Robert).

Charles described his involvement with the audit committee. He did not perceive them as having an advisory role at all:

> 'We … interface with the audit committee probably four times a year, and the two key ones are the interim accounts and the final accounts. Our objective with Lawrence and presumably with Robert was that there should be no issues between us by the time everything gets to the audit committee. So the audit committee's role was to question things and basically to rubber-stamp the decisions that had already been made' (Charles).

He saw the audit committee as a backstop:

> 'I don't think the audit committee should interfere too much in the resolution of issues that have already been worked out between the company and its auditors. Their prime role is of a safety valve, and if the relationship is going well, then they don't really have very much to do' (Charles).

Both Charles and Robert commented on the effect of having experienced accountants on the audit committee. Robert felt there were advantages:

> 'There's a discussion … It is helped by the fact that on our audit committee we have Mr. XX and Mr. YY … so we've got some fairly heavyweight financial people' (Robert).

Charles noticed changes when the accountants joined the audit committee:

> 'In my first year as a partner [*the audit committee*] was the full board. … The difference was between the personalities … the difference came when Mr. XX

became chairman of the audit committee. He obviously understood the rules and their audit committee is heavily staffed by accountants. The level of accounting discussion was pretty high for an audit committee. ... Prior to that it was much more informal' (Charles).

The high level of audit committee accounting expertise had also kept Charles on his toes:

'It's made the quality of our reporting pretty high and you have to concentrate' (Charles).

This did not worry Charles:

'There's no worry because the expertise on our side is of a very high level as well' (Charles).

Charles and Robert both referred to the advantages and disadvantages of audit committees. Robert had mixed views:

'To be honest with you I find it both valuable and irritating ... because there is getting this balance right between the executives managing things and the non-executives not getting involved in too much detail' (Robert).

Robert valued the audit committee's contribution to major issues but did not feel that attention to detail was something an audit committee should concern itself with:

'Where I find it very valuable is where there are key points at issue and they say, "Look, this is the way. We like what you're doing and we think this is meeting the objectives [*the group*] is trying to achieve." ... So if they're bringing forward issues of real importance I'm very happy with it. There are times, I have to say, when they go into too much depth ... I wouldn't have thought that non-executives would want a whole load of detail about stock provisioning. ... I'm not quite sure what the committee would want to do with that information' (Robert).

Charles thought that the audit committee gave the executive directors a more difficult time than they gave the auditors:

'They ask more questions of the management than you would normally get. They don't actually ask the auditors very much' (Charles).

He believed that audit committees helped to keep executive directors under control and the group's committee was particularly effective at this:

> 'I think audit committees have generally been a good thing, because executive directors slightly live in fear of them, particularly the finance director, particularly if you've got a bunch like you've got at [*the group*]' (Charles).

As a matter of course, the auditors met with the audit committee without the executives being present:

> 'For all meetings ... almost every company has the opportunity to meet the audit committee in private and we always go through that and just have a cup of coffee and then the executive directors join. ... It's a formality and you could envisage there might be situations where you'd have to raise something, not with this particular client, but they like that process to be in place so that if you did have to raise something it wouldn't be unusual, ... so we do it every time and talk about the weather or something' (Charles).

He felt that non-executive directors had become more powerful:

> 'I mean it's their jobs isn't it? ... The non-execs have become more powerful over the last five or six years ... you've probably noticed and the executives now feel more answerable to them than they used to do' (Charles).

Charles believes the reason for the increase in non-executives power was economic:

> 'Well, they have the ultimate sanction, don't they? ... They have input over salary with most of them on the audit committee as well' (Charles).

Robert saw the issue rather differently:

> 'I went to lunch the other day where there were a number of finance directors ... you know, some quite big companies and there was quite a long debate about the difficulty of attracting non-execs because of their responsibilities and the onerous nature of being a director. ... They are increasingly, not just here, but across the board getting a bit more nervous' (Robert).

9.8 CONTEXT RC(b): THE WORKING RELATIONSHIPS BETWEEN THE PARTIES AND THE IMPACT ON FEE NEGOTIATION

At the time we interviewed Robert and Charles, Lawrence had only recently left the group. Robert, who had previously been the financial controller, had taken his place. Although he and Charles already knew each other, the relationship was inevitably changing and Charles's own career path was also moving away from audit towards consultancy. Charles and Lawrence had established a relaxed and comfortable relationship with each other and Charles had found the change of finance director difficult, because it was not possible to establish the same relationship with Robert. He found Robert rather more formal. Robert on the other hand felt that Charles and his firm could have been more robust in their advice to the group. Although Robert had concerns that an audit firm's economic dependence on its clients undermined their independence, he nevertheless used the threat of a tender in his own fee negotiations with Charles. Another key issue for both was the need for Charles to rotate off the group's audit within two years and Robert himself looked forward to a change of engagement partner. In the event, this change was accelerated.

Charles gave his perception of the working relationship with the group in the context of the board's conservatism:

'They are a very well-liked company and they don't make many mistakes. So it is really a question of the interpretation of new standards and disclosure that tends to be the focus of the discussions. We try and flag up to them where issues are likely to affect them, where standards are in the pipeline. For example, when a standard or UITF[9] comes out we will try and resolve what the accounting should be whenever it arises in the year. That's the general start and that means reasonably frequent contact' (Charles).

Robert's perception of the way things worked was similar:

'Our relationship with our auditors is very much one of working together, and we don't, frankly, have much negotiation because ... if we've got an issue we will work with them at an early stage ... and work in parallel so that we will reach a mutually satisfactory conclusion rather than saying, "This is what we are going to do and tough if you don't like it"' (Robert).

Robert acknowledged that, despite the group's size, his resources were limited:

'The technical department consists of me and the financial controller' (Robert).

---

[9] The Urgent Issues Task Force (UITF) is a committee of the Accounting Standards Board which it assists with important or significant emerging accounting issues, e.g., where conflicting interpretations have developed or seem likely to develop. Its conclusions, or 'consensus', are published in the form of an abstract and have similar status to accounting standards.

Although Robert and Charles were working together and discharging their responsibilities as finance director and auditor respectively, each had criticisms of the other. Robert believed there was little substance to some of the points raised by Charles at audit meetings and offered an explanation:

> 'The partner would make sure there were a few or he'd have nothing to talk about. ... He's got to earn his fee hasn't he ... that's a serious point ... he has to have something to talk about to the finance director' (Robert).

Charles acknowledged that he had found it easier to work with Lawrence than with Robert:

> 'Robert is relatively new ... Lawrence, who I worked with for five years, he had a sort of coffee morning, a series of meetings for which I just turned up and we'd talk about whatever took our fancy off the file' (Charles).

He found Robert and Lawrence very different:

> 'They are different, totally different individuals. I probably was more comfortable with Lawrence because he was a very relaxed sort of person ... liked informal chat' (Charles).

Discussions with Lawrence had been interesting:

> 'Well, it was all a bit of a game and we both knew when we were having a spat, with two reasonably bright people arguing a point. ... He would start by saying ... the standards are wrong because of this, this and this, and get me to defend the standards, even though he may have thought that I agreed with him. So we would just go round that particular route' (Charles).

But with Robert it was different:

> 'Robert is a slightly more formal individual and slightly more process driven than Lawrence was. I think he just likes to get everything scheduled out and agreements made at the right time' (Charles).

Robert was conscious of the conflict that the auditors had in retaining their client and resisting pressure to breach the regulatory framework:

> 'The key person I deal with is the audit partner, not the senior audit partner who comes in two or three times a year. ... There is one issue ... which is very relevant here and that is the conflict that they have in retaining the audit and resisting any management attempt to try something on in preparation of the accounts' (Robert).

In some ways he was critical of his auditors:

'If I'm disappointed with our auditors, it would be that they don't challenge me enough, and say, "Come on, Robert, you shouldn't, you can't be doing that, that's wrong ... We think it's too clever by half or it actually disagrees with the standard and so on"' (Robert).

But he explained his view of compliance:

'I will always look for the most favourable treatment' (Robert).

However he was not certain whether the lack of confrontation was because no serious issues had come up:

'I've never had a run-in with the auditors and I'm not sure whether that's because there's never really been an issue or because they actually are concerned about losing the audit' (Robert).

Robert would not wish to find himself in front of the Financial Reporting Review Panel:

'I would not want to land there at all, unless it was something the whole board had said, "Right, this is an issue where we do not agree with the standard or whatever it is and we will stick our neck out. I would certainly not want to go in front of them because they weren't happy with this or that disclosure' (Robert).

Charles was aware that the group was an important client to the firm:

'It's not on our blue-chip list, but it's an important client' (Charles).

He explained his position with regard to disagreements over accounting compliance:

'Our reputation is everything ... and unless you're an idiot, you'd never get yourself into a position of dispute with a client without having a second partner, technical department, technical committee, the whole firm either telling you you were wrong and therefore back down, or that you were right in which case the firm would be behind you' (Charles).

Charles did not believe that such a situation could arise with the group. He expressed a very different view to Robert's perception:

'It's inconceivable that it could happen with the group but that would be the principle ... to me it's inconceivable that you'd lose a job over an auditing or accounting issue' (Charles).

Robert considered the problem of the auditor's economic dependence was a profession-wide problem, rather than one for Charles's firm:

> 'I don't think it's the firm. I think it's the profession. I do have a lot of sympathy with them. They've obviously got their livelihood and they know that if they upset the management, the executive management, too much, the executive management will probably turn round to the board and say, "We can't work with these people". Now the board … will have to form a view as to whether they think management are being unreasonable. But it must be at the back of the mind, probably at the front of the mind for the auditors' (Robert).

Despite his sympathy for the profession, he still had a gripe about limitation of liability:

> This is my current irritation … the way auditors are trying to minimise their liability, but we are still paying … the same level of fees. We now have … restrictions on due diligence work, with a cap on their liability. … That's ridiculous … because if they go and do due diligence you're paying for them to get it right … and if they do it wrong they should accept the consequences' (Robert).

Robert openly acknowledged that he used the threat of a tender when negotiating fees:

> 'It is a threat. It's one we've used, dropped hints, and on the due diligence side they know they're not getting the work. They know we are quite capable of turning somewhere else' (Robert).

He explained how he brought these issues into the fee negotiation:

> 'I usually do it in the context of other people, other companies, saying, "Interesting to note that XYZ plc have moved their auditors and gone out to tender." I will drop it in when negotiating the fee … and I will say, "Well, the industry seems to be accepting only one or two per cent and you're proposing five per cent, and no doubt one … of the drivers of the one or two per cent is that tenders are ever increasing". They get the message … let's face it, it's part of the environment in which they operate' (Robert).

Interestingly, Charles did not seem to be aware of the extent to which the group used other advisors:

> 'They try to do it in-house. They have pretty good people. … They tend not to use us for tax advice … due diligence on a big project is done by the finance director. Due diligence on a division-level project is done with the divisional finance director' (Charles).

Robert felt that the economic pressures were greater for a younger partner in an audit firm:

> 'I think it influences their behaviour and I suspect the younger the partner is the less robust he will be to that implied threat. He [*Charles*] is young, he's younger than me' (Robert).

Robert was aware that Charles was planning a permanent change to his career. He was concerned that Charles was no longer particularly interested in audit:

> 'Where I have a problem is that [*consulting*] is much more sexy than doing a standard audit and I suspect he's much more interested in that than he is in doing our audit, and that does create some concern' (Robert).

Charles acknowledged this himself:

> 'As I said earlier, I like this [*consulting*] stuff. It's more buzzy' (Charles).

Discussions were already taking place as to how long Charles should remain as the audit engagement partner:

> 'It's a very current issue, whether it happens this year or not' (Robert).

By the time we interviewed Charles he was no longer the engagement partner for the group and shortly afterwards he left the firm. He did not have many regrets about giving this client up. But he had enjoyed his relationship with Lawrence:

> 'I miss it slightly. I miss Lawrence, who was a tremendous character' (Charles).

9.9   ANALYSIS OF GENERAL CONTEXTUAL FACTORS

The relationship between Robert and Charles was fair. A number of factors served to constrain the overall quality of the relationship:

● there was a moderate lack of respect between them – Robert wanted to show the group's results in a good light, while remaining firmly within the rules, and sought to rely on the auditor as a check on this. Robert felt that Charles was not sufficiently robust on occasions;

- their personalities were not highly compatible – Charles found Robert to be rather too formal in his attitude and manner; he had preferred the style of Robert's predecessor, Lawrence;
- Robert had previously worked for Charles's firm where he had been senior to Charles; and
- the relationship between them had changed – although both had known and worked with each other for some years, Robert was newly promoted to FD.

The contextual influences on the outcomes of the interactions between Robert and Charles are set out diagrammatically in Figure 9.1. These are drawn from general circumstances of the group and the contextual issues set out in sections 9.7 and 9.8 above. The relationship between Robert and Charles was particularly interesting. Both conducted themselves in a properly professional manner. Although there was some lack of mutual respect on a personal level, they recognised the advantages of co-operation, and the need to avoid taking unresolved issues to a highly competent audit committee.

The reporting style of the company was respectable, but Charles was convinced that the board's desire to protect the group's reputation would of itself ensure the integrity of its financial reporting. Robert on the other hand wanted to show the group's results in the best possible light. Although the company was financially healthy, intense competition was making it difficult to sustain profit levels. He was both a comfort-seeker and a resource-seeker for technical advice. As a comfort-seeker, he expected Charles to be more pro-active than he was in making sure that the group did not step over the line. In this respect there was a lack of goal congruence between them. During fee negotiations, Robert undermined Charles by threatening to put the audit out for tender.

9.10   THE SPECIFIC INTERACTIONS AND THEIR OUTCOMES

9.10.1   Interaction RC1: accounting for resale of businesses acquired

This was a financial reporting and measurement issue and a matter of judgement. It related to the valuation of businesses acquired with the intention of quick resale. On acquisition, these businesses had been valued at the net present value of estimated sale proceeds under FRS 7, with a merchant bank providing the estimates. However, by the time the first year-end accounts after acquisition were being prepared, the sale process

205

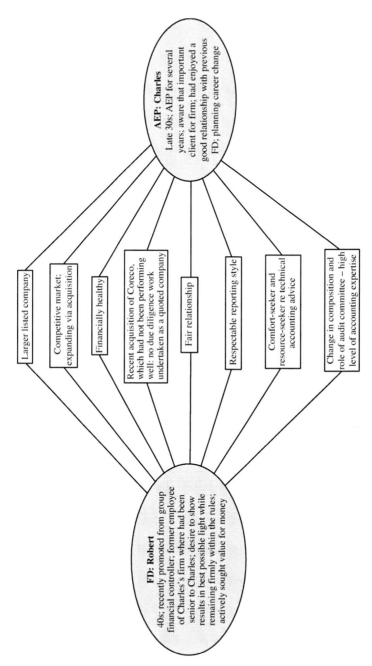

Figure 9.1 Robert and Charles: general context for interactions

was under way and the bids were coming in lower than the estimates. This interaction took place while Robert was still the group financial controller and Lawrence was the FD. It involved only Lawrence, Robert and Charles.

Charles's position was that he wanted to lower the valuations, which had been carried out independently. Lawrence and Robert were initially not keen as it altered the cost profile of the acquisition, and they had accepted the original valuations before the board. The changes would have to be explained to the board and to analysts and this was potentially an embarrassment. However, Charles introduced persuasive arguments. First, he pointed to the clear evidence of over-valuation. Second, he pointed out that any over-valuation not adjusted against goodwill in the current year would, on realisation, hit the profit and loss account the following year. Lawrence and Robert accepted Charles's arguments. It remained only for Lawrence and Charles to present their case to the audit committee to secure their agreement. Figure 9.2 sets out the specific contextual factors in this interaction, together with the parties involved, their specific objectives and the strategies adopted.

The key influences in this interaction were initially a desire on the part of Lawrence and Robert to avoid a change of position in front of the board. However, the possibility of a future charge to the profit and loss account arising from the overvaluation was an even less attractive prospect in their competitive market.

This interaction had a good outcome which was easy for Charles to achieve. His case was supported by strong independent evidence, and the result of non-compliance with his proposals was less attractive to Lawrence and Robert than the result of compliance.

9.10.2   Interaction RC2: agreeing the accounting treatment and the level of provisions for stock and defective products to be brought into the group accounts on the Coreco acquisition

This financial reporting issue involved recognition, measurement and disclosure. It involved a material amount and concerned judgement in respect of the level of provisions, and compliance with the accounting and disclosure requirements of FRS 6. Robert discussed the fair values with Coreco's management, who acknowledged that the provisions were light. As the books had not been closed off at the date of acquisition, he argued that the additional provisions should be put through Coreco's books rather than being treated as fair value adjustments. This did not affect the goodwill on consolidation but made the adjustment less visible. Charles was initially uncomfortable with this proposed treatment as it did not comply with FRS 6 which requires that the book values in the acquired entity's books should be

207

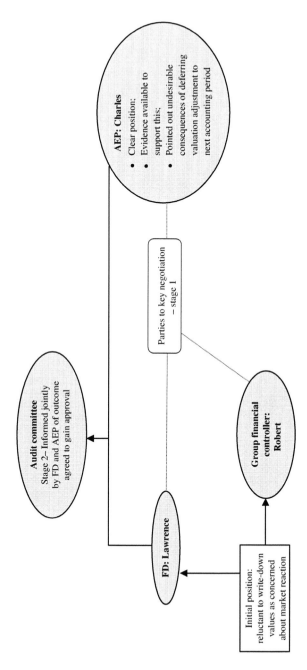

Figure 9.2   Accounting for resale of businesses acquired interaction (RC1)

disclosed before any fair value adjustments are made. He was also concerned that this could be a device to reserve profits for future release into the group. Charles referred the matter to his firm's technical department but did not discuss it with his second partner. He accepted Robert's proposed treatment, on condition that any over-provision identified in the future should not be put through the profit and loss account. Figure 9.3 sets out the specific contextual factors in this interaction, together with the parties involved, their specific objectives, and the strategies adopted.

Although he had got his own way on this matter, after the event Robert felt that Charles had been too soft. Robert was dismissive of Charles's reservation about not releasing provisions to future profits as he did not believe any future claw-backs could be identified to the pre-acquisition period.

This interaction was easy to achieve because Charles and his technical department agreed to Robert's suggestion. It had a poor outcome. Charles allowed material fair value adjustments to be put through the accounting records of Coreco rather than insisting they that they should be properly disclosed as fair value adjustments, contrary to the provisions of FRS 6. The justification that the books had not been closed is an inadequate defence. A further outcome from this interaction was that by agreeing to what Robert knew was a device, Charles undermined his authority.

9.10.3   Interaction RC3: accounting for post-acquisition reorganisation costs

This interaction took place between Lawrence and Charles. It was a financial reporting interaction and concerned recognition and compliance. Lawrence wanted to charge the post-acquisition reorganisation costs associated with the Coreco acquisition to goodwill arising on the acquisition. He believed this to be the logical treatment. FRS 7 states that such costs should not be treated in this way and must be charged to post-acquisition profits. If this adjustment had been charged to goodwill, it would have required disclosure. Although the amount was not material, Charles took a firm stand and threatened to qualify the audit report if Lawrence insisted on this treatment. Lawrence did not insist.

This interaction had a good outcome which was easy to achieve because FRS 7 was quite clear on the issue and Charles took a firm stand at the outset.

9.10.4   Interaction RC4: disclosure of reorganisation costs

This was a financial reporting compliance issue concerning disclosure in a primary statement, and was raised by Robert with the audit committee,

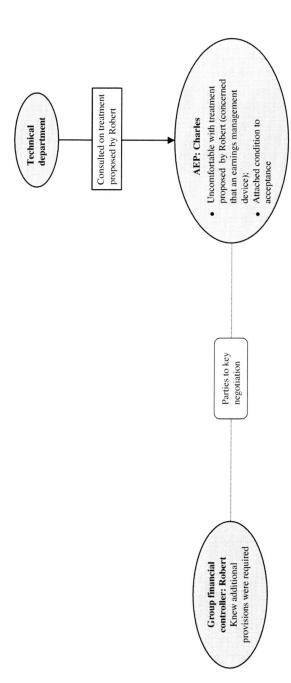

Figure 9.3   Accounting for stock and defective products on acquisition (RC2)

not because there was a disagreement between him and Charles but because he sought their advice. The issue related to FRS 3 and how group reorganisation costs should be presented on the face of the profit and loss account. Robert was suggesting to the audit committee that a third earnings measure should be introduced which showed earnings before reorganisation costs, as he believed this information would help readers of the accounts, particularly the analysts. The audit committee were supportive, and Charles, who was not a prime mover in this discussion, had no objections.

This interaction was easy to achieve as there was no disagreement, merely a discussion of alternative solutions. The information was not presented in a form which would mislead a user and FRS 3 does not prohibit the provision of additional material. This outcome was therefore acceptable.

9.11   CONCLUSION

Some interesting issues emerge from this case in respect of the relationship between Charles and Robert, the role of the second partner, the nature of the unsatisfactory outcome to one of the interactions and the role and composition of the audit committee.

Robert and Charles managed their relationship in a civilised and professional way, but a lack of respect existed between them on a personal level. Charles's attitude to Robert was overshadowed by what had been a much more comfortable relationship with his predecessor. Charles thought Robert was too process-driven. Robert had higher expectations of his auditors than his predecessor. He wanted to be challenged to ensure that nothing was done which could damage the group's reputation, but Charles had not recognised this and had not reacted to it. He trusted his client because he believed that the directors would not risk their own reputation by engaging in doubtful accounting practices. Charles was also at a slight disadvantage as he was younger than Robert and had been his junior when Robert had worked for his firm. As a result, the relationship was unsatisfactory on a personal level. The existence of a relationship problem was recognised by Charles's firm and he did not continue as the engagement partner. This illustrates how a change of one key individual can radically change a relationship.

The group was an important client to Charles's firm. There is little evidence of the involvement of a second partner in the resolution of the issues. The fact of a second partner being assigned to a client in this case did not dictate the extent of the involvement and consultation. It clearly hinged on the personal behaviour of the individuals concerned and the extent to which they chose to consult each other.

Interactions one and three had good outcomes. Charles's position was clearly supported by the regulatory framework, and he took a robust stance. However, in both cases a breach would have been visible in the accounts and could have attracted criticism. Interaction four had an acceptable outcome as there is flexibility in the disclosure requirements within FRS 3 and the disclosure adopted was not misleading.

Interaction two, which had a poor outcome, was not visible in the accounts and Charles had accepted weak arguments in support of the group's case. He was damaged in two ways as a result. First, he lost respect from Robert, and second, Robert had decided to disregard Charles's caveat for future release of the provisions.

Robert's attitude to his auditor was interesting. He wanted to show the group's results in the best possible light. At the same time wanted his auditor to stand up to him robustly, and prevent him doing anything which would bring criticism on the group. However, he still continued to threaten Charles with competitive tenders when he negotiated the fees, a tactic which would undoubtedly make Charles feel vulnerable.

The behaviour of the audit committee in this case is also very interesting. The committee had been reformed to comply with the Cadbury code, in line with the group's conservatism and respectability. It conducted itself on very formal lines in accordance with recognised best practice in corporate governance, and its members included experienced accountants. The existence of this committee, however, did not prevent the poor outcome in interaction two.

10 Dennis and Alan (DA plc)

'They're almost part of the management team'

10.1   BACKGROUND TO THE CASE

This group was originally a family company which had subsequently obtained a listing. It was still controlled by the shareholdings of the family members. A substantial proportion of the publicly owned shares were held by institutions. The group had two main divisions which complemented each other. One was a cash generator and the other needed substantial working capital. The group operated out of a number of sites. At the time of our visit the cash-rich division was experiencing poor trading conditions. Also the board was aware of an impending bid. The head office was a lean operation with most of the accounting done in the two divisions. The board was small, and some of the directors had substantial shareholdings. There were two independent non-executive directors.

The group was going through a period of change and had been divesting itself of peripheral activities and expanding in its two core areas. The introduction of FRS 3 had upset the chairman, a family member, because of the additional disclosures required on acquisitions and disposals.[1] The chairman also resented having to write off goodwill acquired on acquisition, either immediately to reserves or over a period of time through the profit and loss account. This was because the group continued to invest heavily in enhancing its internally generated goodwill. He believed that his inability to show the value of goodwill on the group balance sheet undermined the market's perception of the group's total value. He was particularly unhappy because the market capitalisation of the group was less than the value of its underlying net assets. He attributed this to the non-disclosure of goodwill. Because of its relatively small size, the group also found difficulty in complying with the Cadbury code on corporate governance.

Dennis, the finance director was in his thirties. He had been with the group about two years, having previously worked in a related industry sector. He had limited support in getting the annual accounts prepared and had been using temporary staff to assist him, although he realised that this

---

[1] FRS 3 requires separate disclosure of the results of acquisitions and disposals on the face of the profit and loss account.

was not a long-term solution. He also relied heavily on the auditors both for advice and assistance in preparing the annual report and in the provision of tax advice.

Alan, the audit partner, was also in his thirties. He had previously been the audit manager for the group and had succeeded the previous engagement partner who had retired.

10.2 THE KEY ISSUES FOR DENNIS AND ALAN

Although Alan was familiar with the company, both Dennis and Alan were new to their roles and were to some extent feeling their way in terms of both their new roles and their working relationship with each other. A number of issues were raised which appeared significantly more important to one than the other. This suggests that both had very different priorities. There was also a general recognition by both of the costs that the regulatory framework placed on the smaller listed company.

We interviewed Alan and Dennis separately. Some issues were common to both and others were referred to only or mainly by one. In all we identified six interactions and four contextual influences during the discussions. None of the interactions was regarded by either party as particularly contentious. These are described in the order below to maintain the flow of the story.

- the background to the bid (*context DA(a)*);
- accounting for assets on disposal and acquisition of businesses (*interactions DA1 and DA2*);
- disclosures of acquisitions, disposals and bid costs under FRS 3 (*interaction DA3*);
- last-minute adjustments to the accounts (*interaction DA4*);
- the chairman's attitude to goodwill (*interaction DA5*);
- compliance with the Cadbury Code and other non-mandatory disclosures (*interaction DA6*);
- the role of the audit committee (*context DA(b)*);
- the nature of the company's relationship with its auditors (*context DA(c)*);
- non-audit services and fees (*context DA(d)*).

10.3 CONTEXT DA(a): THE BACKGROUND TO THE BID

The group's share price was low because of the poor performance of one of the core activities. At the time we interviewed Dennis, the board had been notified of a possible bid for the group. When we interviewed Alan the bid had been withdrawn.

Dennis explained how the approach had been made:

'[*Group X*] ... approached us ten days ago, as directors that was, and said they'd like ... to talk to the directors and the shareholders before they made it public' (Dennis).

The board felt exposed because the share price had dropped considerably since the flotation several years earlier:

'It's certainly fallen. ... It's not been a good investment right from the word go' (Alan).

When the bidder's intentions were made known, the directors had to move very quickly. They regarded the bid as hostile:

'We had a meeting and over ... that weekend we talked to those who held [*a majority*] of the shares altogether and the shareholders thoroughly rejected any approaches so far' (Dennis).

The board had doubts about the ability of the bidder to manage the business:

'They've said that the group would be better suited to be part of a larger group and that means that the two main businesses ... would sit inside their group and would be managed by a larger group, presumably doing away with the central function. They have no particular expertise in running either business' (Dennis).

Dennis recognised the threat that this presented to the existing board:

'They would dispense with us here. ... One assumes what they would do is ... break it up and they would sell it on, no doubt for some sort of gain' (Dennis).

The auditors were immediately involved:

'[*Alan's firm*] talked directly to some shareholders on the Monday' (Dennis).

Following the initial approach the bidder then went public:

'Late in the [*Monday*] afternoon, they went public, whether they were forced to or not I don't know. They may have been by the Takeover Panel ... and didn't tell us in advance, which is a bit of a nuisance really. They nevertheless did it, so we obviously had to … get ourselves going' (Dennis).

The group did not find out until very late in the day that the bid had been announced:

'I suppose they would argue that we were on notice, but nevertheless it's a bit frustrating when it happens. We got a phone call from them about six o'clock' (Dennis).

The directors were left with very little time to get up a defence:

'We had to mobilise people to get responses out, and we got a response out the next day … to be honest I thought we did well … because we knew over the weekend that things were happening, we'd already got merchant bank and lawyers … mobilised and PR so at least that was working and the response … was with the shareholders on Wednesday morning. … We've not heard anything so we don't know where we stand now' (Dennis).

Dennis did not think the bid would succeed:

'The family's against it … it depends how far they're prepared to go, to be … honest' (Dennis).

However, the effect of the bid was to make the directors sit up:

'Here we are in a potential … situation. We've got to really get our act together on those sorts of things. That's the way it does work' (Dennis).

Alan described how the matter ended:

'It's gone away, but they wrote a letter with a sting in the tail to … the directors of the company, copy to the major shareholders. It said something like: "We've made you an offer of £X in the pound. We believe this fully values your company. The directors believe that the price you will eventually achieve for your shareholding will be greater by sticking with the current board of directors"' (Alan).

Alan did not think that the bid would come back:

'We will have to see when we look at the results in the year under review … they could [*come back*] but they might not … it's held up extremely well' (Alan).

He made some interesting final observations about the group and the bid:

> 'They've got a marvellous system. The reports, the controls in the market place are actually very, very good. ... I think you can see that bottom line rising. ... One thing that is very pleasing is that the shareholders stood behind them and they made the decision. Yes, it's a hostile bid, and we'll treat it as that' (Alan).

10.4   INTERACTIONS DA1 AND DA2: ACCOUNTING FOR ASSETS ON DISPOSAL AND ACQUISITION OF BUSINESSES

The group had grown very quickly during the boom years of the 1980s and had engaged in a number of diverse activities. After the recession a need to rationalise was perceived and the board decided to concentrate on two core activities and dispose of others. Other businesses in the core areas were acquired and issues also arose in accounting for the assets of these businesses.

10.4.1   Interaction DA1: accounting for assets on disposal of businesses

One disposal which we call SubX proved to be particularly troublesome to Dennis in terms of the timing of the disposal and the asset values. Dennis first explained the background to the decision to rationalise:

> 'The company diversified into all sorts of things. ... We then hit turbulent times. We had all these various businesses. We had ... gone to the market. We thought it was a good idea. There were some ... mistakes with different things at that stage but nevertheless that was what happened ... it was heady days. We then very quickly had to ... take stock of what we'd done ... and reorganised, and decided to, basically, get rid of all these odds and ends as best we could. The last bit of that was really SubX' (Dennis).

SubX was a property-based company and the sale was being negotiated during the time the group accounts for the relevant year were being put together. A problem emerged over the realisability of the book values of the assets. This became apparent during the sale negotiations. Dennis had only just joined the group:

> 'We didn't get too het up on that initially, I didn't have the benefit of having that in advance' (Dennis).

Alan had more of a grip on the situation initially:

'We needed to establish how much we were going to get for some sales ... there were certainly some discussions as to whether the book amounts ... were going to be realised at that level' (Alan).

Historical calculations were carried out to reach an estimate of the values:

'We went back and looked at the proceeds we had received historically ... we looked at proceeds that were received during the year through to the time that we actually signed the accounts and we formed a view. ... We decided that the overall amount that was reflected in the accounts was probably reasonable' (Alan).

Dennis had quickly recognised the problem for the group:

'One of the first things I got involved with when I joined the company in January was to start talking ... about the sale of this business. ... We knew there was a write-down ... so there was no debate about whether or not. ... We certainly talked to [Alan's firm] during that time so it wasn't a surprise' (Dennis).

The issue, therefore, was how it should be disclosed. The sale agreement was not signed until the day before the results were announced so it was treated as an adjusting post balance sheet event:

'We didn't bring the sale in ... we had to make a provision for the sale of the fixed assets, which we sold on the day the results were announced, so that was the adjustment if you like. We would have had to do that anyway because, having got a deal ... if that had gone away we would have still had to write the assets down to that level ... because that was the market level. That was the post balance sheet event' (Dennis).

Alan was slightly more laid back about it. He also gave his views on the materiality of the potential adjustment:

'Overall I don't think the sum was really that material. Even if the estimate had been twenty per cent wrong either way, it would not have been material in the context of the operating profit. It doesn't strike me as something of great concern. Now it might have been sort of slightly different this year, when our retained profit for the half year is [*much lower*] ... it's in rather a different context, but at the time ... certainly well below our materiality level' (Alan).

The combination of putting the accounts together and negotiating the sale of a key business was quite tough for Dennis in his first few weeks with the group. He considered himself fortunate to have found a competent temporary assistant:

> 'Actually that year I had a guy who was working … who was a temp, who was particularly good. I struck lucky. He was just out of the profession himself but had been travelling and was just right. He was a bit raw but he was newly qualified and was just the right sort of guy on that aspect' (Dennis).

The possible sale of SubX running alongside the preparation of the annual accounts had created uncertainty in respect of the preliminary announcement:

> 'It was particularly difficult because we were finalising the sale of SubX at the same time. So in the final throes of producing not so much the glossy version but the prelims which obviously have to be the same … we signed the deal to sell that business at seven o'clock in the morning that we were due to announce results. … We had … two sets of slides ready and all that sort of thing and two sets of prelims' (Dennis).

Another property disposal issue arose as one division of the group had moved into new premises and the original premises were put up for sale. An offer was received which was less than the book value of the property and discussions took place about whether adjustments should be made. This matter was only mentioned by Alan. Dennis did not regard it as significant.

> 'It was standing in the books originally at £X and had been written down by [*30 per cent*]. They received an offer for it of £Y [*80 per cent of the book value*] and … the issue was, if you're going to sell for that, clearly it should be written down even if it doesn't complete until after the accounts are signed … that's an indicative value' (Alan).

However, the board disagreed with the offer value:

> 'The company took the view that they weren't going to accept this offer, that it was a low offer, and they stood by the fact that they were going to keep it in their books' (Alan).

Although he was sympathetic to their position Alan wanted a bit more comfort:

> 'I had some sympathy that probably the right number was in the order of [*the book value*] but we actually asked for at least a verbal assurance from the audit committee that they had no intentions of selling at [*the offer price*] and actually

got a view from the directors that it was a particularly low ball offer. ... It was
certainly of some concern' (Alan).

There was a further development before the accounts were signed,
which allowed Alan to let the book value stand:

'Before we ... signed the accounts they actually got a tenant in part of it ... so at
that stage they were using it for the purposes of the business again, and since
then they have had offers in for part or all of the building which support the
valuation' (Alan).

10.4.2   Interaction DA2: accounting for assets on acquisition of businesses

At the same time that disposals of non-core businesses were effected,
acquisitions were made to expand the core activity and Alan was not comfortable with the group's approach to accounting for depreciation on the
fixed assets acquired. A number had been acquired in the financial year
before Dennis joined the group. Alan was unhappy that proper asset registers were not maintained.

Dennis acknowledged that dealing with the accounting treatment of the
assets acquired had been left very late:

'If I'd been there from the beginning ... before the year-end itself, I sometimes
think that ... would have been sorted. We left it too late. I mean, I joined in
January' (Dennis).

Alan had a particular problem with the acquisitions and was slightly
critical of Dennis:

'I don't think that he gave quite the right amount of time and importance to it
that he should have done' (Alan).

Alan's problem related to depreciation:

'The area was really ... putting a valuation on the fixed assets ... and the policy
that was chosen was to allocate the purchase price and then ... depreciate the
fixed assets as though they were new on the day that they were bought. ... Our
concern was that some of these assets were so many years old and therefore
there was inconsistency in depreciation policy between businesses that had been
set up from scratch that were being depreciated over three, five, seven or ten
years, whatever it happened to be, and the fact that ... the same policy was used,

three years for one thing, five years another, seven years for another. ... These items were arguably part way through their lives' (Alan).

Alan felt this was an important matter:

'We thought that was a very important issue because we wanted to be comfortable, clearly that the assets were able to last.... What we wanted them to do was actually to prepare an asset register' (Alan).

The problem affected two consecutive years:

'It hit in both 19XX and 19XY. They were acquired late in 19XX. During the 19XX audit we weren't that concerned because they were only going to hit a month or two depreciation anyway, and the deals really weren't all finalised till the audit was going on, so we were more relaxed' (Alan).

Alan did some calculations to establish the size of the possible adjustment:

'I did a calculation ... saying what would be the impact on depreciation if you took one of these [*assets*] and said, "Well it's four years old and you depreciate it over seven years rather than three years. So instead of taking a third hit each year you're only taking a seventh, what's the difference?" There was a reasonable size number there. So I thought it actually critical that ... that I see ... that they weren't going to end up with a relevant asset that ultimately wasn't depreciated when the assets had no further enduring benefit to the business' (Alan).

His concerns were such that he took the matter to the audit committee, but did not entirely get his own way because of the cost to the group of complying with his wishes:

'We presented that to the audit committee. Where we ended up was that ultimately it was agreed that an exercise was carried out to check that all the major items of plant and equipment would have a life at least as long as they were being depreciated over ... but the company wouldn't actually go back and list every item of fixed assets and allocate individual values to it and I think at the end of the day we formed the view that probably the time and expense of actually doing the full exercise was disproportionate to the benefits they would achieve' (Alan).

Although the group agreed to deal with the assets acquired on acquisition Alan discovered that assets acquired since had not been separately logged:

'We presented it more to bring home the point that this was a serious issue ... and no fixed asset register had been done for additions since the plant and machinery additions when the [*additional businesses*] were bought, and they were just left in one particular account' (Alan).

Alan was not happy about finding this:

'We could see that it would just roll on from year to year and we wouldn't have any specific costs allocated to any fixtures, fittings, plant and equipment' (Alan).

However, the group did agree to improve things in the future:

'What they did was start a new fixed asset register for all fixed assets acquired after [*an agreed date*]' (Alan).

But Alan intended to check that this had been done:

'We're going to go in and have a look. We've actually just gone in at the interims at the moment. … That'll be one area I just want to see under tight control' (Alan).

Interestingly, as if to bear out Alan's concern that Dennis paid little attention to this matter, Dennis made no reference to asset registers in his interview.

10.5 INTERACTION DA3: DISCLOSURE OF ACQUISITIONS, DISPOSALS AND BID COSTS UNDER FRS 3

The group's acquisition and disposal activity required extensive disclosure under FRS 3. This caused some questioning by Dennis and other board members about the relevance of the FRS 3 disclosure requirements to groups which regularly acquired businesses in their core areas. Dennis also raised materiality issues in respect of the disposal of SubX.

Dennis first complained about the complexity of the FRS 3 profit and loss account presentation which in his view did not emphasise the most important issues:

'I am not convinced that the average reader of the accounts really understands. I mean tucked away in the notes is the split on the business issues which in many respects is much more important' (Dennis).

He felt he was able to give out much more useful information in his preliminary announcement:

> 'What we give out, I believe, when we announce our results to the world … is in many respects more user friendly because you're not quite tied by the same rules as this. … Most of this stuff really, truly is irrelevant' (Dennis).

Dennis believed that too much of the group's routine activity was caught by the definitions of continuing and discontinued businesses:

> 'I mean, the other thing of course in here is continuing and discontinuing businesses. My interpretation of what was meant by that was that it was only going to be very exceptional items that would go into discontinued. The truth is every company has discontinued or new businesses every year now, so it doesn't entirely help the reader because he doesn't really know what is continuing any more … if you admit you are going to have five new businesses next year. … I don't think they're new businesses. I think they will go into continuing operations; they'll just get added in. But if we bought five businesses as a going concern they'd probably go into new businesses' (Dennis).

As some of the activity had already been disclosed at the half year Dennis was stuck with year-end disclosures:

> 'We were hampered slightly because the half-year results had two of those events already, and they'd been disclosed so we had to follow the book. It wasn't so much a frustration with them, it was more a frustration with the rules. … As far as I was concerned the big issue was really not what had happened as far as the businesses that had gone but what was happening to the businesses that we were keeping. I still think that's the major issue' (Dennis).

Dennis objected to the blocks on the face on the profit and loss account which he felt distorted the overview of the accounts:

> 'We find ourselves putting a big block on the front page of the accounts showing the profit impact of those three businesses and the sale of those three businesses, and we tuck away in the notes the split between the main products. It's that area which is ongoing, is used to evaluate whether the business is going to do well or not' (Dennis).

FRS 3 also annoyed the chairman:

> 'Our chairman has an absolute bee in his bonnet about FRS 3' (Dennis).

Dennis was frustrated by the time which was spent in working out the presentation of the profit and loss account:

'It's the minutiae actually that takes the time ... a lot of it isn't a very big decision. A lot of it is how you lay these accounts out in the most appropriate form. I mean for instance in the exceptional items area we've already got four lines, in year 19XX which I think is gross overkill in all respects' (Dennis).

He engaged in lengthy discussions with Alan on the presentation:

'I mean there were different ways of showing this thing as well, whether it's columns. It was that sort of nitty gritty ... we debated for instance whether we could get that on the front page ... because I think we waste space on the accounts ... in some respects it's probably not a good idea because it makes the front page so cluttered' (Dennis).

Dennis was not very keen on using boxes[2] on the profit and loss account:

'I still think that box there was just overkill but it was ... a compromise ... when I look back on it, it was all rather small-fry stuff' (Dennis).

Alan however was rather more enthusiastic about boxes:

'It depends on how far you actually go with this presentation. I think you can use it constructively as a benefit to the reader. However I've seen examples where it's been used to mislead' (Alan).

He was planning to suggest putting a box on the profit and loss account in a subsequent year's accounts to indicate what the profit would have been without the exceptional costs associated with the bid:

'It's slightly grey, what we want to do is a box presentation above our operating profit, and essentially what it does is ... without drawing a line ... brings ... to the attention of the reader, once you take out the aborted bid costs, what the profit would have been had they not been in there. ... I'm actually quite comfortable with it ... to highlight an item which I actually believe is exceptional but clearly doesn't fall within the definition given in the section' (Alan).

---

[2] *Boxes on the profit and loss account*: placing figures in a box on the face of the profit and loss account is a way of showing the make-up of a particular item which the company wishes to emphasise, e.g., the effect of one-off costs or expenses on the profit. As is suggested, it can be used to include items additional to those suggested in FRS 3 but can also in some circumstances draw the user away from the mandatory disclosures.

Dennis felt that accounts production involved complex arrangement of space:

> 'These accounts had a lot more information than the previous year's accounts. …
> We always had the option of taking out the back page and putting it into a sepa-
> rate page … but we did squeeze some things up and those are the sort of things
> you have to plan for' (Dennis).

This was one reason why early discussion with the auditors was important:

> 'That's why the discussions with the auditors are important. It'll save you get-
> ting caught out. If you get caught out in March, April time, it's uncomfortable to
> have to disclose that we haven't got room in these accounts' (Dennis).

10.6   INTERACTION DA4: LAST-MINUTE ADJUSTMENTS
TO THE ACCOUNTS

Dennis complained about the way the group's accounts were sent to the technical department at a very late stage in the reporting cycle. Some last-minute
amendments were required and Dennis was annoyed about being caught up
in an unexpected rush which had also involved weekend work with no prior
warning. Alan was very much in favour of technical reviews and believed it
was a valuable exercise. Dennis and Alan both had views on the importance
of technical compliance and how best to deal with issues which arose:
Dennis believed that auditors needed to understand commercial reality:

> 'They have to … understand that this is the commercial reality of the world
> when they sign off accounts and what the management is really about. I don't
> think management is about trying to fool anybody, but you do have to watch
> what you say, of course' (Dennis).

He felt that Alan's firm's technical department was somewhat mysterious:

> 'One of the biggest areas of debate … comes from when you get a technical guy.
> It's not so much the people you see. The people you see are fine, by and large.
> They understand what you are trying to achieve and they will be realistic. But
> they send the accounts off to a technical panel in a room … somewhere … as far
> as I can see they never emerge … talk about grey suits' (Dennis).

He wasn't enthusiastic about their activities:

> 'They analyse everything based on what the numerous accounting standards
> deal with and that's the problem' (Dennis).

Alan, however, was more supportive of technical reviews having spent time working in his firm's technical department:

> 'I sent the accounts to our technical department because I spent a year and a half working in it, so I know a lot of people there' (Alan).

As a newly appointed partner, he found input from the technical department reassuring:

> 'It was my first year as a partner, better to be safe than sorry … certainly I like a technical review particularly as there were a number of presentational issues' (Alan).

Because of the shortage of accounting resources in the group, they were reliant on their auditors for technical expertise:

> 'As always you can't get these things reviewed by the technical people because there's no point until you're virtually here at this stage … we don't employ anyone here whose got enough knowledge to do that' (Dennis).

However, Dennis did not want to rely on his auditors for accounting assistance as he wanted to be in control of this himself, but he did need their technical support:

> 'We've used temps to help us through this … period of producing the accounts. I'd rather do that than pay the auditors to do it for us. … I don't think we get the independence we want … so the auditors sent if off to their own technical department' (Dennis).

Dennis thought that there were only one or two issues, and that Alan was basically happy with the accounts:

> 'I think there might have been one or two questions that they had, but … they were basically happy with the thing' (Dennis).

However, Alan's technical department raised a number of points which led to a last-minute rush:

> 'I remember sitting in the office next door on a Saturday morning going through them. … It was to do with the cash flow and the disclosure of finance leases' (Dennis).

Dennis acknowledged that the points raised by the technical department were right:

> 'We had to make a change and they were right about that ... but the frustrating thing about that was that no one else had picked it up. ... They should have done the previous year and maybe the year before that as well, because it wasn't something that was different' (Dennis).

Alan was away at the time and as time was so short Alan's firm had passed the technical department's comments straight to Dennis:

> 'There were other things in there which we should never have seen because the audit partner, who ... wasn't around that particular twenty-four hours, would have sorted out those issues, and we'd never have seen the response' (Dennis).

He thought the fact of Alan's firm passing on the letter showed the strength of the relationship:

> 'That's an example of us working very well with our auditors ... because they trusted us and we trusted them enough to be able to work it through ... but maybe we got involved a bit too much ... on an issue that they'd probably ... have solved ... with their own technical people before it got to us' (Dennis).

Dennis's main gripe was that he had already prepared his presentation to the city analysts:

> 'The heartache that I had was more to do with the presentation I was about to make to the analysts in the city, because we'd got slides and so on for that ... and we'd got a cash flow done and they were almost ready to go, and we had to change that at the last minute' (Dennis).

Interestingly, when asked about this particular problem, Alan did not recall it, possibly because he had not been involved, but he acknowledged that accounts were not sent to the technical department until printer's proof stage:

> 'I have to say about the particular issue regarding finance leases, certainly I didn't come in over the weekend with it, so I'm a little bit surprised. There is a possibility of things coming out late in the day ... in this case we'd only got the printer's proof probably something like the end of March, so there's only a couple of weeks probably for them to go backwards and forwards, and we'd want to send quite a reasonable proof up to our advisory people' (Alan).

Dennis also had a few words on the burdens that the current framework imposed on smaller listed companies:

> 'One area I have a little beef about in terms of reporting requirements, probably more to do with the stock exchange than accounting problems in many respects ... We're not exactly enormous. We've got a shareholder base that's predominantly family, but nevertheless we've got ... shares in the public domain and those shareholders have every right to see those accounts produced in the right way and I wouldn't want to do anything else, even if we had a larger proportion of family shareholders ... but there are certain requirements that are just too damned expensive to put into practice' (Dennis).

Dennis was not convinced that investors benefited:

> 'We are getting quite nit-picky these days in the way we produce accounts ... the amount of time it takes to produce the accounts. I don't like the presentation of accounts particularly. ... I don't think the cash flow helps the average investor understand the business any better. ... He sees something of the cash flow from operating activities. He's got to go into the notes to find it and if he's not very good at that he'll never find the profit' (Dennis).

10.7 INTERACTION DA5: THE CHAIRMAN'S ATTITUDE TO GOODWILL

The chairman of the group, who was a member of the family and had no accounting background, felt that the group was undervalued because of the need to write off goodwill on acquisition of new businesses. Both David and Alan had tried to convince him that nothing could be done to address his concerns, but his concerns had been aggravated by the hostile bid which he also believed had undervalued the business. Alan had the most to say on this subject. He explained the background to the chairman's concerns:

> 'The audit partner before, I know, had several discussions on internally generated goodwill. The chairman has an issue that his company is worth more than the balance sheet value. He believes that' (Alan).

The chairman believed that the group's inability to show both acquired and internally generated goodwill on the balance sheet undermined its share price. Alan was not so sure:

> 'One could actually say that of course the value of the company is reflected in the share price ... if you look at the share price what does it matter what the

assets are. But even then the company's discounted by something like twenty per cent … to what he believes the real net asset value of the company to be' (Alan).

Alan explained the chairman's arguments:

'His view is quite simple. We put effort in over all these years. The company's worth more than that. We have written off goodwill to reserves over the years. Arguably we shouldn't have done that. We should put it back on the balance sheet. I'd like to increase the life on my goodwill' (Alan).

It had been made clear to the chairman that at the time this was not possible:

'Some things we know we can't do. Sorry, the accounting standards make it absolutely clear … I forget what it is that's coming in that may allow us to change the life of goodwill and lengthen it, but at the present time there's nothing we can do about that' (Alan).

Alan felt that Dennis had been rather caught by this issue shortly after he joined the group:

'Dennis was caught in the middle of those discussions and the discussions had gone on for some time … because of the pressure from the chairman, he came back and spoke to me about the subject … and at the end of the day there was nothing that we could do to help him' (Alan).

The bid had increased the chairman's frustration over this issue:

'He will want to revisit that subject and particularly as we've had this hostile takeover bid that's come in. If the balance sheet had actually reflected that they might have offered £XX instead of £YY. But there was really no scope to increase the net asset value of the company, which is one of the things the chairman wanted to do and we did discuss a number of ways' (Alan).

Alan felt personally that there was little to be gained from putting intangibles on the balance sheet:

'If an analyst was to look at the company, if you stuck an intangible on the balance sheet that suddenly appeared out of nowhere. … All an analyst is going to do is put his pen through it anyway. So I didn't actually believe it was going to be of any benefit' (Alan).

But it took a long time and much effort to convince the chairman:

'There was a discussion between Dennis and myself and then the chief executive ... had discussed the issue with the former partner. It had been decided I think it must be back in 199X that nothing could be done. It was revisited in 199Y and during 199Y we did a presentation to the whole board of our findings during the audit. ... This was an issue that was on the agenda and they wished us to summarise our findings. So we'd already had the meetings with the executive directors and we'd presented a paper to the audit committee meeting so that the non-execs were aware of the issues as well' (Alan).

The auditors were helped out by one of the independent non-executive directors:

'It was very interesting in that one of the non-executive directors, Keith, assisted us in this and actually guided the chairman to take [*Alan's firm's*] advice. He'd clearly been down this route with one or two other companies and realised that you couldn't put internally generated goodwill on the balance sheet. Keith also stated that it's not necessary to reflect the full value of your company in your net assets on the balance sheet' (Alan).

Alan felt that the independent non-executive director had carried the day:

'Now it's fair to say that the two other non-execs on the board ... had quite a large interest in the company, and it was very much Keith that was the calming influence, if you like, a professional non-exec. Keith appreciates the responsibilities of directors and you know, the activities of the remuneration committee, audit committee etc.' (Alan).

The possibility of revaluing the properties was considered, but was not believed to be helpful, as Alan ruled out selective revaluation:

'We've certainly reviewed the property portfolio ... and had a great deal of discussion on those, because they haven't been revalued since 19XX, and it was very much my view that if there was a revaluation it wouldn't necessarily be upwards ... on certain properties. Now the one thing that I felt very strongly about is that if there was going to be a revaluation ... then all would need revaluing ... some of which would need a third party valuation to be carried out. Whereas I think there was an initial view by the company, "Why couldn't we pick this particular site?" ' (Alan).

In the end the revaluation was not carried out:

> 'As far as the company was concerned, I don't think it was a satisfactory out-come. They'd have liked a solution to the problem … but in the event I felt that there was nothing that we could do for them along those particular lines' (Alan).

Dennis felt that the chairman would never change his view, and was rather disparaging:

> 'If he was sitting here now he would still say the same thing. We're talking about the valuation of our businesses and what they are really worth as far as he is con-cerned, not what we paid for them. He would say the balance sheet doesn't reflect their true worth because we wrote all this goodwill off' (Dennis).

10.8   INTERACTION DA6: COMPLIANCE WITH THE CADBURY CODE[3] AND OTHER NON-MANDATORY DISCLOSURES

The group had expanded considerably in the year before Dennis joined and until then had been fairly casual about compliance with the Cadbury Code. Until Dennis was appointed the role of finance director had been filled by a temporary appointment. It was becoming apparent to the board that they needed to take Cadbury disclosures much more seriously and they sought advice from Alan about best practice. At the same time the board also decided to improve other disclosures in the accounts. They did not want to be at the forefront of reporting practice. Alan provided exam-ples of what other companies were doing but was not prepared to draft the disclosures himself. A considerable amount of discussion arose about the internal control disclosures.

Dennis explained why the board felt it needed to improve its accounts:

> 'We'd acquired a lot of businesses during 199Y and … all of a sudden, if you like, the company had become much more public in its stance and I think we all felt that we had to … be whiter than white … . We had to follow these things and follow these rules' (Dennis).

He nevertheless found some of the changes excessive for a group of their size:

> 'At the same time for a small company to get involved in all the aspects, I think was, in some cases, overkill, but we felt we should do it' (Dennis).

---

[3] See footnote 4 in Chapter 5.

They decided to expand the non-statutory disclosures and tidy up the Cadbury disclosures:

'We would try and break up the reports so that we had a Chairman's Statement, Chief Executive's Review and a Finance Review. ... The other area that changed was around this Cadbury thing and we had to find the words' (Dennis).

However they did not want to go too far with the disclosures, and felt that the timing was against them:

'The reporting season was just getting under way ... and we didn't want to be at the forefront of that ... particularly being a minnow, but there weren't enough examples around of companies that had fully complied' (Dennis).

Dennis found that Alan's firm were not prepared to draft the disclosures for him:

'What they were loath to do, I found, was to actually draft for you. They wanted you to do something' (Dennis).

He did not feel that Alan's firm had sorted out a style of its own, and appeared to expect more help than Alan was willing to provide:

'You always seem to be waiting for somebody to put out something that says this is the way you do it, or the auditors to put out. They hadn't decided what their style was and that was the frustration there' (Dennis).

However, Alan believed that he had contributed significantly by providing examples of other cases:

'Essentially we did the Cadbury thing for him. I went off to our technical advisor and just pulled out a lot of examples ... what was best practice at the time, and what we did was let him take the choice, in what he ... really wanted to say' (Alan).

Alan described the discussion on internal control disclosures:

'One thing that he wanted was to make a statement that he'd got good internal controls and that they were totally satisfactory and adequate, rather than give a description of what they were, but not actually conclude on internal controls. ... That's quite a difficult discussion we had on that' (Alan).

Internal control disclosure was a subject that Alan's firm had taken a position on in advising clients:

> 'We formed a view ... that there would be a misinterpretation if you actually said that internal controls were up and working. ... I mean you can be satisfied that you reviewed your systems of internal controls, and you can describe what they are. That's actually fine but of course nothing's perfect. ... I think going back three or four years there was a small fraud' (Alan).

Alan, nevertheless, believed that the group's internal controls were very strong:

> 'When I reported to the audit committee I was very positive about internal controls because we did a separate report on the cash system. I was very impressed with them, but equally an appropriate caveat was required' (Alan).

Dennis acknowledged that the exercise in the end had not been too difficult:

> 'I didn't find it terribly difficult to pull that together because I pinched other people's at the end of the day ... the time angle was in trying to agree the words' (Dennis).

Alan believed that sorting out the corporate governance disclosures was an important issue for Dennis:

> 'Corporate governance, Cadbury, it was important. They actually took it very seriously, and although probably we didn't start out together as to what was going in the accounts. ... It was quite a good statement, I think, that went in, in the end, and that was important' (Alan).

Following the year-end accounts the group also revised its approach to the interim statements, but they became concerned about the cost benefit:

> 'When we did the release of the interim announcements and the executives ... had gone pretty well full bore with cash flows and notes. ... It was getting about that thick, and we always realised that we were unlikely to get more than two lines in the FT if we were extremely lucky' (Alan).

The independent non-executive director suggested that they were going too far, in terms of their size:

> 'Keith ... is actually a non-exec of some quite large PLCs. ... He did turn round to [the group] and say. "You know, you're not ICI here, please appreciate that.

Let's give them something that's in keeping with our size and … the coverage we are actually going to get." … If one had gone back to the chairman it would have been all singing, all dancing, and really, quite frankly it wasn't appropriate for them to do it because the shares are quite closely held anyway' (Alan).

10.9 CONTEXT DA(b): THE ROLE OF THE AUDIT COMMITTEE

Dennis described in some detail how the group's audit committee operated. His description provides insights into the impact of corporate governance recommendations on the smaller family controlled group. He first explained how the meetings worked:

'The audit committee in principle doesn't include all the board, but in practice we tend to have one meeting that is the board and the audit committee. Keith's experience is better than anybody else I know. So he's the right guy to do these things and he's much more familiar with the routines and so on. The committee meets once and sometimes twice a year. It doesn't always meet for the interim results' (Dennis).

Sometimes the committee didn't meet for some time:

'It didn't formally meet this year to be honest. The timing wasn't right and the board felt quite happy' (Dennis).

Part of the reason for not meeting was the difficulty of isolating the business:

'The accounting requirements as regards all the committees and so on for a company of our size rather disregard the fact that there's a board of directors. I think for a small company of our size we're embarrassed as far as having non-execs and independent non-execs. … Two of the directors are family shareholders … but the feeling is that we feel we only really need to meet with the auditors once a year … but it's difficult at times to try and isolate. What is an audit committee, what's the function?' (Dennis).

Confusion had arisen about this in the last round of meetings:

'Last year we tried to run it as two separate meetings and it didn't really work, because we … had the audit committee meeting and the auditors joined us for that section and then we found ourselves discussing the year end accounts after that without them present. So this year … we started it at the normal time. We went through the numbers without the auditors being there so that everyone was up to speed and then we pulled the auditors in to discuss. They present their paper ... which admittedly the chief executive and I have had a chance to go through with them ... and those issues are discussed' (Dennis).

Despite the apparent lack of formality, Keith, the independent non-executive director, who chaired the audit committee (but not the board), insisted that the executives left the room to give the auditors the opportunity to speak to the other members of the board:

> 'At the end of that Keith throws the execs out ... so he takes the chair and then it gives them a chance to talk direct if there's anything that has to be said without us being present. ... What exactly is said I don't always know though I do if they ask me to minute something. But that's quite simply how it works' (Dennis).

Dennis, however, felt sure that Alan would take matters to the audit committee in his absence if he felt the need:

> 'I'm absolutely convinced that our partner who looks after us, if he felt that there was something that we were doing that he wasn't happy with ... he would then go to the ... chairman of the audit committee. I'm quite convinced of that' (Dennis).

He was also confident that such a situation would never arise:

> 'We work closely enough together for me to be absolutely confident that it would never arise, because I couldn't let it happen. ... I think if a genuine mistake had been made I think he would treat that differently. ... But if it's matters of principle. ... I don't think we'd ever get to that point anyway' (Dennis).

10.10   CONTEXT DA(c): THE NATURE OF THE COMPANY'S RELATIONSHIP WITH ITS AUDITORS

Being a small group with limited resources, the board relied on the auditors for advice, particularly on technical areas. Dennis also made some interesting observations on the nature of the relationship which existed and changes that he had observed in the way Alan's firm was operating. He believed it was becoming much more commercial. Dennis first commented on the previous engagement partner, who had since left the firm. He felt his departure reflected a change in the firm's attitude:

> 'There was a change in partner ... he has actually since left ... he wasn't old by any means. A lot of partners seemed to have moved on in the last two or three

years … there's a whole new breed of partners looking after the audit side' (Dennis).

Dennis doubted that the partner in place at the time he joined the group was totally up to date:

'I don't think he was as clued up as to what we had to show … been on this audit for several years and knew the company far better than I did. He was a bit of the old school and maybe he just wasn't so familiar with things' (Dennis).

At the time Alan was the senior manager and Dennis felt that the partner relied too heavily on his subordinates:

'He was relying on his senior guy who's now the partner and … the manager who's now the senior manager' (Dennis).

Dennis also felt that the relationship was not very good:

'We didn't have a very good, very strong working relationship simply because we hadn't worked together before' (Dennis).

He was now much more comfortable with Alan:

'We've almost grown up together on this audit because he's been partner for now for about twelve to fifteen months or something like that' (Dennis).

Although Dennis had criticised the activities of the firm's technical department he found it valuable that Alan had spent time there. He had also observed how Alan had matured since and how the relationship had developed:

'Funnily enough, he came from the technical department … so he's one of those boffins, but it's interesting how they change, you know. … I've had conversations with him since about that and he's quite enlightening to listen to, because he knew what he had to do when you're in that sort of box, ticking away. … Probably that's the best experience because they can see both sides of it and understand where the client's coming from as well as where the committees are coming from, but it's been easier since and it's probably down as much to the relationship as it is to anything else' (Dennis).

Dennis had also observed how the senior manager had matured:

'The manager was new to the audit … his rule book, if you like, at that level is much more black and white as to what you can and can't do. As they become more senior but also more confident … they feel they can deal with those situations without referring to others and maybe see the more commercial aspects of it' (Dennis).

He felt that the manager was now much more relaxed about things, as he matured and the relationship developed:

'The guy who looked after us in 199X, he's still with us today. He's now the senior manager on the audit and there's a marked difference in two years. But he's now much more relaxed about certain issues. He probably knows us and knows me especially, what we're after' (Dennis).

Dennis went on to explain how the relationship now worked:

'I don't regard the auditors as a bunch of people who come in twice a year and check what you've done and then go away again. From my point of view, dare I say it, they're almost part of the management team.

He did not tell the auditors everything:

'We're obviously careful what we say and don't tell them things … that would blow back in our face at some later stage or whatever' (Dennis).

However, he used them as a sounding board:

'I use them a lot to bounce ideas off, to get their views on things, because it's at that point that it matters. I mean you can't decide when it comes to March/April time when you announce results, "Oh God, I've got to disclose this thing. … If I'd thought of that at the time I might have approached it perhaps differently." So what we tend to do is to talk to them beforehand about various things, and we miss a few things' (Dennis).

In Dennis's view the group was far more reactive than he would like:

'I'm afraid we're far more reactive to a situation than we'd like. I think we'd like to think we are much more in control than we are. … In an ideal world we would plan these things and take them through' (Dennis).

He recognised that it was inevitable, given the size of the group, that they would rely on the auditors:

'I think the size of the company would do that anyway … When it comes to the real nitty-gritty you need somebody. At the end of the day the only people who can do that are the auditors' (Dennis).

Despite the closeness of the relationship and the firm's growing commerciality, Dennis respected his auditors' independence:

'I know they wouldn't compromise their own position. I'm positive about that. They're not those sort of people, but nevertheless they do tend to have quite a good back way of balancing what would be fairly commercial with what is being required' (Dennis).

10.11 CONTEXT DA(d): NON-AUDIT SERVICES AND FEES

Although Dennis was reasonably comfortable with the audit service he was getting from Alan's firm, he was less happy with the tax service and the way in which charges were made. He preferred the fixed fee arrangement on the audit service. He also found the need to disclose all the non-audit fees an embarrassment. Dennis believed that Alan was well aware of his views on the differences between the quality of the service he received on audit and tax:

'He knows my views about this thing, about the commercial attitude of the guys. ... I find it strange, because our auditors are supposedly independent and they have to retain their independence ... irrespective of what they tell us and yet we get better advice, really and truly, from them than we do from the tax guys' (Dennis).

He explained the relationship further:

When we're trying to find a solution to something, I can pick up the phone to Alan and we can discuss it and find a way through it. ... He'll be pretty clear and he might have to come back to me and stuff like that. But it's a much easier relationship, and again it may be the individuals' (Dennis).

He thought the problem arose because some of the tax people came from the Inland Revenue:

'It sounds simplistic. I think one factor is that [*Alan's firm*] certainly have a lot of guys now who come in from the Inland Revenue. ... I feel they still have a slight sort of auditor type attitude, typical auditor attitude, hiding behind that instead of being open with us and helping us to get the charge down and finding ways of doing it' (Dennis).

Dennis could find no excuse for this as they were working for the group:

'They are working for you and they are charging you a commercial fee to do that and there's no conflict of loyalty there. As far as I'm concerned they're part of the team. We happen to be paying them a fee to do it rather than employing someone' (Dennis).

Dennis also doubted the accounting competence at times:

'They don't quite understand all those little companies. ... If I rather naively ask the tax partner what the tax charge is going to be next year, he'll tell me what the corporation tax people will put in, but he won't tell me what the deferred tax will be.[4] He doesn't understand deferred tax, or doesn't profess to understand it. ... I find it weird actually' (Dennis).

The tax staff were very smart at marketing tax-avoidance schemes:

'They are very good at selling you extra products, if they find what may be construed as a loophole that one could take advantage of. They will always do that ... but they are less quick to tell us what's going on, literally under our noses, if you like' (Dennis).

There were also different ways of charging fees. The audit fee was agreed each year and Dennis felt more comfortable with this:

'We negotiate the audit fee every year and we do have built into that an element of advice. When we have conversations it's all part of the fee. If it got heavy then we would have some special fee. ... We get on well enough ... in that way. Both the old partner and the new partner have said, "Well, If you're happy to leave it that way. If it becomes onerous, we'll tell you"' (Dennis).

But the tax charging was different, and the advice not as good, although it was improving:

'I know with the tax guys the meter is ticking from the moment you pick up the phone, and of course you need those guys probably more, in many respects than the audit guys. ... I just feel that the advice is not as good, although it has improved. I have to say, and they are much more approachable these days. A change of tax partner has helped' (Dennis).

Dennis thought that the tax staff had been told to be more client friendly:

'He comes here now. He never used to come here. ... It was an ivory tower thing really. ... I get the distinct feeling they've been told they've got to be more

---

[4] Deferred tax is represents tax accelerated or deferred by the effect of timing differences arising as a result of the allocation of items to different periods for taxation and accounting purposes, e.g., the variation between capital allowances and depreciation.

personable with clients, because they'll make more money from the clients by being approachable' (Dennis).

He was also using the services of other firms:

'One of the other firms is particularly good. It's much more approachable. I can talk to them about it. They seem to be prepared to do work without costs initially. [*Alan's firm*] are not, yet they are our auditors already' (Dennis)

He was embarrassed about the size of the fees that had to be disclosed:

'One of the acute embarrassments in the accounts of course is that you have to disclose their fees and their fees are high, very high for a company of our size. ... It's an embarrassment because it's one of the only things you disclose. I mean why don't you disclose what you pay to your merchant bank or to another firm of accountants? (Dennis).

Dennis felt the issue was about value for money, because they needed the advice:

'I have far less of a problem with the audit than I do with the rest of the work. I understand why we make the disclosure, but again, it comes back to value for money to some degree. ... You have to get advice from somewhere. You have to get advice from somebody you can trust. ... We don't spend very much on other firms because I've tended to work on the basis that it's easier to use the one firm, to be honest' (Dennis).

10.12   ANALYSIS OF GENERAL CONTEXTUAL FACTORS

The relationship between Dennis and Alan was good for a number of reasons:

- they were of similar age and were both newly appointed to their roles;
- both had high integrity;
- mutual respect and trust existed between them although they did not know each other very well; and
- because the group was listed and had outside shareholders, and was growing in size, both felt it was essential that accounting practices in the company should be respectable despite the resistance of the chairman to new FRSs.

The general contextual influences on the interactions between Dennis and Alan identified in the interview material are shown diagrammatically in Figure 10.1. These are drawn from the general circumstances of the group, the specific circumstances in which Dennis and Alan found themselves and the contextual issues described above. Although the relationship between Dennis and Alan was in its early days, they had already established mutual trust and respect. Because of the relatively small size of the group, Dennis was a resource-seeker and relied heavily on Alan's firm for advice. The poor performance of the group's shares and the emergence of the bid had made the board more conscious of its vulnerability, and the controlled expansion also increased its desire to project a respectable image in its attitude to compliance although some aspects of compliance were felt to be onerous. Although the audit committee consisted of the entire board, the group had a strong independent non-executive director, who chaired the audit committee and who made an effective contribution to the corporate governance and decision-making of the board.

10.13   SPECIFIC INTERACTIONS

10.13.1   Interaction DA1: accounting for assets on disposal of businesses

Two financial reporting measurement issues arose in respect of assets which were being disposed of. Both were matters of judgement. The first issue concerned the book values of the assets of a property company whose sale was being negotiated as the year-end accounts were being finalised. Dennis and Alan agreed that the book values of the assets would have to be written down, whether or not they were disposed of, and provisions had already been made in advance of the sale. As the sale actually took place just before the results were announced, on the basis of the evidence obtained, the disposal was treated as an adjusting post-balance sheet event. There was no disagreement in reaching this solution. It was a good outcome and was easily achieved.

The second issue was potentially more difficult. An offer had been received for a property which the directors believed was below its realisable value. It had already been written down by 30 per cent. This offer was indicative to Alan of a potential need to write the property down further, but the directors were reluctant to do this because they believed the offer was unrealistically low. Alan had some sympathy with their view but was

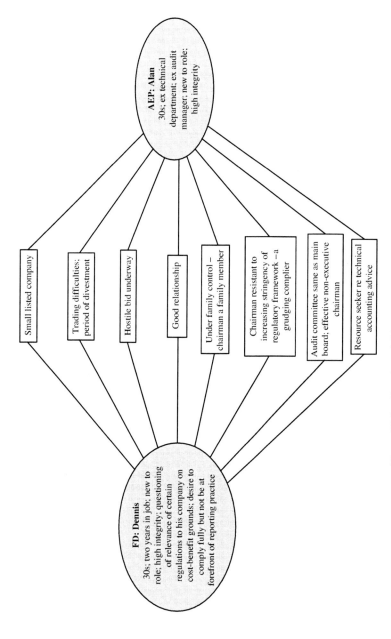

Figure 10.1 Dennis and Alan: general context for interactions

not prepared to accept no further write-down without assurances from the board and the audit committee that they would not sell the property at the offer price. In the event, the property was partially let and further offers came in to justify the directors' views.

There was no tension in reaching this outcome. It was a good outcome and was easily reached, but was influenced by Alan's determination to get assurances on the value of the properties.

10.13.2 Interaction DA2: accounting for assets on acquisition of businesses

This financial reporting interaction concerned the measurement of depreciation on assets acquired and the adequacy of the accounting records for fixed assets, which were material to the group. It was a judgement issue. It continued through two accounting periods. Figure 10.2 sets out the specific contextual factors in this interaction, together with the parties involved, their specific objectives, and the strategies adopted.

A number of businesses had been acquired around the year-end immediately before Dennis had joined the group. Alan was particularly concerned about this issue. The first stage of the negotiation arose because Alan realised that the fixed assets in the businesses acquired were being depreciated as if they were brand new, when they were not. He was concerned that their useful lives could be shorter than the period over which they were being depreciated and the depreciation charge could therefore be understated. Alan had taken the view for the first year-end that the amounts were not material because only one or two months' depreciation was involved and some of the businesses had been acquired after the year-end. He realised that the issue was material for the next year and needed to be sorted out. He also felt that the group should keep a proper asset register. Alan gathered evidence to support his argument that the impact was material. He believed it was a serious issue and escalated the negotiation by taking his arguments to the audit committee to seek their support.

The audit committee recognised the point that Alan was making but were not prepared to set up a historical asset register for all assets already acquired because of the time and cost involved. They agreed to confirm the useful lives of the major assets and also agreed to set up an asset register for all future assets acquired.

A follow on to this interaction arose the following year when Alan discovered that the group had not, as had been agreed, set up the asset register.

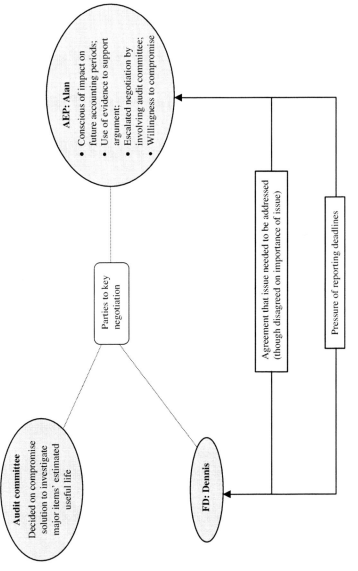

Figure 10.2 Accounting for assets on acquisition of businesses interaction (DA2)

He insisted that this was done and a commencement date was agreed. Alan was determined to ensure that this was carried out.

This outcome represented something of a compromise. Alan did not get everything he wanted at the first stage and had to go back and insist a second time to ensure the original agreement was met in full. However, the material issues were addressed. Dennis, while not being obstructive, did not provide strong support to Alan as he simply did not see the cost benefit of the amount of management time needed to meet all Alan's requests. This was a relatively good and realistic outcome. It was relatively easy to achieve due to the willingness of the parties to reach a compromise.

10.13.3   Interaction DA3: disclosure of acquisitions, disposals and bid costs under FRS 3

This financial reporting issue concerned classification in a primary statement – a compliance issue. The board accepted that they had to comply with FRS 3 but resented it. Dennis and the chairman were particularly uncomfortable about the acquisition and disposal disclosures required by FRS 3 because the group frequently acquired and disposed of businesses as part of its regular business. They therefore did not see the relevance or benefits of FRS 3 disclosures to the reader of their accounts. In an effort to reduce their level of frustration, Alan suggested a presentation using boxes on the face of the profit and loss account. Dennis was less enthusiastic about these boxes than Alan, who felt that when they were applied responsibly they could be helpful to the reader. A further box disclosure was used to show the costs of defending the bid.

These outcomes were relatively good and were easily reached. The board had a culture of rather grudging compliance and it was felt the regulations were directed at larger groups. Their frustration surrounding the issue was directed at the regulators, not at Alan.

10.13.4   Interaction DA4: last-minute adjustments to the accounts

This financial reporting interaction concerned the accounting treatment of leases, a measurement and judgement issue. No negotiation was involved, but the interaction did affect the overall relationship between the group and its auditors. Alan had not sent the accounts for technical review within his firm until the printers' proof stage. He appeared not to have made it sufficiently clear to Dennis that further changes could arise from the review. Dennis had, therefore, prepared his analysts' presentation by the time the required adjustments were communicated to him. Dennis was put out about having to work unexpectedly over a weekend, when Alan himself was away, to make the necessary changes and revise his analysts' presentation. He accepted the points raised and was appreciative in Alan's absence that his firm had passed their technical review comments direct to him.

Better communication between Dennis and Alan could have avoided this situation. In particular, Alan should have made it clear to Dennis that he should not consider the accounts agreed until the technical department review had been completed, and possibly he should have referred the accounts slightly earlier.

This interaction had a good outcome. It was easily achieved, as Dennis did not disagree with the points raised and got on with making the changes, but he felt put out about the timing of it.

10.13.5   Interaction DA5: the chairman's attitude to goodwill

This financial reporting issue concerned recognition and was a compliance issue involving a material amount. It was a curious interaction because Dennis and Alan were in complete agreement regarding the correct accounting treatment which was clear-cut. The issue only arose and escalated because of the chairman's strong views and reluctance to accept the regulatory requirement that goodwill on acquisition should be written off, and internally generated goodwill could not be capitalised. Figure 10.3 sets out the specific contextual factors in this interaction, together with the parties involved, their specific objectives, and the strategies adopted.

The issue had been discussed by Alan with third parties within the company (the chief executive and the audit committee) to get these higher authorities to understand the issue and help to convince the chairman that he had no choice. In the end agreement was reached by the actions of the independent non-executive director, Keith, who was the chairman of the audit committee. He was able to persuade the chairman, using various arguments, to accept the proposed treatment. Keith was an experienced and respected independent director and was on the board of several large PLCs. It appears that his views were accepted by the chairman as a consequence.

A strategy to mitigate the impact of this treatment on the balance sheet was proposed and considered by the board, which was to revalue some of the properties. However, Alan made it clear that he would not accept selective revaluation. If it were done at all, it would have to include all properties. The board decided that this may not improve the balance sheet overall and so abandoned the idea.

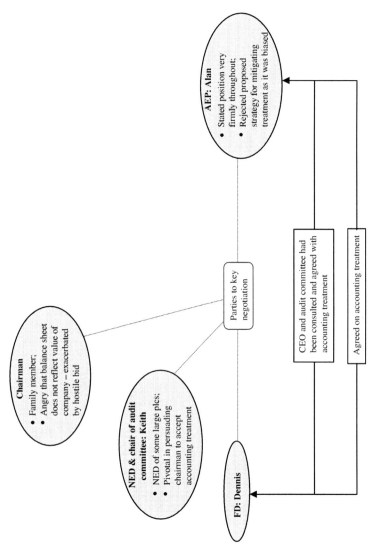

Figure 10.3   Chairman's attitude to goodwill interaction (DA5)

The outcome was good, and could never have been in doubt, but was very difficult and time-consuming to reach because of the chairman's attitude.[5]

10.13.6 Interaction DA6: compliance with the Cadbury Code and other non-mandatory disclosures

This issue concerned disclosure and was a compliance issue. Dennis wanted Alan to suggest suitable draft Cadbury disclosures and was a little unhappy that Alan stated firmly that he was not prepared to do this. Alan did offer technical advice, having consulted with the firm's technical advisor, by giving examples of good practice. The interaction that took place involved simply an attempt by Dennis to get Alan to provide more specific advice, but Alan was determined not to do this. He appears not to have made the position as clear as he could have done to Dennis that ownership of these disclosures rested with the group.

In addition, the company initially wanted to comment on the quality, rather than just the existence, of their internal controls. Although the audit opinion does not cover these statements by directors, Alan thought the action to be ill-advised and said so. His argument that no controls can give complete assurance persuaded the company to adopt a more moderate form of words.

This interaction had a good outcome. It is not the auditor's role to prepare these disclosures as they are the responsibility of the board. It was achieved relatively easily.

10.14 CONCLUSION

This group was a small family-controlled company but did have a number of institutional investors. Dennis recognised that the return for the outside investors had not been very good and the bid for the company made the board realise that they could not be complacent. Had the bid succeeded they would all have been dispensed with. This demonstrates the influence that external forces can wield over poorly performing shares.

Having got over the worst of the recession by selling off non-core businesses, the group then started to expand in one of its core areas and also recruited Dennis to its much under-resourced accounting function. He then

---

[5] It is interesting to note that FRS 10, issued after the interviews were carried out, now permits purchased goodwill to be kept on the balance sheet without amortisation where it is regarded as having an indefinite useful economic life.

found himself reliant on temporary staff to produce the accounts. Despite its expansion, the group remained heavily dependent on its auditors for technical advice, i.e., it continued to be a resource-seeker. However, the board wanted to enhance its standing with outside investors. One strategy for doing this was to take compliance with the corporate governance code more seriously, a mechanism which would signal greater respectability.

The board experienced some difficulty in complying with corporate governance best practices because of its small size. The audit committee and the board were one and the same body with a different chairman, and two of the non-executive directors were substantial shareholders, and therefore not independent. The audit committee had a limited role, meeting only twice a year, but the presence on the board of one very experienced and competent non-executive director made all the difference. He helped to convince the non-accountant chairman of the need to comply with accounting regulations which the chairman regarded as uncommercial and damaging to his share price, and he made sure that the auditors had an opportunity to talk to the audit committee without the executives being present. Thus the effectiveness derived from an individual rather than the structure itself.

The developing relationship between Dennis and Alan is interesting. Although still at an early stage, they already had mutual respect both for each other's personal integrity and for their relative responsibilities. Neither hesitated to criticise the other but this was done in a positive and dispassionate way. Dennis knew that Alan would go to the audit committee if he felt things were wrong, but he recognised that if this were to happen he would have failed himself in some way. Alan showed himself willing to take a reasonable view, within the constraints of materiality, on the cost benefit of setting up a comprehensive asset register, but was not going to allow Dennis to go back on what had been agreed. Alan also made his position clear on issues from the outset and did not dither on his advice.

FRS 3 disclosures emerge as a problem area. The group had some difficulty in accepting the relevance to their particular circumstances of the disclosures for continuing and discontinued businesses and did make use of boxes to provide additional information.

The problems of late adjustments are particularly highlighted in this case. Where a late adjustment in respect of the disposal of a business had been anticipated, Dennis had prepared alternative presentations. He was put out by the very late and unexpected changes which Alan's technical department produced. Although he recognised that the changes were necessary, he nevertheless found himself under pressure to process the changes through all the necessary channels. The timing of audit firm's in-house technical reviews and the processing of late adjustments clearly put a strain on relationships.

Interesting insights also emerge about non-audit services and independence. The group was a resource-seeker from Alan's firm but Dennis did not see the provision of non-audit services or the recognised commercialism of Alan's firm in some of its non-audit activities as a problem to Alan's independence. He judged each service on its separate merits, and shopped around. In this case he found the audit advice of better quality than the rest. Because of his extensive use of the resources he was embarrassed by the need to disclose these services when services from other providers were not disclosed.

Part III
The Analysis and Conclusions

11 The Grounded Theory Process

11.1 OVERVIEW

The broad approach taken to the analysis was outlined in sections 4.6 to 4.9. Before embarking on the cross-case analysis in the next chapter, this chapter describes more fully the grounded theory methodology that will be used (and which also underpins the within-case analysis presented in Chapters 5 to 10).

11.2 THE ANALYTICAL PROCESS

11.2.1 The nature of grounded theory

Analysis of the transcribed interviews was undertaken using grounded theory procedures and techniques (Strauss and Corbin, 1990). Grounded theory refers to the process of building theory inductively by means of the qualitative analysis of data. General theories of negotiation, such as Gulliver's framework described in section 4.2 above, may have some applicability to the audit setting. There are, however, important specific circumstances associated with the audit context that suggest that any general framework will be conceptually underdeveloped and will need special adaptation and extension. In particular, there is the regulatory environment in which the negotiation takes place, together with the professional connections of the main participants.

The research question being addressed can be stated as follows: *How do companies and their auditors resolve important audit issues?*

In exploring this phenomenon, there are three principal ways in which we developed theoretical sensitivity to this research question. First, our awareness of the relevant theoretical literature (reviewed in Chapter 2) helped us to maintain an awareness of the subtleties of meaning of data. This literature suggested concepts and relationships that can be assessed against the data collected, as we sought to adapt and extend the generic theory of negotiation. Second, our combined years of professional experience

253

also helped. Third, the rigorous procedures and techniques used in the analytical process were expressly designed to build theory.

11.2.2   Procedures and techniques

The analytical process involved coding of various forms, as the data was read and reread. This went far beyond the mere descriptive summarisation of data. Three types of coding were used. First, open coding, in which concepts were identified, labelled and categorised. Concepts are the basic unit of analysis in grounded theory – it is a name that represents a phenomenon and therefore can be used at a higher level of generality than the raw data. Concepts were identified by asking questions of the raw data and by comparing phenomena so that like phenomena are given the same name. Once concepts began to emerge from this coding, we began to group concepts that appeared to relate to the same phenomenon, thus forming categories. These categories were also labelled, using higher-level names than those of the concepts grouped under it.

In order to identify and understand the relationships between categories in the later stages of analysis, it was necessary to establish the attributes of the categories (i.e., their properties) and also the dimensions of these properties.

Whereas open coding focused on the breaking down of data, the second type of coding, axial coding, focused on putting the data back together again in a different way, by making connections between each category and its sub-categories. This process allowed categories to be developed beyond their properties and dimensions. Elements of this type of coding inevitably creep into open coding, for as the data is broken apart it is natural to begin to put it back together in a relational form.

The third and final type of coding, selective coding, concerns the final theory development phase of analysis. It involved the selection of a core category, followed by a process of systematically relating all other categories to it at a high level of generality.

As the data was read and reread, all three types of coding took place, although open coding dominated early coding sessions while axial and selective coding dominated later sessions. Moreover, all early coding was viewed as provisional, as concepts and categories evolved and changed as new data was read and compared. Many iterations were required before a stable set of concepts and categories emerged.

During coding, notes were written containing the products of the three types of coding, such as concept labels, sub-categories and relationships. Diagrams that visually represent the relationships between concepts and categories were particularly useful. These were modified continuously as

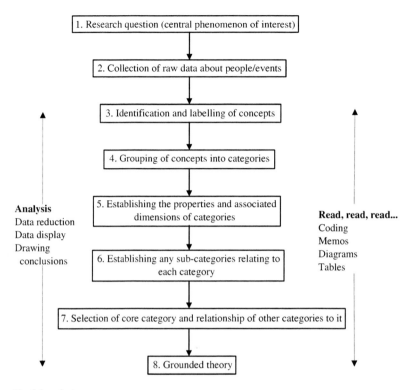

1. Research question (central phenomenon of interest)

2. Collection of raw data about people/events

3. Identification and labelling of concepts

4. Grouping of concepts into categories

5. Establishing the properties and associated dimensions of categories

6. Establishing any sub-categories relating to each category

7. Selection of core category and relationship of other categories to it

8. Grounded theory

Analysis
Data reduction
Data display
Drawing
 conclusions

Read, read, read...
Coding
Memos
Diagrams
Tables

Useful techniques:
  – asking questions: Who? When? How? Why?
  – memos
  – coding
  – making comparisons between cases/events
  – the analysis of action/interaction as a process (i.e., a related sequence of events) in relation to conditions ranging from close to distant and to consequences
  – diagrams/tables

Figure 11.1   The grounded theory research process

the analysis of the data progressed and new insights emerged. Figure 11.1 presents an overview of the analytical process adopted.

Chapters 5 to 10 and Chapter 12 include the final versions of the tables, diagrams and notes that emerged during the within-case and cross-case analysis. We hope that by doing this, the reader will be able to see how we bridged the 'huge chasm' that often separates data from conclusions (Eisenhardt, 1989, p. 539).

12 Cross-Case Analysis and Theory Development

12.1 INTRODUCTION

Early on in the analytical process, it became clear that the core category (the central phenomenon) was the interaction itself. In fact, this was the only category that involved action at all. All other categories related to this at some level. This chapter presents the principal categories and sub-categories and loosely establishes their relationship to each other in terms of their proximity to the core interaction. Thereafter, each category is discussed in turn, beginning with those most distant to the interaction. For each category, relevant concepts are identified, as are the properties and dimensions of the category.

Next, a grounded theory is presented in which categories are systematically related to the core category. In particular, this offers a model that can be used to explain the *outcome* of the interaction in terms of its quality and ease of attainment. Finally, we identify and describe four empirically-based AEP (seller) types.

12.2 INTRODUCING THE PRINCIPAL CATEGORIES

During the analytical process, many distinct categories gradually emerged. Before looking at each individually, it is useful to present them in groups, with each group representing a set of conditional features bearing upon the core interaction, with some groups quite distant to the interaction and others very close to it. These groups are shown in Figure 12.1 as a series of embedded rectangles. This figure is a useful analytical aid for considering the wide range of conditions and, to a lesser extent, consequences related to the phenomenon under study. Strauss and Corbin (1990, ch. 10) refer to it as a 'conditional matrix'.

At the outermost level, reflecting the weakest and most indirect influence on the interaction, lies the global regulatory climate. This category refers to the tone of pronouncements and policies on accounting and auditing emanating from the Securities and Exchange Commission (SEC) in the US and the EC. Although none of our interviewees specifically mentioned

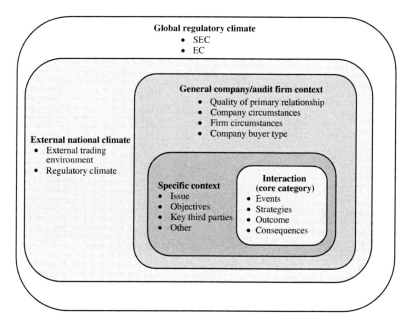

Figure 12.1   Principal analytical categories

these bodies, the global regulatory position influences the national regulatory position and most of the interviewees would be aware of this link.
Most of the case companies had overseas operations.

Next closest to the periphery lies the external national climate, encom-
passing the economic trading environment (economic growth, interest
rates, exchange rates) and the national regulatory climate. The influence of
the regulatory bodies in particular was mentioned by interviewees – the
impact of the Accounting Standards Board (ASB) in curtailing aggressive
accounting practices; the desire not to be investigated by the Financial
Reporting Review Panel (FRRP); and the need to comply with the
Cadbury corporate governance requirements.

Moving one level further towards the core, we come to the general context of the company and the audit firm. This context impacts upon all
interactions between these two parties. There are four distinct categories to
consider here: the quality of the primary relationship; the company circumstances; the audit firm circumstances; and the company buyer type.

Closest to the core comes the specific context of the interaction. This
concerns features of the interaction that vary from interaction to interaction, moderating the general contextual factors. We identified four distinct

categories: the interaction issue; the objectives of the individual parties; the key third parties; and other factors.

Finally, there is the core category, i.e., the interaction itself. We identified four categories involved in the processual sequence of related actions: events, strategies, outcome and consequences.

12.3   A DETAILED EXAMINATION OF EACH PRINCIPAL CATEGORY

12.3.1   Quality of primary relationship

The influence of this category on the nature and outcome of interactions was critical in many cases. The single dimension of this category was, obviously, quality, measured on a scale of very poor to very good. The six cases covered a wide range of relationship qualities: one poor; one fair; one good; and three very good. Table 12.1 sets out the concepts that are grouped into this category. From the cases analysed, there appear to be key determinants of relationship quality. Two of these concepts appeared to have a negative relationship with quality–age gap and Finance Director's (FD) previous employment with audit firm in a position senior to Audit Engagement Partner (AEP). Clearly, not all of these concepts are independent of each other, e.g., compatible personalities will tend to be associated with mutual trust and respect.

Table 12.1   Quality of primary relationship

Concepts	Category	Dimension

Mutual objectives
Mutual trust and respect
Compatible personalities
Experience/competence
Level of professional
  integrity of FD relative
  to AEP
Age gap
FD's previous employment
  with audit firm in a
  position senior to AEP
Length of relationship
	**Quality of
	primary
	relationship**
		Very poor–very good

While the professional integrity of the two individuals (especially the AEP) impacts very directly on the interaction, it appears that it is the level of professional integrity of one *relative* to the other that influences the interaction indirectly through its impact on the quality of the primary relationship. The direct impact of integrity is considered below under other categories.

12.3.2 Company circumstances

This category was also a critical influence on the nature and outcome of interactions in most cases. The concepts grouped under this category are set out in Table 12.2. We identified three dimensions to this category: (i) the importance of the company to the client portfolio; (ii) the general audit risk associated with the company; and (iii) the level of technical support required by the company. The six cases covered a wide range of circumstances.

The risk factors were of two general types: those related to the corporate culture and those related to the company's current financial and trading

Table 12.2   Company circumstances of relevance to interactions

Concepts	Category	Dimensions
Size of company		Importance of company to client portfolio
Ownership structure		- - - - - - - - - - - - - - - - -
Company reporting style, i.e., Board attitude to:		
• matters of fact (compliance culture)		
• matters of judgement (aggressive vs. conservative)	**Company circumstances**	Audit risk of client
Professional integrity of FD		
Effectiveness of audit committee		
Financial position (healthy/in difficulties)		
Growth position (expansion/contraction)		
Bid risk/possibility of sale		
Level of technical accounting		- - - - - - - - - - - - - - - - -
expertise within company		Level of technical support required

circumstances. It was apparent that in some cases the corporate culture was not internalised by all key parties within the company and this lack of consensus was, not surprisingly, problematic. In particular, the position of the FD was important, as he is one of the primary parties.

Buyer types were discussed in section 2.8. Essentially, the buyer type of the company is determined by the company's attitude to each of five issues: the overall value of the audit and the importance of four general, independent auditor characteristics (integrity/competence/reputation of auditor; auditor's acceptability to third parties; quality of working relationships with auditor and auditor efficiency; and non-audit services provided by auditor). Our case companies were predominantly comfort-seekers, as most were larger listed companies. The two smaller listed companies were, to a greater or lesser extent, grudgers. While several companies relied on the auditor for technical accounting advice (i.e., resource-seekers), there were no status-seekers among the group.

Clearly, buyer type is associated with both company reporting style and the professional integrity of the FD (both of which are identified as concepts related to company circumstances). However, the category of buyer type goes beyond these features – it captures the company's view of what the auditor can contribute to the company.

The position of the FD may, of course, not be in tune with that of the board as a whole (in reality, the company position tends to be the view held by key, dominant board members such as the chairman). The two buyer types that are incompatible with each other are that of grudger and comfort-seeker. It is unlikely that the FD will be a grudger if the company is a comfort-seeker, as it is in the FD's interests to adopt the company position unless it compromises his professional integrity (which in this case it would not). It is more likely that the FD will be by nature a comfort-seeker while the company is a grudger. This is a very difficult position for the FD as he will always be at risk of compromising his professional integrity in order to satisfy the demands of his employer. This situation existed in DA plc and, to some extent in NS plc, where the new chairman, despite wanting to move towards reporting respectability, was a grudger. In the other four cases, the company exhibited a consistent buyer type across senior management.

12.3.3   Firm circumstances

Unfortunately, the interviews do not provide much detail regarding the audit firm circumstances. Ideally, we would have liked to have been able to analyse information on the nature of the support and monitoring infrastructure

Table 12.3   Firm circumstances

Concepts	Category	Properties and dimensions
Support and monitoring infrastructure		Structures, procedures, schemes
Partner incentives		
Professional integrity of AEP		- - - - - - - - - - - - - - -
		Low–high
Personal integrity of AEP		- - - - - - - - - - - - - - -
Buyer type:		View of value added by audit;
grudger		Importance of integrity/
comfort-seeker	**Firm**	competence/reputation of
resource-seeker	**characteristics**	auditor;
status-seeker		Importance of auditor's acceptability to third parties;
		Importance of quality of working relationships with auditor and auditor efficiency;
		Importance of non-audit services provided by auditor

(e.g., second partner review; technical review, peer review) and the AEP's incentives (e.g., compensation tied to office vs. firm revenues). However, the need to preserve the anonymity of the audit firm precludes such analysis. Nevertheless, the two most critical factors on the audit firm side of the interaction appear to be the personal characteristics of the AEP (one of the primary parties) and the infrastructure within the firm. We distinguished two key features of the AEP's personal code of behaviour – professional integrity and personal integrity. Personal integrity is how we refer to behaviour that goes beyond the standard required by professional ethics. These concepts are set out in Table 12.3.

12.3.4   Interaction issue

Seven classes of interaction issue were identified, as explained in section 4.8.3 and shown in Table 12.4. Of the twenty-four interaction issues arising from the six cases, one relates to a fundamental principle, one to corporate governance, seven to recognition, twelve to measurement, three to classification, three to disclosure, and two to audit matters (three have double codes and one has a triple code).

Table 12.4   Interaction issue

Concepts	Category	Properties and dimension
Fundamental principle		Fact vs. judgement;
Recognition		
Measurement/valuation	**Interaction**	One-off vs. continuing;
Classification in a primary statement	**issue**	
Disclosure		Visible vs. not visible;
Corporate governance		
Audit-related matters		Materiality

Table 12.5   Objectives of individual parties

Concepts	Category
Desire to minimise effect and/or visibility of issue	
Earnings management	
Revenge	
Face-saving:	
– own	**Objectives of individual**
– another individual	**parties**
– organisation	
Secrecy	
Keep out of trouble	
Avoid escalation	
Avoid confrontation	

We identified three properties of the interaction issue. The first was whether the issue was a matter of fact (e.g., treatment of reorganisation costs on acquisition) or a matter of judgement (e.g., valuation of stock). The second was whether the treatment adopted impacted only on the financial statements of the current period or whether future periods were also affected. The third was whether the issue was visible on the financial statements or not. In addition to these properties, a critical dimension of many issues was that of materiality, a concept that has particular significance in auditing.

12.3.5   Objectives of primary parties

It was possible to identify a range of objectives of the individuals who took an active part in the interactions. These are set out in Table 12.5. No particular properties or dimensions of this category emerged.

12.3.6   Key third parties

In addition to the FD and AEP, various individuals and groups were influential in the interactions (see Table 12.6). These parties were company management, part of the audit firm, or an external party. The nature of their involvement ranged from passive, indirect involvement (as in the case where the primary parties were concerned about the impact of an outcome on analysts' perceptions of the company) to active, direct involvement (as in the case where a chairman or CEO engaged in an interaction with the AEP).

12.3.7   Other specific contextual factors

A small number of other features of specific interaction settings were identified from the cases, as shown in Table 12.7. No particular properties or dimensions of this category emerged.

12.3.8   Interaction events

Interaction events are things that take place during an interaction. They can be distinguished from interaction strategies, which are plans. Of course, the

Table 12.6   Key third parties

Concepts	Category	Properties and dimensions
Chairman		Affiliation: company, audit firm; external;
Individual non-executive director		
CEO		Influence direct or indirect via primary party;
Board of directors		
Audit committee		
Senior management (not main board level)	**Key third parties**	Active involvement vs. passive influence;
Second partner		
Technical partner		Nature of involvement:
Technical department		• provide information or opinions/assurance
Regulator		
Specialist advisor		• be informed
Shareholders		• give approval/agreement
Analysts		• participate in negotiation
Lenders		• take action

Table 12.7   Other specific contextual factors

Concepts	Category

Party raising issue:
  – FD
  – AEP
  – both
Agreement between primary parties that issue
  needs to be addressed
Negotiation conducted under time
  pressure/reporting deadlines
History of issue, i.e., need to take a tougher
  stance due to:
  – regulatory climate
  – new evidence
  – change in company risk profile
Impact of other current interactions
Impact on future accounting periods
	Other specific contextual factors

Table 12.8   Interaction events

Concepts	Category

Provision of information by auditor
Primary party seeks advice/opinion of third party
Withholding of information from third parties
Search for solution to avoid an undesirable
  outcome for company (e.g., reduce
  visibility)/assessment of alternative outcomes
Change of position
Acknowledgement of mistake
	Interaction events

two categories are closely related, as the adoption of a strategy often gives rise to events, but not necessarily those planned. We identified six events from our cases, as shown in Table 12.8. No particular properties or dimensions of this category emerged.

12.3.9   Interaction strategies

A wide range of strategies was used during the various interactions studied. These are shown in Table 12.9, classified according to their type. The particular mix of strategies used determined certain properties of the interactions, in particular, the number of parties involved, the number of stages, and the level of escalation.

Table 12.9   Interaction strategies

Concepts	Strategy type	Category[1]
State position very firmly at outset	Assertiveness	
Tender/auditor change threat made	Sanction	
Escalate or threaten to escalate negotiation by involving additional parties	Sanction	
Qualification or threat of qualification made	Sanction	
Take blame (to achieve desired outcome)	Ingratiation	**Interaction**
Use evidence to support argument	Reason	**strategies**
Use reasoned argument	Reason	
Willingness to compromise	Bargaining	
Strategic give and take across issues	Bargaining	
Agreed strategy for handling third parties	Coalesce	
Get third party on side to secure agreement	Coalesce	

Seek confirmation and authority:
  – for own position
  – for other party's position
	Higher
	authority	

Apply conditions to acceptance of other party's position	Conditions	

[1] The principal properties of this category are the number of parties involved, the number of stages and the degree of escalation.

The concept 'willingness to compromise' had two distinct forms. The compromise could take place either within the rules or outside the rules. For example, in many cases the primary party did not state their position very firmly at the outset, perhaps because the 'answer' was not clear-cut. In these cases, the views/suggestions of the other primary party were influential in forming their own view (e.g., CRA4). On the other hand, there were a few cases where a primary party was prepared to bend the rules (e.g., TJ1).

12.3.10   Interaction outcome

It is the dimensions of the outcome of the interaction that are of critical importance (see Table 12.10). What is of primary interest to external parties is the *quality* of financial reporting by the company, i.e., does the outcome

Table 12.10   Interaction outcome

Category	Dimensions
Outcome of interaction	Quality of accounting: poor/not compliant–good/fully compliant;
	Ease of agreement: very difficult–easy

Table 12.11   Interaction consequences

Concepts	Category
Impact on other current accounting interactions	
Impact on future accounting periods	**Consequences of**
Impact on fee negotiations	**interaction**
Impact on quality of primary relationship	
Impact on third parties	

reflect 'good' or 'bad' accounting from a public interest perspective? This is essentially a dichotomous variable for compliance issues (matters of fact), although, as discussed in section 1.3, there is often scope for creative compliance. It is a continuous variable for matters of judgement.

In addition, for the parties involved directly in the interaction, the ease with which the agreed outcome is reached is important. For a given outcome, it is rational to prefer an easy interaction to a difficult one. This outcome dimension is also a continuous variable. It captures issues like number of parties involved, number of stages, and the extent to which strategies were used that undermine ongoing relationships.

The focus of section 12.4 will be to try to understand those factors that are most influential in determining these two dimensions of the final outcome, including the identification of critical moderating variables. This will require an understanding of the *process* of interaction. These two dimensions of outcome (quality and ease of agreement) can be perceived as capturing the effectiveness and efficiency of the audit, respectively.

12.3.11   Interaction consequences

Interactions can have a number of consequences (see Table 12.11). Most obviously, interactions can impact directly upon other ongoing accounting interactions (CRA1) and/or future accounting periods (TJ1, CRA4, RC1,

RC2 and DA2). An outcome can also impact upon fee negotiations (TJ2 and TJ3). Interactions can also impact indirectly upon future interactions by affecting the quality of the primary relationship or indeed the relationship between the audit firm and the company more generally (TJ plc and RC plc). Finally, the outcomes of interactions may affect the perceptions, and thereby potentially the actions, of third parties such as regulators, shareholders, lenders, and analysts.

12.4   GROUNDED THEORY OF INTERACTION OUTCOMES

As part of the process of developing the grounded theory, we undertake in this section a cross-case analysis of the six cases presented in Chapters 5 to 10. At this point, we are attempting to identify and understand the key links between context, strategy and outcome. These key categories and links are shown in Figure 12.2.

Of the 24 interaction issues emerging from the six cases, two relate to audit, leaving 22 with a financial reporting outcome. The within-case analysis of each of these 22 interactions was reviewed to identify the *critical* contextual factors, the strategies adopted and the dimensions of the outcome. The results are shown in Table 12.12.

The primary contextual factors affecting the strategy adopted and the nature of the outcome appeared to be general, rather than specific. In particular, the integrity of the AEP influenced the quality of the outcome – high integrity ensured an outcome quality above a certain threshold, although the ease of agreement depended upon other factors. The quality of the primary relationship impacted directly upon both the quality of the outcome and (in those cases where the position of the FD was in tune with that of the board) the ease of agreement. Where the position of the FD was *not* in tune with that of the board, difficult interactions could still arise despite a good primary relationship (CRA3, CRA5 and DA5).

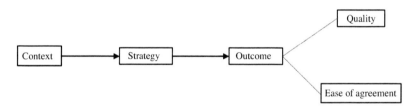

Figure 12.2   Key links between context, strategy and outcome

Table 12.12 Cross-Case analysis of critical contextual factors, strategies adopted and financial reporting outcome dimensions

Case ref.	General context	Interaction ref.	Issue type[1]	Specific context	Strategy	Outcome Quality	Outcome Ease of agreement
NS plc	Very good relationship; Integrity on both sides; Severe financial difficulties; Chairman a grudger; Desire/need to moderate aggressive reporting style.	NS1	FP	Agreement to address.	AEP stated his position very firmly.	Good	Easy
		NS2	C	History of issue: regulatory change, change in risk profile; Agreement to address.	AEP stated his position very firmly; FD & AEP get third party on-side.	Good	Easy
TJ plc	Poor relationship; Small, family-controlled company; Chairman a dominant grudger; Possible sale.	TJ1	J & C	Agreement to address; Evidence available.	AEP willing to compromise; AEP escalated.	Poor	Slightly difficult
		TJ2	C	–	Chairman escalated.	Creative compliance	Very difficult
		TJ3	C	–	AEP took blame; AEP willingness to compromise; AEP seeks confirmation and authority of his position.	Creative compliance	Very difficult
MP plc	Very good relationship; Integrity on both sides;	MP1	J	Agreement to address; AEP use of evidence to support argument.	AEP stated his position very firmly; AEP seeks confirmation and authority of his position.	Good	As easy as could be

Company	Description	Code	J	Factors	AEP/FD behaviour	Outcome	Difficulty
	Very conservative, compliant culture.	MP2	J	AEP use of evidence to support argument.	AEP stated his position very firmly; AEP seeks confirmation and authority of his position.	Good	Relatively easy
CRA plc	Very good relationship; High integrity of AEP; Senior accountants fairly aggressive; Possible hostile bid; Respectable, mild comfort-seeker.	CRA1	J	Impact of other current interactions.	FD strategic give and take.	Good	Easy
		CRA2	J	Agreement to address.	FD and AEP seek confirmation and authority of their positions; FD and AEP use of evidence and reasoned argument; FD and AEP willingness to compromise.	Good	Easy
		CRA3	J	–	FD stated his position very firmly; AEP escalated.	As good as could be	Slightly difficult
		CRA4	J	Agreement to address; Impact on future accounting periods; Time pressure.	FD and AEP willingness to compromise	Good	Easy
		CRA5	J	–	AEP stated his position very firmly; AEP escalated.	As good as could be	Slightly difficult
RC plc	Fair relationship; Respectable comfort-seeker.	RC1	J	Impact on future accounting periods.	AEP use of evidence and reasoned argument.	Good	Easy
		RC2	J	Impact on future accounting periods.	AEP applied conditions to acceptance.	Poor	Easy

Table 12.12 Continued

Case ref.	General context	Interaction ref.	Issue type[1]	Specific context	Strategy	Outcome Quality	Outcome Ease of agreement
RC plc		RC3	C	–	AEP stated his position very firmly; AEP threatened to qualify.	Good	Easy
		RC4	C	–	AEP willingness to compromise.	Acceptable	Easy
DA plc	Good relationship; Integrity on both sides; Small, family-controlled company;	DA1	J	Agreement to address.	FD and AEP use of evidence.	Good	Easy
		DA2	J	Impact on future accounting periods.	AEP use of evidence; AEP escalated; AEP willingness to compromise.	Relatively good	Relatively easy
	Chairman grudger; Hostile bid under way.	DA3	C	–	AEP willingness to compromise.	Relatively good	Easy
		DA4	J	Time pressure.	N/App.	Good	Easy
		DA5	C		AEP stated his position very firmly; FD and AEP get third party on-side.	Good	Very difficult
		DA6	C	–	AEP stated his position very firmly.	Good	Relatively easy

[1] FP = fundamental principle; J = judgement issue; C = compliance issue

These two factors (integrity of AEP and quality of primary relationship) did appear to be correlated, in practice, insofar as all of the good or very good primary relationships involved AEPs with high integrity (Simon, Paul, Andrew and Alan). There were other general contextual factors that critically influenced both outcome characteristics – the company type and situation (e.g., conservative or aggressive, the possibility of a bid); the effectiveness of corporate governance arrangements in the company (e.g., powerful, dominant chairman); the clarity of the accounting rules relating to the interaction issue; and the support and quality control procedures of the audit firm. These relationships are shown in Figure 12.3.

It was also observed that some contextual factors served to constrain the possible outcome to within certain bounds (e.g., AEP integrity), while others acted more as moderating variables (e.g., quality of company's corporate governance arrangements). The strategy adopted by, in particular, the AEP, is an intervening variable in these relationships. In general, assertiveness, reasoning, coalition and sanction strategies were associated with good outcomes, although whether they were attained easily or not depended on other contextual factors. By contrast, ingratiation and conditional acceptance were

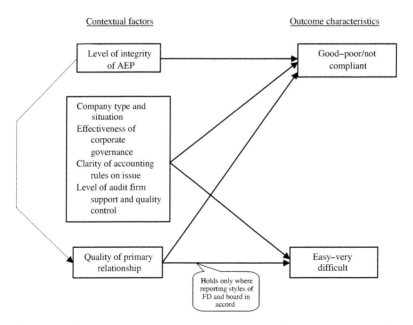

Figure 12.3   Relationships between contextual factors and outcome characteristics

associated with poor outcomes. The use of bargaining and authority strategies were associated with outcomes of varying quality and so no stable relationships emerged.

We then looked to see if there were any common reasons for certain
types of outcome. For example, what leads to good, easy outcomes? At the
other extreme, what leads to poor outcomes and difficult negotiations? To
assist in this task, we created a visual representation of the 22 outcomes
using a two-dimensional map (Figure 12.4). Both dimensions can vary
across a range of values (good – poor/not compliant; easy – very difficult),
however, measurement as such is not possible as no scales exist. In our
analysis, we have, however, used descriptive labels to distinguish several
points on each dimension that are capable of ordinal ranking. For example,
on the quality dimension, we have used good > relatively good > acceptable > poor for judgemental issues and fully compliant > creative compliance > not compliant for compliance issues. On the ease of agreement
dimension, we have used easy > relatively easy > as easy as could be >
slightly difficult > very difficult. If the interaction escalated at all, we
judged that the ease of outcome could not be 'easy'. The distance between

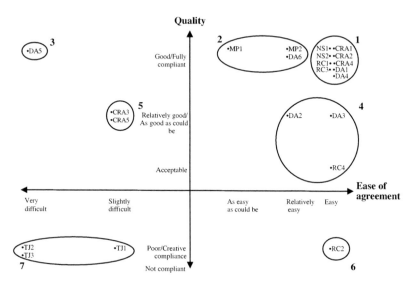

Figure 12.4   Visual representation of interaction outcomes in
two dimensions, showing seven clusters

each point on the scale is clearly subjective and we make no particular claims in this regard.

It is clear from this mapping that the 22 interactions cluster into seven broad groups. Using Table 12.12, the *critical* contextual factors and strategies adopted in each cluster are explored.

Cluster 1: Good outcome, attained easily

This cluster, representing the ideal outcome, contained the highest number of outcomes. The nine outcomes are drawn from four cases. The quality of the relationship ranged from fair to very good, with five interactions being characterised by a very good relationship. Where the relationship was only 'fair' (RC plc), the company was a respectable comfort-seeker, and the availability of evidence (RC1) and clear accounting rules/guidance (RC3) were instrumental to the outcome. Where the relationship was 'good' (DA plc), the company context was not favourable (a powerful, grudging chairman and a hostile bid). The outcome was critically influenced by the integrity of the AEP and the strategies adopted (reason, bargaining and sanctions).

Cluster 2: Good outcome, attained relatively easily/as easy as could be

The three outcomes in this cluster come from two different cases. The AEPs involved were characterised by high integrity and the primary relationship was either good (one interaction) or very good (two interactions). The common strategy adopted was one of assertiveness, in that the AEPs stated their position very firmly at the outset. In the MP plc case, the company had a very conservative, compliant reporting culture.

Cluster 3: Good outcome, attained with difficulty

The cluster contained only one outcome (DA5), but one that was clearly different in nature from the rest. The difficult outcome was entirely attributable to the corporate governance characteristics of the company – a grudging, dominant chairman who simply would not agree to comply with the accounting rules, despite the fact that the FD, AEP, CEO and audit committee were all agreed. The company context was, as noted above, not favourable and the existence of clear accounting rules became critical to the outcome. The non-executive director chairman of the audit committee was instrumental in finally resolving this dispute.

Cluster 4: Relatively good/acceptable outcome, attained easily/relatively easily

The three outcomes in this cluster come from cases DA plc and RC plc. As the company context of DA plc was not favourable and the quality of the primary relationship fell short of 'very good', it is not surprising that some outcomes from this case were less than ideal. However, the integrity of the AEP, combined with a willingness to compromise within the rules, ensured that outcomes were of reasonably high quality.

In the case of RC plc, where the relationship was fair, and the company circumstances were favourable, the AEP was willing to compromise within the rules in the absence of a clear prohibition and accede to the client's preferred treatment.

Cluster 5: As good as could be, slightly difficult

The two outcomes in this cluster come from the same case (CRA plc). The difficulty arose because, despite a very good relationship between the primary parties, the senior accountants were fairly aggressive in their reporting style, perhaps influenced by the possibility of a hostile bid. Although the proposed accounting treatments were not outside the rules, the AEP felt that they were inappropriate/wrong and, given his high level of integrity, escalated the interactions.

Cluster 6: Poor outcome, attained easily

The single outcome in this cluster comes from RC plc. Despite a favourable company context, the relationship was only fair. This was, arguably, because Charles was not sufficiently challenging as he trusted the company not to compromise their own reputation. The AEP was prepared to accept the client company's preferred treatment (albeit with conditions attached).

Cluster 7: Poor/creative compliance outcome, attained with a degree of difficulty

The three outcomes in this cluster all come from the same case (TJ plc). In this case, the relationship is poor, partly because the inexperienced AEP, faced with a difficult client, sought to appease them rather than be assertive. Moreover, the audit firm appeared disorganised. This is a dangerous and volatile set of circumstances that led to low quality accounting.

Because the relationship between the FD and AEP was so poor, the option of coalescing to face the chairman was closed off. Another possible strategy for an AEP in this situation would be assertiveness, but James's lack of experience did not lend itself to this course of action.

It is also worthwhile to take a broader view of the distribution of outcomes in Figure 12.4. On the left-hand side of the figure, clusters 3, 5 and 7 together represent outcomes that are, to a degree, difficult, irrespective of the quality of the outcome. The three cases giving rise to these six interactions had certain common characteristics: two were small, family-controlled companies where the chairman was a grudger and two involved hostile bids (the third was considering a sale). They also had one critical characteristic not in common, as a mix of relationship qualities was represented – from poor to very good. However, in those cases where the relationship was at least good, the FD and the board were not in harmony in their reporting style, and it is this that contributed to the difficulty.

At the bottom of the Figure 12.4, clusters 6 and 7 together represent outcomes that are of low quality (either poor or creative compliance). Both cases giving rise to these four interactions involved AEPs who exhibited moderate rather than high levels of integrity and where the primary relationship was less than good. In none of these four interactions did the AEP state their position firmly, and the failure to use this assertiveness strategy seems to have contributed significantly to the poor outcomes.

12.5   AEP (SELLER) TYPES

It is clear from section 12.4 that the AEP him/herself is, not surprisingly, a central determinant of the strategy adopted and the outcome. The characteristics of the AEP have a major direct influence on the quality of the outcome and, via the quality of the principle relationship, on the ease with which this outcome is attained. In this section, we focus on the AEP, and identify four distinct 'seller types', which are represented by the cases covered in this book. The seller type determines the AEP's basic negotiating position and influences the strategies likely to be adopted. This development of seller types, grounded as it is in empirical evidence, complements the development of the four distinct buyer types that were outlined in section 2.8.

The nature of each seller type is both based upon the AEPs stated attitudes and beliefs, taken from the direct interview evidence, and also inferred from their behaviour given the context of the interaction. A summary of these types is given in Figure 12.5.

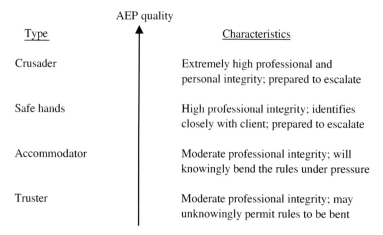

Note: In addition to these four seller types that were observed in our six case studies, there is the theoretical possibility of two others: the incompetent and the rogue (described in section 12.5.5).

Figure 12.5   A hierarchy of AEP (seller) types and thier characteristics

12.5.1   The 'crusader'

We identify two AEPs, Paul and Andrew, whom we label 'crusaders'. Both exhibit an extremely high level of professional and personal integrity. In other words, they display a social conscience as well as a professional conscience. They were prepared to take their responsibilities beyond their strict statutory duty if they felt that it was the right thing to do.

12.5.2   The 'safe pair of hands'

We classify Simon and Alan as 'safe hands'. We would expect most AEPs to fall into this type, because of the nexus of incentives and controls faced by AEPs. Both Simon and Alan display a high level of professional integrity and their actions were designed to ensure that the company's financial reporting complied not only with the letter of the regulatory framework, but with the spirit. While both identified strongly with the client company, and acted as advisors to it, they did not compromise themselves in any way.

12.5.3   The 'accommodator'

We classify James as exhibiting characteristics of an 'accommodator' in some interactions. An accommodator is an AEP who may have a moderate level of professional integrity. In other words, although they comply with the letter of the rules, they are prepared, under certain circumstances, to bend the rules, i.e., to condone creative compliance, certain types of non-compliance and rather aggressive accounting treatments. The circumstances might be pressure from the client company, historical 'baggage' relating to the issue that make it difficult to insist on what is known to be the 'right' accounting outcome, or immaturity as a partner. Above all else, they want to be helpful to the company where possible. This approach can, however, easily backfire if the client company loses respect for the AEP.

12.5.4   The 'truster'

We classify Charles as exhibiting characteristics of a 'truster' in some interactions. A truster is an AEP who, when dealing with a client company that is known to have a conservative reporting style and to be concerned to preserve its reputation, adopts an attitude that is insufficiently critical and questioning given their role as auditor. They take the company to be fire-proof and are not sufficiently sceptical. While their underlying professional integrity may be high, this trusting attitude serves to 'dilute' their effective level of professional integrity.

Both the accommodator and the truster can exhibit 'do-it-yourself' characteristics, in that they do not consult appropriately within their firm. This behaviour could arise for a number of reasons: it may be that the AEP thinks that they know it all, or that they are doing something that they know they should not be doing, or because of personal style. Both the crusader and the safe pair of hands do, however, consult when appropriate.

It should also be noted that not all of the seller types are mutually exclusive. In particular, it would be possible for an AEP to display accommodator and truster characteristics.

12.5.5   Other possible seller types: the 'incompetent' and the 'rogue'

Although we found no examples of these AEP types among our cases, the theoretical possibility clearly exists that an AEP lacking the necessary level of technical competence could attain the position of AEP. The likelihood of this occurring is, however, likely to be small, and sound internal appraisal and quality control procedures within the firm would reduce this to a remote possibility. The incompetent can be characterised as someone with a low level of professional integrity, who is insufficiently aware of the regulatory framework to secure good outcomes in cases where the client company is ignorant or non-compliant.

The theoretical possibility of the 'rogue' type also exists. Rogue AEPs have no sense of professional integrity. They will knowingly flout the regulatory framework for personal gain if they think that they can get away with it. The well-publicised US case of ESM provides an example of this AEP type (*Wall Street Journal*, 1987). The engagement partner stated that the loss of status within the partnership, were he to lose the client, was one of the reasons that he acquiesced to the client's fraudulent accounting practices.

12.6   COMPARISON WITH EXTANT THEORY

Our grounded theory of auditor–client interactions is broadly consistent with the generic negotiation model proposed by Gulliver (1979). We do find, however, that the specific features of the audit setting (e.g., the regulatory environment) exert a strong influence on the nature and outcome of the interactions.

We also find Kohlberg's stage model of moral development and ethical cognition (outlined in section 2.10.5) to be reflected in the seller types. The accommodator and truster exhibit the pre-conventional level, the safe pair of hands exhibits the conventional level, while the crusader exhibits the post-conventional level. In contrast, we do not find the AEPs in the six cases fit into Windsor and Ashkanasy's (1995) three styles of auditor decision-making (and levels of moral reasoning) very well. While the crusader maps onto the autonomous style, the mapping of the other three seller types is less clear. This is perhaps because the Windsor and Ashkanasy model does not include economic variables such as penalties and the visibility of the breach.

We find that the range of strategies used by the primary parties are very similar to those identified by Kipnis and Schmidt (1982) (see section 4.3).

Finally, we note that the interaction issue types to emerge in the six cases reflect those most frequently cited during the questionnaire stage of this study (see section 3.3).

13 Conclusions

13.1 OVERVIEW

In this final chapter we first summarise our findings and then draw conclusions. From this, we derive policy recommendations and set out the issues for audit firms and regulators to consider. Finally, we address the implications for future research.

13.2 SUMMARY OF FINDINGS

Our findings arise from the case studies themselves and from our grounded theory analysis of them. The five key issues to emerge are listed below:

- factors which influence the company's predisposition towards earnings quality;
- the influence of ownership structure and corporate culture on attitudes to regulatory compliance;
- factors which influence the outcomes of financial reporting interactions between FDs and AEPs;
- the effectiveness of sanctions available to FDs and AEPs and the impact of materiality on their application; and
- partner types and the effectiveness of quality control procedures in audit firms.

13.2.1 Factors which influence the company's predisposition towards earnings quality

It is clear that some companies are much more conservative than others in their approach to accounting. Earning quality is a function of where a company's attitude to financial reporting lies on a scale between ultra conservative and very aggressive. (The expression 'creative', much used in the 1980s has been replaced by 'aggressive'.) The ASB's accounting standards have closed off a number of opportunities for abuse. In our case studies we have found examples of creative compliance (interactions TJ2 and TJ3), but no non-compliance which is visible on the face of the accounts.

Companies and auditors run the risk of visible breaches being picked up by the FRRP, which is perceived as a deterrent to non-compliance, particularly by the larger, more conservative companies. These companies do not want the reputation damage associated with an FRRP adverse finding. Breaches which are not visible in the published accounts are beyond the investigatory authority of the FRRP. These may be breaches of accounting standards or failure to adhere to fundamental principles of accounting.

Areas of accounting judgement which can have a major impact on profits (e.g., property and stock valuations, bad debt provisions and fair value provisions) cannot be precisely defined in standards. The outcomes of judgemental decisions are not usually visible to the external user of audited financial statements, other than in the general description of accounting policies. These judgemental decisions and their outcomes are dependent on the company's attitude to earnings quality.

A key driver of aggressive accounting is found to be financial difficulty, and particularly the need to stay within debt covenants. This emerges in three of our six cases. In interaction NS1, the company itself is in difficulty. In interactions MP1 and RC2, the holding company has found aggressive accounting in newly acquired subsidiaries, to such an extent in MP1 that the group auditors disclaim on the subsidiary's opening position in their audit report. (This indicates the wide range of opinion which can arise among auditors in respect of earnings quality.) In both interactions, the holding company is concerned not to appear to have overpaid for the acquisition.

Earnings quality can change rapidly as a company's circumstances change. Apart from the problem of staying within debt covenants, a decline in profitability can lead to a reluctance to make adequate provisions at the time they should be made (interaction TJ1). A further influence is the expectation of a hostile bid where the board may be motivated to make the company look as strong as possible (CRA plc).

It is possible that shareholders and others who rely on information which is on public record may not be fully aware of these issues.

13.2.2   The influence of ownership structure and corporate culture on attitudes to regulatory compliance

Ownership structure and corporate culture have a major influence on attitudes to corporate governance and financial reporting. DA plc and TJ plc, although listed, are family controlled. The FDs of both companies complain that the regulatory framework is too onerous for companies of their size. In both of these companies the chairman is also the chief executive, despite the Cadbury recommendations, and with his family interests effectively controls the company as well as the board. The chairman could easily remove the auditor. Both companies have only one non-executive director. In DA plc the non-executive director is effective. By contrast, TJ plc has no institutional investors, no audit committee and the non-executive director is the chairman's poodle. The non-family shareholders have little protection in this company. The influence of institutional investors and lenders on corporate governance is apparent in NS plc where a change of board, and improved corporate governance, is made a condition for the provision of further funding.

RC plc and CRA plc are both very respectable companies who comply with the Cadbury code. Both want to show their results in the best possible light, without attracting criticism, yet RC plc's high-powered audit committee does not prevent the poor outcome in interaction RC2. (An interesting consequence of this outcome was the FD's request to the AEP's firm for a change of audit partner, as, on reflection, he was uncomfortable with the outcome himself.) In interaction CRA5, the board and the audit committee do not support the AEP's position. This is different from interaction MP2, where the auditors' position is supported. Thus, compliance with corporate governance best practice does not necessarily lead to good financial reporting outcomes in all cases.

13.2.3 Factors which influence the outcomes of financial reporting interactions

Using grounded theory methodology we analyse twenty-two financial reporting interactions between FDs and AEPs. These interactions show both the importance of the quality of the primary relationship itself and the complexity of the influences on the issues on which agreement is reached. From our analysis, it is clear that these interactions are multi-dimensional and complex, particularly as they are subject to regulatory influences. Existing negotiation models (e.g., Gulliver, 1979; and Nicotera, 1993) do not adequately encompass all dimensions of these interactions.

Eighteen interactions have outcomes which comply fully with the regulatory framework for financial reporting and auditing as it stands. The other four interactions have low-quality outcomes. Interactions TJ2 and TJ3 result in creative compliance. Although the outcomes of these two interactions demonstrate no clear breach of the regulatory framework, in our view the presentation adopted was intended to misdirect readers of the accounts. The outcomes in TJ1 and RC2 breach accounting standards as a result of poor judgement on the part of the AEPs. TJ1 overstates the reported profit for the year in contravention of SSAP 9 as the stock overvaluation is written off over three years instead of being recognised immediately. RC2 fails to disclose the fair value adjustments on an acquisition in a fair value table as required by FRS 6. We have no evidence to suggest that any stakeholders in TJ plc or RC plc were disadvantaged in any way as a result of the low-quality outcomes.

Fully compliant outcomes are easier to achieve where the company board has a conservative attitude to financial reporting and where there is a good working relationship between the FD and the AEP. Good relationships occur where there is mutual trust and respect and where both parties have a high level of integrity.

Fully compliant outcomes are more difficult to achieve where one or more of the following circumstances exist: the board's culture is less conservative; the issue is a sensitive one within the company; the issue arises at a late stage in the financial reporting cycle; the buyer type is a grudger; or the firm is disorganised. To achieve a fully compliant outcome in these more difficult circumstances, the AEP should take a firm position from the outset. Additional useful strategies are for the AEP to call on other parties in his firm for support and also seek support from the company's audit committee. Support from the audit committee is not necessarily forthcoming. A well-researched argument grounded in the regulations greatly helps the AEP to carry his point. Where the issue is a matter of judgement rather than a straightforward matter of compliance with a regulation, the AEP may find it more difficult to get his point of view accepted. An important mechanism for avoiding confrontation is for the FD and the AEP to maintain a continuous, interactive relationship, so that issues are resolved as they arise. Late interventions from an audit firm's technical reviews cause irritation to FDs. Proposed last-minute adjustments to accounts create undue time pressure and have the potential to lead AEPs to compromise the outcomes.

Interestingly the four low quality outcomes arise in cases where the relationship between the FD and the AEP (i.e., the primary relationship) is not good. Poor relationships may arise because the FD and AEP do not trust and respect each other and lack goal congruence. Contributory factors to this situation occur where the FD has previously been in a position senior to the AEP in the same audit firm (which appears to put the AEP at a disadvantage) or where there is a significant age and experience gap between them.

None of the AEPs in our cases was prepared to condone any form of visible non-compliance. The two non-compliant outcomes were invisible but the two examples of creative compliance were clearly visible.

13.2.4   The effectiveness of sanctions available to FDs and AEPs and the impact of materiality on their application

The key sanction available to a company board is to remove an auditor, subject to legal process. This puts economic pressure on the audit partner. Another form of economic pressure is to try and get the audit fees reduced. The key sanction available to an auditor is to qualify the audit report (or, in extremis, to resign and draw attention to the reasons for the resignation). There is strong awareness among FDs and AEPs of the possibility of these sanctions being applied.

The threat of putting the audit out to tender, which is normally the first step in the auditor change process, can be used either for the purpose of intimidating an auditor and/or as a means of getting a fee reduction. The threat is used by the FD in RC plc for both purposes i.e., as a mechanism to undermine the AEP for whom he has little respect, and as a means of keeping the audit fee down. A tender threat is also used in NS plc by the recently appointed chairman, who has no established relationship with the AEP. This tender threat is solely a mechanism to try and get the audit fees reduced. Fee pressure is used as a form of retaliation (interaction TJ3) to cause embarrassment to the AEP for a major last-minute problem. In a highly competitive market, the AEP is in a weak position in fee negotiations and in our cases the clients' demands for fee reductions were accepted. It is theoretically possible, however, for a company board faced with a serious disagreement to threaten to put the audit out to tender. Unless this were to be done in the year the disagreement arose, the underlying reasons for the change would not be disclosable under the current regulatory framework.

In two interactions, TJ3 and MP2, the AEPs feel that there is a possibility of losing their client. Both are prepared to accept this rather than to back down from a position which they firmly believe to be right. AEPs generally express a belief that they would not lose a client over a technical disagreement. We have no evidence that the extent of non-audit services influenced the behaviour of the partners faced with the possibility of losing a client. The issue for the AEP is the loss of the client rather than the mix of the fees arising from the engagement.

The possibility of a qualified audit report is taken very seriously by FDs who do not want their accounts qualified. Faced with a qualification, FDs back down (interaction RC3). However, regulatory clarity and materiality can influence an AEP's ability to use this sanction. The AEP in interaction CRA5 disagrees with the company's accounting treatment but there is no clear support for the issue in the regulatory framework, and the amount involved is not regarded as material enough to justify a qualified audit report. Therefore the ultimate sanction is not effective. In this case, resort to lesser sanctions, being reference to the audit committee and the main board, does not change the accounting treatment, as they decide to support the FD.

A further curious dimension to the issue of materiality emerges in interaction TJ1, where the overvaluation of the stock is not adjusted in one accounting period because the figure is considered too large. Interestingly, materiality appears to have upper as well as lower boundaries.

13.2.5   Partner types and quality control in audit firms

From our analysis we classify AEP's into four key categories: the *crusader*, the *safe pair of hands*, the *accommodator* and the *truster*. Crusaders have very high integrity and are the conscience of their clients. They seek to protect their clients and are prepared to take their responsibilities beyond their statutory duty as auditors. *Safe pairs of hands* have high integrity and they ensure that their clients' financial reporting is fully compliant with the regulatory framework. Crusaders and safe pairs of hands seek advice and consult where necessary and they also comply fully with their firms' internal quality control procedures.

Accommodators are prepared, under some circumstances, to bend or infringe the rules to accommodate the wishes of their clients. They may also be more likely to give in to fee pressures. *Trusters* believe their client to be low risk and fireproof and are not sufficiently sceptical of their motives. A characteristic of both accommodators and trusters is that they are inclined to be 'do-it yourselfers', in that they do not always consult appropriately within their firms and follow all the quality control procedures.

All the audit firms in our cases have in-house quality control procedures in place, such as technical departments, consultation procedures and second partners assigned to the clients. However, the extent and timeliness of the use of these resources appears to lie in the hands of the AEPs. Critically, the ones who most need to consult appear to be the least inclined to do so.

13.3   THE POLICY IMPLICATIONS OF OUR FINDINGS

13.3.1   The auditor's influence on the quality of financial reporting

This study goes behind the audit report to show how the audit process actually works in practice. It presents the outcomes of interactions between the key parties to the primary relationship, the FD and the AEP, and clearly demonstrates the significant contribution the audit process makes to the quality of financial reporting. Audit is found to be a complex, interactive and judgemental process, which requires a high level of technical knowledge, integrity and interpersonal skills from the AEP. The outcome of each interaction in our study is found to be influenced by a range of factors which emanate from the specific circumstances of each case, the nature and significance of the issue and the clarity of the regulatory framework surrounding it.

13.3.2 The key to auditor independence

One finding which stands out from this study is the extent to which the outcomes of interactions depend on the personal integrity, conviction and courage of the individual AEPs, at times in the face of complex judgemental issues and considerable pressure from directors to back down. Possibly for the first time, this study provides direct evidence of auditors demonstrating independence in fact. Because the fact of independence is not usually observable, regulators have concentrated their efforts on developing a framework to protect the *appearance* of independence. Although such a framework is essential to maintain confidence in the audit process, independent behaviour in individual cases appears to be much more closely linked to the personal characteristics of the AEP than to the influence of the regulatory framework.

There is a widely held perception that the level of non-audit services (NAS) undermines auditor independence. We have found no evidence that our AEPs were influenced by the level of NAS in the way they conducted their interactions with clients. The economic risk for the auditor has more to do with the loss of an important client rather than the proportion of audit to non-audit fees. Furthermore in a competitive market, the FDs are discriminating buyers and shop around for the non-audit services they require. They are not locked in to their auditors for all types of non-audit services, although some companies make a policy decision to rely on their auditors for high-level technical accounting advice in preference to employing people themselves. The perceived adverse effect of the provision of non-audit services on independence is not supported by the facts of this study.

13.3.3 Creative compliance

We have found no examples of breaches of accounting standards which could be identified from published financial statements. However, despite the best efforts of the ASB, creative compliance still exists, and unless the standard setters move to a much higher level of formalism than is currently applied, this will continue to some extent. The cost–benefit of a heavier rule-based framework is, however, difficult to justify, for wherever the rules are set, there will be manoeuvring at the margin. Nevertheless, it must be recognised that clear rules strengthen the auditor's position in a difficult negotiation. There are, however, no rules which can effectively regulate some of the more complex judgemental issues that auditors deal with.

13.3.4   Substance and form of corporate governance

Although Cadbury and subsequent corporate governance recommendations are believed to have improved corporate governance generally, it is worth reiterating that it is the quality of the individuals on a board of directors and the culture of the company which dictates the real quality of its corporate governance. We make the slightly cynical observation that corporate governance appears to work best where it is least needed.

13.4   PROPOSALS AND ISSUES FOR REGULATORS AND AUDIT FIRMS TO CONSIDER

This study provides evidence of the successes which arise from the audit process. Because of confidentiality constraints between auditors and their clients such evidence usually remains hidden, whereas the small number of failures, which do reach the public domain, inevitably attract a great deal of attention. In a perfect world, all the interactions in our study would have fully compliant outcomes, but it is not a perfect world and there is always room for improvement. We now make a number of suggestions for change and raise issues for regulators and audit firms to consider.

13.4.1   Regulators

Earnings quality and debt covenants

Judgement plays a key role in accounting decisions. This can lead to wide differences in earnings quality. Earnings quality can deteriorate when a company is in financial difficulty and trying to keep within its debt covenants.

- We suggest that the terms of debt covenants and the company's own ratios relative to them should be disclosed in preliminary announcements, interim statements and annual reports.

- We suggest that consideration be given to identifying other mechanisms for investors better to understand the extent to which judgement can influence accounting numbers.

Family-controlled companies which are listed

We are concerned about the position of external shareholders in family-controlled companies which are listed. A chairman who also controls the company has too much power.

- We suggest that consideration be given to insisting that, where companies float, a majority of the shares should not be closely held and an independent chairman should be required.

Detecting invisible non-compliance

Non-compliance which is visible in published financial statements is subject to regulatory oversight by the FRRP. Invisible non-compliance is much more difficult to detect. If it is condoned by an AEP, it can only be picked up by the audit regulation regime or by quality control procedures within an audit firm. We have found two instances of invisible non-compliance in our study.

- We suggest that, in the light of cost–benefit issues, consideration be given to whether the current regulatory procedures for detecting invisible non-compliance are adequate as they stand. (We make recommendations in respect of quality control in audit firms below.)

The effectiveness of sanctions available to auditors

An audit report qualification is taken very seriously by directors. We suggest that it may be taken *too* seriously by both directors and auditors, with the result that only issues which are really substantive are likely to attract a qualification and FDs will fight very hard to avoid one. Therefore lesser issues of poor quality accounting or non-compliance do not come to the attention of investors. Because they are not regarded as material in audit terms, the auditor has no means of drawing attention to them. Such issues, however, can be a key indicator of a company's attitude to compliance and its quality of earnings.

Our cases also show that proposals to change the accounting numbers and disclosures are more strongly resisted when they arise close to the reporting date. Thus materiality may increase as this date approaches.

We suggest two possible solutions to this.

- We suggest that the currently accepted materiality constraint on an audit report could be radically changed so that all breaches, other than those which are genuinely minutiae, become reportable.
- *Alternatively*, we suggest that a lesser sanction of disclosure, but not in the audit report, be introduced for less serious breaches.

In either case, we believe that the possibility of disclosure, even of a relatively minor breach, would ensure better compliance and therefore improve overall earnings quality. It would also mitigate the resistance to late adjustments.

Competition

There is no doubt that the ability of a company board readily to replace an auditor in the current highly competitive environment has the potential to undermine the incumbent auditor and lead to poor outcomes, particularly if the AEP is an accommodator. The threat of a tender may be used as a means of driving down fees, as a means of threatening an auditor who will not back down, or both. In fee negotiations the balance of power undoubtedly lies with the company board, as the auditor has no sanction. It is theoretically possible for a robust auditor to be replaced through the tender process, in a year following a major disagreement, using a fee reduction as an excuse.

- We suggest that the current provisions for depositing statements of circumstances associated with auditor changes be reviewed so that the distinction between changes solely associated with fee reductions and those associated with more serious issues are distinguished.

Given the effective control that directors have over the auditor appointment process:

- We suggest that consideration be given to the deposition of a statement by the directors, setting out their reasons for proposing change.

13.4.2   Audit firms

Partner selection and training procedures

Our identification of partner types indicates how vital it is that audit firms ensure their partner selection procedures are sound.

• We suggest that partner selection procedures must minimise the possibility of individuals who have inherent tendencies towards accommodating and trusting behaviour being appointed audit partners.

As high levels of personal and professional integrity are key attributes of crusaders and safe pairs of hands, a continuing training programme in ethical development for all audit staff is of fundamental importance.

• We suggest that the use of case studies such as those presented in this book might provide useful material for a continuing training programme in ethical development.

Risk management

The risk profile and earnings quality of a company can change very quickly.

• We suggest that risk profiles are constantly reviewed.

The critical importance of the primary relationship and the appropriate allocation of partners to clients

The quality of the primary relationship between the FD and the AEP emerges from our analysis as a fundamental influence on the outcome of interactions.

• We suggest that it is essential that audit firms take great care in the matching of AEPs to FDs.

For example, it is not a good idea to allocate a young, inexperienced partner to a client (TJ plc) where the FD is much older and there is a dominant chief executive. A further danger is that where a company is considered to be low risk, a truster can take advantage of the risk profile by assuming nothing can go wrong and permitting non-compliant outcomes.

The need to ensure the effectiveness and timeliness of in-house consultation and review procedures

In all our case studies the AEPs' audit firms have back-up procedures in place for second partner reviews and technical support. However, the existence of these resources does not mean that they are used properly. The partners who are most likely to put their firms at risk by agreeing to non-compliant outcomes are less likely to avail themselves of advice. It is not sufficient for audit firms to make resources available.

- We suggest that audit firms must ensure that mechanisms are in place to confirm the operation of quality control in this area.

Although there are cost–benefit issues to be considered, we believe that an independent, hot review of the two cases where there was invisible non-compliance would have uncovered the problems and possibly prevented them happening.

In concluding this section, it is worth comparing our findings in the UK with those of the Panel on Audit Effectiveness in the US (see section 2.13). The Public Oversight Board (POB) (2000) report was published just as we were submitting our manuscript to the publishers. Two of the comments in the POB report struck a particular chord with us as they reflect our own findings very well. They conclude that 'our report demonstrates that both the profession and the quality of its audits are fundamentally sound' (POB Press Release, 7 June 2000) and note 'the importance of the individual professional auditor who is the ultimate backstop in furthering audit quality' (POB, 2000, p. xi).

13.5 IMPLICATIONS FOR FUTURE RESEARCH

13.5.1 Further verification of grounded theory

Our grounded theory of interaction outcomes was set out in section 12.4. The theory comprises hypothesised relationships (sometimes with conditions or moderating variables) between the major categories uncovered, which have been validated against the data contained in the six cases. Although the six cases were selected carefully to ensure that a wide variation of real-life settings was sampled, it is possible that they do not represent the full range of variation that exists. The hypothesised relationships could be stated as formal propositions and subjected to further testing. This could provide further confidence in the validity of the theory. The general rule in grounded theory research is to sample until theoretical saturation of each category is reached. The relationships presented here may require alteration or expansion to accommodate additional and specifically different conditions (Strauss and Corbin, 1990, pp. 188–190).

Moreover, all six cases were drawn from the UK, and it would be of great interest to conduct similar studies in other jurisdictions where some of the general contextual factors will be different. This would allow the influence of these factors on the nature and outcome of the interactions to be explored.

Another approach to verification of the grounded theory would be the use of multiple methods, allowing the triangulation of findings (Jick, 1979). In particular, we encourage researchers to undertake experimental studies that focus on subsets of the critical variables to emerge from the grounded theory. These variables are: integrity of AEP; quality of primary relationship; reporting styles of FD and board; hostile bid/financial health; effectiveness of corporate governance; clarity of accounting rules; and level of audit firm support and quality control.

13.5.2 Further development of grounded theory

The grounded research presented in this book has focused on the FD and the AEP, these being the parties to the primary relationship. In some inter-actions, other parties had a critical influence upon the nature and outcome of the interactions (e.g., the chairman in TJ plc, the senior technical part-ner in TJ3, the audit committee in CRA5, and the non-executive chairman of the audit committee in DA5). It would be interesting to extend the focus of the analysis to these key secondary parties, to explore their attitudes, beliefs and motivations in order to understand more fully their behaviour.

A further potentially useful direction for further research relates to the attributes of the AEP. It was found that the integrity of the AEP was criti-cal to the quality of the final outcome. In section 12.3.3 we distinguished two key features of the AEP's personal code of behaviour – professional integrity (i.e., behaviour that meets the standards required by professional ethics) and personal integrity (i.e., behaviour that exceeds the standards required by professional ethics). We also saw that personality characteris-tics, such as predisposition towards self-reliance, confrontation and scepti-cism, can sometimes also play a part. Further clarification of these personal attributes (how to identify and measure them) and their role would be valuable.

13.5.3 Implications for related areas of research

It is interesting to consider our findings in relation to the study by Behn *et al.* (1997) (see section 2.7). That study found a negative association between auditor scepticism and client satisfaction. Our findings endorse this – in RC2, although the FD got his own way, he felt that the AEP had been too soft, resulting in a loss of respect. This was a case where the FD had a moderately aggressive reporting style (he wanted to show the company's results in the best possible light, while remaining firmly within the rules), while the company overall was a comfort-seeker. Whether this relationship between between auditor scepticism and client satisfaction would persist in cases where the FD had a complete disregard for the rules (however unlikely this is in a listed company), we cannot say from our evidence.

Our findings have particular relevance to research into auditor independence (see section 2.10). The complexity of this concept is well illustrated by our six cases. Purely economic definitions, such as DeAngelo's (1981b), are shown to be too simplistic, as whether or not a discovered breach is reported is shown to depend upon materiality and judgement.

Our cases find no evidence that breaches remain undiscovered by the auditors; however, some are not reported for reasons that have little to do with a lack of independence. Further research is required into the types of breach that auditors do not report and the reasons for non-reporting. This research could either use experimental methods or investigate actual cases.

Our cases also provide no evidence that the provision of NAS by the auditor affects their behaviour in any way. The issue was never mentioned directly by any of the parties and no link can be inferred from the data collected. Yet NAS provision is an issue of great concern to users and policy-makers (see section 2.10.3). While there may be a perception problem, we find no evidence that actual independence is impaired. There needs to be more studies into independence in fact, so that *mis*perceptions (if that is what they are) can be corrected.

Finally, our cases suggest that the quality of corporate governance tends to be inversely related to the need for it. Nothing much will be learned from studying corporate governance in financially healthy companies with boards that have a conservative, compliant reporting culture. We suggest that future research concentrates on (a) companies in some financial distress, (b) companies where the board culture is aggressive and resistant, and (c) companies where both circumstances apply.

13.5.4   In closing …

This research has used a method (grounded theory) that is not common in the field of auditing research. This lack of popularity can be attributed to a number of factors: the large amount of time required to undertake such a study relative to, say, a quantitative study; a lack of relevant training and skills; the difficulty of publishing studies of this type in the leading academic journals (perhaps because of the difficulties of demonstrating, within the space constraints of this form of output, how one got from the mass of data to the final grounded theory). It *should not* be attributed to either an inappropriateness of the method or a lack of rigour inherent within the method (although qualiphobes may claim this). We advocate the use of mixed methods in auditing research, as we believe that this will advance knowledge most effectively. This echoes the general pleas made by writers on research methods and methodology and of researchers in many social science disciplines. We hope that the detailed exposition of our study presented here will encourage other auditing researchers to explore the rich insights that the grounded theory method supports and help guard against theoretical stagnation within the field.[1]

---

[1] The issues discussed in this sub-section are explored more fully in Beattie (2000).

Bibliography

Accountancy (1999) October, pp. 8–9.

—— (2000) 'Davison to Head Independence Review', May.

Accountancy Age (1999) 'Ahead of the Rest', 24 June, pp. 20–1.

Accounting Education News (1999), Early Fall Issue, pp. 25–6.

AICPA (1978) *Commission on Auditors' Responsibilities: Report, Conclusions, and Recommendations* (Cohen Commission) (New York: American Institute of Certified Public Accountants).

—— (1979) *Public Oversight Board Report: Scope of Service by CPA Firms* (New York: American Institute of Certified Public Accountants).

—— (1986) *Division for CPA Firms SEC Practice Section: SECPS Manual* (New York: American Institute of Certified Public Accountants).

—— (1992) *Professional Standards* (New York: American Institute of Certified Public Accountants).

—— (1997) *Serving the Public Interest: A New Conceptual Framework for Auditor Independence* (New York: American Institute of Certified Public Accountants).

Anderson-Gough, F., Grey, C. and Robson, K. (1999) *Making Up Accountants: The Organizational and Professional Socialization of Trainee Chartered Accountants* (Aldershot, Hampshire: Ashgate).

Antle, R. (1982) 'The Auditor as an Economic Agent', *Journal of Accounting Research*, 20(2), pp. 503–27.

—— (1984) 'Auditor Independence', *Journal of Accounting Research*, 22(1), pp. 1–20.

—— (1999) 'Accounting Firms, the Accounting Industry, and Accounting Research', *British Accounting Review*, 31(1) (March), pp. 1–13.

APB (1994) *The Audit Agenda* (London: Auditing Practices Board).

—— (1995) *Objectives and General Principles Governing an Audit of Financial Statements*, SAS 100 (London: Auditing Practices Board).

—— (1996) *The Audit Agenda – Next Steps* (London: Auditing Practices Board).

—— (1998a) *Corporate Governance Reporting and Auditors' Responsibilities Statements*, Bulletin 1998/10 (London: Auditing Practices Board).

—— (1998b) *Communication Between External Auditors and Audit Committees*, Audit Briefing Paper (London: Auditing Practices Board).

—— (2000) *Quality Control for Audit Work*, Proposed Statement of Auditing Standards 240 (London: Auditing Practices Board).

Ashkanasy, N.M. and Windsor, C.A. (1997) 'Personal and Organizational Factors Affecting Auditor Independence: Empirical Evidence and Directions for Future Research', *Research on Accounting Ethics*, 3, pp. 35–48.

Barkess, L. and Simnett, R. (1994) 'The Provision of Other Services by Auditors: Independence and Pricing Issues', *Accounting and Business Research*, 24(94), pp. 99–108.

Bartlett, R.W. (1993) 'A Scale of Perceived Independence: New Evidence on an Old Concept', *Accounting, Auditing & Accountability Journal*, 6(2), pp. 52–67.

Beattie, V. (2000) 'Mixing Quantitative and Qualitative Research: A Case Study on Auditor Negotiations', Paper presented at the Gregynog Conference, 30–31 May.

—— and Fearnley, S. (1995) 'The Importance of Audit Firm Characteristics and the Drivers of Auditor Change in UK Listed Companies', *Accounting and Business Research*, 25, pp. 227–39.

—— (1998a) *What Companies Want (and Don't Want) From Their Auditors* (London: Institute of Chartered Accountants in England and Wales).

—— (1998b) 'Auditor Changes and Tendering: UK Interview Evidence', *Accounting, Auditing & Accountability Journal*, 11(1), pp. 72–98.

——, Brandt, R. and Fearnley, S. (1998) 'Auditor Independence and the Expectations Gap: Some Evidence of Changing User Perceptions', *Journal of Financial Regulation and Compliance*, 6(2), pp. 159–70.

—— (1999) 'Perceptions of Auditor Independence: U.K. Evidence', *Journal of International Accounting, Auditing and Taxation*, 8(2), pp. 67–107.

—— (2000) 'Behind the Audit Report: A Descriptive Study of Discussions and Negotiations Between Auditors and Directors', *International Journal of Auditing*, 4(2) (July), pp. 177–202.

Beck, P.J., Frecka, T.J. and Solomon, I. (1988) 'An Empirical Analysis of the Relationship Between MAS Involvement and Auditor Tenure: Implications for Auditor Independence', *Journal of Accounting Literature*, 7, pp. 65–84.

Behn, B.K., Carcello, J.V., Hermanson, D.R. and Hermanson, R.H. (1997) 'The Determinants of Audit Client Satisfaction Among Clients of Big Six Firms', *Accounting Horizons*, 11(1) (March), pp. 7–24.

Bell, T., Marrs, F., Solomon, I. and Thomas, H. (1997) *Auditing Organizations Through a Strategic-Systems Lens* (KPMG Peat Marwick LLP).

Brandt, R., Fearnley, S., Hines, T. and Beattie, V. (1997) 'The Financial Reporting Review Panel: An Analysis of its Activities', in *Financial Reporting Today: Current and Emerging Issues – The 1998 Edition* (Milton Keynes: Accountancy Books), pp. 27–54.

Brass, D.J. and Burkhardt, M.E. (1993) 'Potential Power and Power Use: An Investigation of Structure and Behaviour', *Academy of Management Journal*, 36(3), pp. 441–70.

Brown, S.M. (1992) 'Cognitive Mapping and Repertory Grids for Qualitative Survey Research: Some Comparative Observations', *Journal of Management Studies*, 29(3), pp. 287–307.

Cadbury, A. (1992) *Report of the Committee on the Financial Aspects of Corporate Governance* (London: Gee & Company).

CAJEC (1999) *Revision of the Guide to Professional Ethics*, White Paper (London: Chartered Accountants Joint Ethics Committee).

Carcello, J.V., Hermanson, R.H. and McGrath, N.T. (1992) 'Audit Quality Attributes: The Perceptions of Audit Partners, Preparers, and Financial Statement Users', *Auditing: A Journal of Practice & Theory*, 11(1) (Spring), pp. 1–15.

CCAB (1988) *The Making of Accounting Standards (The Dearing Report)* (London: Combined Committee of Accounting Bodies).

—— (1998) *Modernising Regulation: Becoming Accountable to Stakeholders – the Proposals of the Leading Accountancy Bodies* (London: Combined Committee of Accounting Bodies).

Collier, P. (1996) 'The Rise of the Audit Committee in UK Quoted Companies: A Curious Phenomenon?', *Accounting, Business and Financial History*, 6(2), pp. 121–40.

Committee on Corporate Governance (1998) *The Combined Code* (London: Gee Publishing).

Conyon, M. (1995) 'Cadbury in the Boardroom', *Hemmington Scott Corporate Register*, April, pp. 5–10.

DeAngelo, L.E. (1981a) 'Auditor Independence, "Low Balling", and Disclosure Regulation', *Journal of Accounting and Economics*, 3(2), pp. 113–27.

―― (1981b) 'Auditor Size and Audit Quality', *Journal of Accounting and Economics*, 3, pp. 183–99.

De Ruyter, K. and Wetzels, M. (1999) 'Commitment in Auditor–Client Relationships: Antecedents and Consequences', *Accounting, Organizations and Society*, 24, pp. 57–75.

Dopuch, N. and King, R.R. (1991) 'The Impact of MAS on Auditors' Independence: An Experimental Markets Study', *Journal of Accounting Research*, 29, Supplement, pp. 60–98.

―― and Simunic, D. (1980) 'The Nature of Competition in the Auditing Profession: A Descriptive and Normative View', in J.W. Buckley and J.F. Weston (eds), *Regulation and the Accounting Profession*, (Lifetime Learning Publications).

―― (1982) 'Competition in Auditing: An Assessment', Fourth Symposium on Auditing Research, University of Illinois.

DTI (1998) *A Framework of Independent Regulation for the Accountancy Profession*, A Consultation Document (London: Department of Trade and Industry).

Dye, R.A. (1991) 'Informationally Motivated Auditor Replacement', *Journal of Accounting and Economics*, 14, pp. 347–74.

Dykxhoorn, H.J. and Sinning, K.E. (1982) 'Perceptions of Auditor Independence: Its Perceived Effect on the Loan and Investment Decisions of German Financial Statement Users', *Accounting, Organizations and Society*, 7(4), pp. 337–47.

EC (1996) *The Role, the Position and the Liability of the Statutory Auditor within the European Union* (Brussels: European Commission).

―― (1998) *The Statutory Audit in the European Union: The Way Forward*, Communication (Brussels: European Commission).

―― (2000) *Statutory Auditor's Independence*, Committee on Auditing (Brussels: European Commission).

Eisenhardt, K.M. (1989) 'Building Theories from Case Study Research', *Academy of Management Review*, 14(4), pp. 532–50.

Farmer, T.A., Rittenberg, L.E. and Trompeter, G.M. (1987) 'An Investigation of the Impact of Economic and Organization Factors on Auditor Independence', *Auditing: A Journal of Practice & Theory*, 7(1) (Fall), pp. 1–14.

FEE (1995) *Audit Independence and Objectivity*, Position Paper (Brussels: Fédération des Experts Comptables Européens).

―― (1998) *Statutory Audit Independence and Objectivity: Common Core of Principles for the Guidance of the European Profession*, Initial Recommendation (Brussels: Fédération des Experts Comptables Européens).

Fellingham, J.C. and Newman, D.P. (1985) 'Strategic Considerations in Auditing', *The Accounting Review*, October, pp. 634–50.

Firth, M. (1980) 'Perceptions of Auditor Independence and Official Ethical Guidelines', *The Accounting Review*, 55(3) (July), pp. 451–66.

Fisher, J., Schatzberg, J.W. and Shapiro, B.P. (1996) 'A Theoretical and Experimental Examination of Strategic Auditor–Client Interaction', *Advances in Accounting*, 14, pp. 135–60.

Gibbins, M. and Newton, J.D. (1994) 'An Empirical Exploration of Complex Accountability in Public Accounting', *Journal of Accounting Research*, 32(2), Autumn, pp. 165–86.

——, Salterio, S. and Webb, A. (1999) 'Evidence about Auditor–Client Management Negotiation Concerning Client's Financial Reporting', Working Paper.

Goldman, A. and Barlev, B. (1974) 'The Auditor–Firm Conflict of Interests: Its Implications for Independence', *The Accounting Review*, 49 (October), pp. 707–18.

Gray, R.H. with Bebbington, J. and Walters, D. (1993) *Accounting for the Environment* (London: Paul Chapman Publishing Ltd.).

Greenbury, R. (1995) *Report of a Study Group on Directors' Remuneration* (London: Gee Publishing Ltd.).

Griffiths, I. (1986) *Creative Accounting* (London: Unwin Paperbacks).

—— (1996) *New Creative Accounting: How to Make Your Profits What You Want Them To Be* (London: Macmillan).

Gronroos, C. (1990) 'Relationships Approach to Marketing', *Journal of Business Research*, 20, pp. 3–11.

Gulliver, P.H. (1979) *Disputes and Negotiations: A Cross-Cultural Perspective* (New York: Academic Press).

Gundlach, G.T., Achrol, R.S. and Mentzer, J.T. (1995) 'The Structure of Commitment in Exchange', *Journal of Marketing*, 59, pp. 78–92.

Hampel, R. (1998) *Committee on Corporate Governance, Final Report* (London: Gee Publishing).

Hansen, C.D. and Kahnweiler, W.M. (1993) 'Storytelling: An Instrument for Understanding the Dynamics of Corporate Relationships', *Human Relations*, 46(12), pp. 1391–409.

—— and Watts, J.S. (1997) 'Two Models of the Auditor–Client Interaction: Tests with United Kingdom Data', *Contemporary Accounting Research*, 14(2) (Summer), pp. 23–50.

Hatherly, D. (1997) 'Beware Consultancy', *Accountancy Age*, 17 April, p. 17.

—— (1999) 'The Future of Auditing: The Debate in the UK', *European Accounting Review*, 8(1), pp. 51–65.

——, Nadeau, L. and Thomas, L. (1996) 'Game Theory and the Auditor's Penalty Regime', *Journal of Business Finance and Accounting*, 23(1) (January), pp. 29–45.

Hughes, R. (1999) 'The Rise and Rise of the Audit Committee', *Accountancy*, February, p. 69.

ICAEW (1991) *Audit Regulations and Guidance* (London: Institute of Chartered Accountants in England and Wales).

—— (1995) *Report to the Council of the ICAEW of the Working Group on Competitive Pricing* (London: Institute of Chartered Accountants in England and Wales).

—— (1999) *Internal Control: Guidance for Directors on the Combined Code* (London: Institute of Chartered Accountants in England and Wales).

ICAS (1993) *Auditing into the Twenty-First Century*, W.M. McInnes (ed.), Discussion Document (Edinburgh: Institute of Chartered Accountants of Scotland).

Jensen, M.C. and Meckling, W.H. (1976) 'Theory of the Firm: Managerial Behavior, Agency Costs and Ownership Structure', *Journal of Financial Economics*, 3 (October), pp. 305–60.

Jeppesen, K.K. (1998) 'Reinventing Auditing, Refining Consulting and Independence', *European Accounting Review*, 7(3), pp. 517–39.

Jick, T.D. (1979) 'Mixing Qualitative and Quantitative Methods: Triangulation in Action', *Administrative Science Quarterly*, 24 (December), pp. 602–11.

Kadous, K., Kennedy, J. and Peecher, M.E. (1999) 'Auditors' Judgments of the Acceptability of Client-Preferred Accounting Methods', Working Paper.

Kalbers, L. and Fogarty, T. (1993) 'Audit Committee Effectiveness: An Empirical Investigation of the Contribution of Power', *Auditing: A Journal of Practice and Theory*, 12(1) (Spring), pp. 24–49.

Keasey, K. and Wright, M. (1993) 'Issues in Corporate Accountability and Governance: An Editorial', *Accounting and Business Research*, 23(91A), pp. 291–303.

Kinney, W.R. (1975a) 'A Decision Theory Approach to the Sampling Problem in Auditing', *Journal of Accounting Research*, Spring, pp. 117–32.

—— (1975b) 'Decision Theory Aspects of Internal Control System Design/ Compliance and Substantive Tests, *Journal of Accounting Research*, Supplement, pp. 14–29.

Kipnis, D. and Schmidt, S.M. (1982) *Profile of Organizational Influence Strategies* (San Diego, CA: University Associates).

—— (1983) 'An Influence Perspective on Bargaining Within Organizations', ch. 17 in M.H. Bazerman and R.J. Lewicki (eds), *Negotiating in Organizations* (Beverly Hills, CA: Sage Publications).

——, Schmidt, S.M. and Wilkinson, I. (1980) 'Intraorganizational Influence Tactics: Exploration in Getting One's Way', *Journal of Applied Psychology*, pp. 440–52.

Kleinman, G., Palmon, D. and Anandarajan, A. (1998) 'Auditor Independence: A Synthesis of Theory and Empirical Research', *Research in Accounting Regulation*, 12, pp. 3–42.

Knapp, M.C. (1985) 'Audit Conflict: An Empirical Study of the Perceived Ability of Auditors to Resist Management Pressure', *The Accounting Review*, 60(2) (April), pp. 202–11.

Levitt, A. (1998) 'The Numbers Game', Speech at the NYU Center for Law and Business, New York, 28 September (www.rutgers.edu/Accounting/raw/aaa/newsarc/pr101898.htm visited on 20 October 1998).

Lindsay, D. (1990) 'An Investigation of the Impact of Contextual Factors on Canadian Bankers' Perceptions of Auditors' Ability to Resist Management Pressure', *Advances in International Accounting*, 3, pp. 71–85.

——, Rennie, M., Murphy, G. and Silvester, H. (1987) 'Independence of External Auditors: A Canadian Perspective', *Advances in International Accoun-ting*, 1, pp. 169–89.

Magee, R. and Tseng, M. (1990) 'Audit Pricing and Independence', *The Accounting Review*, April, pp. 315–36.

Magill, H.T. and Previts, G.J. (1991) *CPA Professional Responsibilities: An Introduction* (Cincinnati, OH: Southwestern Publishing Company, Inc.).

Manson, S., McCartney, S. and Sherer, M. (1994) *The Usefulness of Management Letters*, Certified Research Report 38 (London: Chartered Association of Certified Accountants).

Mastenbroek, W. (1989) *Negotiate* (Oxford: Basil Blackwell).

Matsumura, E.M. and Tucker, R.R. (1995) 'Second Partner Review: An Analytical Model', *Journal of Accounting, Auditing & Finance*, Winter, pp. 173–200.

Mautz, R.K. and Matusiak, L.W. (1988) 'Concurring Partner Review Revisited', *Journal of Accountancy*, March, pp. 56–63.

Mautz, R. and Sharaf, H. (1961) *The Philosophy of Auditing* (Sarasota, FL: American Accounting Association).

McBarnet, D. and Whelan, C. (1991) 'The Elusive Spirit of the Law: Formalism and the Struggle for Legal Control', *Modern Law Review*, 54(6) (November), pp. 848–73.

—— (1992) 'Regulating Accounting: Limits in the Law', chapter 7 in *Accounting and the Law*, M. Bromwich and A. Hopwood (eds) (London: Prentice Hall) pp. 99–111.

—— (1999) *Creative Accounting and the Cross-Eyed Javelin Thrower* (Chichester: John Wiley & Sons).

McCarthy, P.S., Kannan, P.K., Chandrasekharan, R. and Wright, G.P. (1992) 'Estimating Loyalty and Switching with an Application to the Automobile Industry', *Management Science*, 38(10), pp. 1371–93.

McMullen, D.A. (1996) 'Audit Committee Performance: An Investigation of the Consequences Associated with Audit Committees', *Auditing: A Journal of Practice and Theory*, Spring, 15(1), pp. 87–103.

Moizer, P. (1994) Review of Recognised Supervisory Bodies: A Report to the Department of Trade and Industry on the Audit Monitoring Process (London: Department of Trade and Industry).

NACD (2000) *Report of the NACD Blue Ribbon Commission on Audit Committees: A Practical Guide* (Washington, DC: National Association of Corporate Directors).

Nichols, D.R. and Price, K.H. (1976) 'The Auditor–Firm Conflict: An Analysis Using Concepts of Exchange Theory', *The Accounting Review*, 51 (April), pp. 335–46.

Nicotera, A.M. (1993) 'Beyond Two Dimensions: A Grounded Theory Model of Conflict-Handling Behavior', *Management Communication Quarterly*, 6(3), pp. 282–306.

NYSE/NASD (1999) *Report and Recommendations of the Blue Ribbon Committee on Improving the Effectiveness of Corporate Audit Committees* (New York: New York Stock Exchange/National Association of Securities Dealers).

Pany, K. and Reckers, P.M.J. (1980) 'The Effect of Gifts, Discounts, and Client Size on Perceived Auditor Independence', *The Accounting Review*, 55(1) (January), pp. 50–61.

Pearson, M.A. (1987) 'Auditor Independence Deficiencies & Alleged Audit Failures', *Journal of Business Ethics*, 6, pp. 281–7.

Percy, J.P. (1997) 'Auditing and Corporate Governance – a Look Forward into the 21st Century', *International Journal of Auditing*, 1(1), pp. 3–12.

POB (2000) Panel on Audit Effectiveness, Exposure Draft (Public Oversight Board). (www.pobauditpanel.org/ visited on 16 June 2000).

Ponemon, L.A. and Gabhart, D.R.L. (1990) 'Auditor Independence Judgments: A Cognitive-Developmental Model and Experimental Evidence', *Contemporary Accounting Research*, 7(1), pp. 227–51.

Roush, P.B., Jacobs, F.A. and Shockley, R.A. (1992) 'The Effects of Non-Audit Services and Auditor Independence', Working Paper presented at the American Accounting Association conference.

Schroeder, M.S., Solomon, I. and Vickrey, D. (1986) 'Audit Quality: The Perceptions of Audit–Committee Chairpersons and Audit Partners', *Auditing: A Journal of Practice and Theory*, 5(2) (Spring), pp. 86–94.

Schulte, A.A. (1965) 'Compatibility of Management Consulting and Auditing', *The Accounting Review*, July, pp. 587–93.

Schuetze, W.P. (1994) 'A Mountain or a Molehill?', *Accounting Horizons*, 8(1) (March), pp. 69–75.

Sharma, D.D. (1991) *International Operations of Professional Firms* (Lund, Sweden: Studentlitteratur).

—— (1994) 'Classifying Buyers to Gain Marketing Insight: A Relationships Approach to Professional Services', *International Business Review*, 3(1), pp. 15–30.

Short, H., Keasey, K., Wright, M. and Hull, A. (1999) 'Corporate Governance: From Accountability to Enterprise', *Accounting and Business Research*, 29(4), pp. 337–52.

Smith, T. (1992) *Accounting for Growth: Stripping the Camouflage from Company Accounts* (London: Century Business).

Spira, L. (1998) 'An Evolutionary Perspective on Audit Committee Effectiveness', *Corporate Governance: An International Review*, 6(1), pp. 29–38.

St Pierre, K. (1984) 'Independence and Auditor Sanctions', *Journal of Accounting, Auditing & Finance*, 7(3), pp. 257–63.

—— and Anderson, J. (1982) 'An Analysis of Audit Failures Based on Documented Legal Cases', *Journal of Accounting, Auditing & Finance*, Spring, pp. 229–47.

Stamp, E. and Moonitz, M. (1978) *International Auditing Standards* (London: Prentice-Hall International).

Strauss, A. and Corbin, J. (1990) *Basics of Qualitative Research: Grounded Theory Procedures and Techniques* (Newbury Park, CA: Sage Publications).

Sweeney, J.T. and Roberts, R.W. (1997) 'Cognitive Moral Development and Auditor Independence', *Accounting, Organizations and Society*, 22(3/4), pp. 337–52.

Teoh, H.Y. and Lim, C.C. (1996) 'An Empirical Study of the Effects of Audit Committees. Disclosure of Non-Audit Fees, and other Issues on Auditor Independence: Malaysian Evidence', *Journal of Accounting, Auditing and Taxation*, 5(2), pp. 231–48.

Thompson, P. (1988) *The Voice of the Past: Oral History* (Oxford University Press).

Tricker, R.I. (1984) *Corporate Governance* (Vermont: Gower).

Tucker, R.R. and Matsumura, E.M. (1997) 'Second-Partner Review: An Experimental Economics Investigation', *Auditing: A Journal of Practice & Theory*, 16(1) (Spring), pp. 79–98.

Turner, L. (2000) 'Shifting Paradigms in Self-Regulation', Speech at the 27th Anniversary Securities Regulation Institute, 27 January. (www.sec.gov/news/speeches/spch340.html visited on 24 March 2000).

Tweedie, D.P. and Whittington, G. (1990) 'Financial Reporting: Current Problems and Their Implications for Systematic Reform', *Accounting and Business Research*, 21(81), pp. 87–102.

Wall Street Journal (1987) 'Auditor's Downfall Shows a Man Caught in Trap of His Own Making (ESM Case)', 4 March.

Wallace, W.A. (1980) 'The Economic Role of the Audit in Free and Regulated Markets', The Touche Ross and Co. Aid to Education Program (reprinted in *Auditing Monographs* (1985) (Macmillan Publishing Company).

Whittington, G. (1989) 'Accounting Standard Setting in the UK after 20 Years: A Critique of the Dearing and Solomons Reports', *Accounting and Business Research*, 19(75) (Summer), pp. 195–205.

Williamson, M. (1998) 'Audit Add-Ons? Leave it Out', *Accountancy Age*, July, pp. 34–6.

Windsor, C.A. and Ashkanasy, N.M. (1995) 'The Effect of Client Management Bargaining Power, Moral Reasoning Development, and Belief in a Just World on Auditor Independence', *Accounting, Organizations and Society*, 20(7/8), pp. 701–20.

Yin, R.K. (1984) *Case Study Research: Design and Methods* (Newbury Park, CA: Sage Publications).

Index

Note: finance directors and audit engagement partners have not been indexed as they appear throughout the text.

Index